THE EASTERN FRONT, 1941–45, GERMAN TROOPS AND THE BARBARISATION OF WARFARE

THE EASTERN FRONT, 1941–45, GERMAN TROOPS AND THE BARBARISATION OF WARFARE

Omer Bartov

St. Martin's Press   New York

ISBN 0–312–22486–9

Library of Congress Cataloging-in-Publication Data
Bartov, Omer.
The eastern front, 1941–45.
Bibliography: p.
Includes index.
1. World War, 1939–1945—Campaigns—Eastern.
2. Germany.   Heer—History—World War, 1939–1945.
3. World War, 1939–1945—Atrocities.   4. Soldiers—
German—History—20th century.   5. Sociology, Military—
Germany—History—20th century.   I. Title.
D764.B233   1986   940.54′13′43   85–14600
ISBN 0–312–22486–9

To my Mother and Father

Jen, or humaneness, is a way to be followed
  'In fear and trembling
  With caution and care,
  As though on the brink of a chasm
  As though treading thin ice' (Confucius, *Analects,* 5:3)

'The era of the Hitler regime, with its gigantic, unprecedented crimes, constituted an unmastered past . . . for the rest of the world, which had not forgotten this great catastrophe in the heart of Europe either, and had been unable to come to terms with it.'

(H. Arendt, *Eichmann in Jerusalem,* p. 283)

Geschichte: Staub und Altäre, Jammer und Notzucht.
Und jeder Ruhm ein Spott auf seine Opfer.
Wahrhaftig: Schöpfer, Schöpfung und Geschöpf sind widerlegt durch Auschwitz.
Das Leben als Idee ist tot.
Das könnte der Angang einer grossen Umkehr sein, einer Erlösung vom Leid.
Es gibt nach dieser Einsicht nur mehr eine Schuld: Fluch dem, der Leben schafft.
Ich schaffe Leben ab, das ist die aktuelle Humanität, die einzige Rettung vor der Zukunft.

(R. Hochhuth, *Der Stellvertreter,* p. 198).

Contents

Contents

List of Tables

Preface

When I began reading German history, I was struck by the great elasticity of meaning which some key terms assumed in the hands of historians, particularly regarding the Third Reich. 'The Germans', for example, were portrayed either as all Nazis or as having had almost nothing to do with the 'criminal clique' which had somehow succeeded in coming to power; 'the generals' were either counted in with the Nazi leaders of the state or, on the contrary, depicted as the last bastion of resistance to National Socialism; 'the Eastern Front' featured in some accounts as the main theatre of the war, where the Russians had sacrificed millions of their people in pushing back the Nazi invader set upon enslaving and destroying them, whereas for many West Europeans and Americans it remained an unclear and baffling sideshow. It was often much more convenient to remember what were perceived as the chivalrous battles in the West and in North Africa, where there had apparently been decent chaps on both sides, though unfortunately some were led by rather more unpleasant characters than others.

This was a very disturbing state of affairs for a young student of history. The memoirs of German generals insisted that they had put up a fair and professional fight; Western military historians thought that they were even better behaved than during the First World War; the Russians described them as beasts. I felt increasingly confused. Moreover, there seemed to be much disagreement on the character of the German army. Who, for instance, represented it – the generals, the officer corps, the rank-and-file? What was the relationship between the army and the Nazis? Was it an ideologically committed, fanatic party army, or was it a professional, cool, aloof organisation, efficient, disciplined and 'correct' in its dealings with the enemy?

It would be, of course, unjust to claim that other historians have ignored this problem till now. On the contrary, many recent and excellent studies have dealt precisely with the question of who supported the Nazis, what did the Third Reich look like seen from within, how many people knew about or were involved in the genocidal policies of the regime, how influential anti-Semitism was and so forth. But the army was neglected; it was left either to the military historians who were concerned with its tactics and armaments, or to the political historians who focused on the relations between the generals and the regime. The soldiers were forgotten, subjected only once in a while to generalisations which nobody could prove or correct.

This is the reason why it seemed to me appropriate to write a study based on a 'view from below' of the German army in the East, in an attempt to reach down as far as possible to the lowest levels of the military, and to analyse carefully all the data found there with the aim of tackling such questions as the attitudes, education and conduct of the soldiers as they manifested themselves on the battlefield itself. This, then, can almost be seen as a regional study of the military; instead of concentrating on a town, or a district, I have selected a number of combat formations which fought on the Eastern Front and tried to learn about them as much as was possible from their own divisional and personal files. Although limited in scope, I hope that this study will shed light on some issues which have till now remained rather obscure.

This study was first written as a DPhil thesis at St Antony's College, submitted to Oxford University in April 1983. I have, however, made some substantial revisions in most parts of this work, particularly in Chapter 3 and the Conclusion. A great number of scholars have rendered me their assistance both in the writing of the dissertation and in its subsequent revisions. First and foremost I would like to take this opportunity to thank my supervisors, Dr Tim Mason and Mr Tony Nicholls, without whose wisdom and friendship I could never have even launched this project. Mr John Ridge gave me much of his time and expertise in working with the computer. My examiners, Professors Michael Howard and Volker Berghahn, made numerous helpful suggestions for revisions of my thesis. Dr David Blackbourn and Dr Richard Bessel kindly invited me to deliver a paper on my work at the London Institute of Historical Research where further useful comments were made. In the Federal Republic of Germany, the members of the Militärgeschichtliches Forschungsamt in Freiburg, and particularly Dr Wilhelm Deist, have all shown much interest in my progress, as has Professor Klaus-Jürgen Müller of the Bundeswehr Hochschule in Hamburg. Special thanks are due to Dr Bernd Wegner and his wife as well as to Mrs Kwiet and her son, Professor Konrad Kwiet. In Israel I would like to extend my thanks to all members of the Department of History at Tel-Aviv University, and particularly to the Chairman, Professor Zvi Yavetz, as well as to Professor Shlomo Ben-Ami, Walter Grab, Yehuda Wallach, Saul

Friedländer and Shula Volkov. This research could not have been undertaken without the friendly co-operation of the staffs of the Bundesarchiv-Militärarchiv in Freiburg, the Bundesarchiv-Zentralnachweisstelle in Kornelimünster, the Deutsche Dienststelle (WASt) in Berlin and the Berlin Document Centre. Financial support was given me by Tel-Aviv University, the German Historical Institute in London, the German Academic Exchange Service (DAAD), the Rothschild Foundation and the Fulbright Educational Exchange Grant; I wish to thank them all.

This book was written at Princeton University, to which I had been kindly invited as a Visiting Fellow in the Shelby Cullom Davis Center for Historical Studies. I would like to thank all the members of the History Department for their friendship and advice, and especially Professors Lawrence Stone, Arno Mayer, Theodor Rabb, David Abraham and Sheldon Garon. Notwithstanding this long list of friends and advisers, I hasten to add, of course, that they should bear no responsibility for the opinions expressed in this book. Any attempt to express in a few words the great debt which I owe to those who have helped me most is doomed to failure; let me just say that only they, Mary J. Picone and my parents, know how much they deserve my gratitude.

Princeton   O.B.

List of Abbreviations

AFS	*Armed Forces and Society*
AJS	*American Journal of Sociology*
BA-MA	Bundesarchiv-Militärarchiv, Freiburg i. B.
Dulag	Durchgangslager (POW transit camp)
GD	Grossdeutschland (Regiment, later Division)
Gen.Lt.	Generalleutnant (Lieutenant General)
Gen.Maj.	Generalmajor (Major General)
Gen.Oberst	Generaloberst (Colonel General)
GFP	Geheime Feldpolizei (Secret Field Police)
Hiwis	Hilfswillige (Russian volunteers in the Wehrmacht)
HJ	Hitlerjugend (Hitler Youth)
Hptm.	Hauptmann (Captain)
HWJ	*History Workshop Journal*
I.D.	Infanteriedivision (Infantry Division)
I.R.	Infanterieregiment (Infantry Regiment)
JCH	*Journal of Contemporary History*
JMH	*Journal of Modern History*
Lt.	Leutnant (Second Lieutenant)
MFO	Mitteilungen für das offizierkorps (Information for the Officer Corps)
MFT	Mitteilungen für die Truppe (Information for the Troops)
MGM	*Militärgeschichtliche Mitteilungen*
NSDAP	Nationalsozialistische Deutsche Arbeiterpartei (National Socialist German Workers' Party)
NSFO	Nationalsozialistischer Führungsoffizier (National Socialist Leadership Officer)
Oblt.	Oberleutnant (Lieutenant)
Obstlt.	Oberstleutnant (Lieutenant Colonel)
OKH	Oberkommando des Heeres (High Command of the Land Forces)
OKW	Oberkommando der Wehrmacht (High Command of the Armed Forces)
POQ	*Public Opinion Quarterly*
P&P	*Past and Present*
PSQ	*Political Science Quarterly*
Pz.Div.	Panzerdivision (Armoured Division)

RAD	Reichsarbeitsdienst (Reich Labour Service)
Rgt.	Regiment
SA	Sturmabteilung (Storm Troops of the Nazi Party)
SD	Sicherheitsdienst (Secret Police of the SS)
SS	Schutzstaffel ('Defence Squad' of the Nazi Party)
VfZ	*Vierteljahrshefte für Zeitgeschichte*

Introduction

The main question posed by this study is what were the causes of the barbarisation of German troops on the Eastern Front during the Second World War? More specifically, this book is an attempt to examine the relationship between the conditions at the front, the social and educational background of the junior officers and political indoctrination on the one hand, and the criminal activities of the army in the East on the other hand. That a research of this kind is necessary, both from the factual and the methodological points of view, can be demonstrated by a brief survey of the available literature dealing with these issues.

Under Hitler's regime, and particularly after the collapse of the Third Reich, the German generals tried to justify their collaboration with the Nazis by invoking two main arguments. The first was that the junior officer corps and the rank-and-file of the army had already been infiltrated by National Socialism to such a degree that it would have been impossible to find the 'divisions' with which to stage a coup; the second argument emphasised the long tradition of *'Überparteilichkeit'* in the army and its professional duties at the front which hindered any interference with the political leadership of the Reich. Thus, for example, von Manstein wrote in his memoirs that

> The preconditions for a *coup d'état* would have been . . . the following of the whole Wehrmacht and the agreement of the majority of the population. Both did not exist during the years of peace in the Third Reich as well as during the war (with the exception perhaps of the very last months).

On the other hand, von Manstein was quick to add the second argument, according to which the staging of a Putsch during peacetime would have resulted in a civil war, whereas during the war itself it would have meant

> that the military leaders had brought about the collapse of the fronts and the defeat with their own hands.

1

This, he claimed, was quite an impossible demand from the German soldier, whose whole tradition was based on a 'selfless devotion to the service of the state, Reich and Volk'.[1]

Thus the German generals sought to clear themselves of the charge of collaborating with the regime and implementing its policies by laying claim to a set of moral values which stood in stark contradiction to their actions. Alongside the impressive list of apologetic and self-righteous memoirs, the early post-war years saw the appearance of numerous divisional chronicles, written by the veterans themselves and aimed at presenting their history as a tale of courage, patriotism and sacrifice. The uglier aspects of the war were generally ignored, or at best seen as mere 'excesses'.[2] Similarly, military historians, German and non-German alike, were far more interested in the operational and strategic events of the war, and consequently took the assertions of the generals regarding their conduct at face value. A good example of this attitude is Liddell Hart's description of von Blomberg who, we are told, 'became almost lyrical in discoursing the appeal of "gentlemanliness" in war', and seems to have led the British historian to the astonishing conclusion that 'The German Army in the field on the whole observed the rules of war better than it did in 1914–18.'[3]

The relations between the senior officers of the army and the political leadership of Germany have been dealt with by a number of valuable and comprehensive works.[4] The debate on this issue was given further impetus by the controversy over the Putsch attempt of July 1944 and the moral questions involved in the problem of whether treason against a criminal regime was a crime or a virtue.[5] The main shortcoming of these studies is that they tell us a lot about a few generals, and precious little about the majority of the officers and soldiers who composed the German army. When they come to the question of how Nazi the army really was, and how far it was involved in carrying out National Socialist policies, they return to the accounts of the generals themselves which, as has already been noted, are far from unbiased. As to the Putsch itself, it must be stressed that the number of those involved was even more restricted and their moral and political insight even more unrepresentative of the great multitude of officers and men. No one was more aware of this fact than the organisers of the Putsch, as can be clearly seen from Stauffenberg's words shortly before 20 July, often quoted as proof of the resisters' courage, but rarely as a condemnation of the army's widespread loyalty to Hitler:

It is time that something is done. But whoever dares to act must realise that he will probably go down in German history as a traitor. Yet if he fails to act, he will be a traitor before his own conscience.[6]

The collaboration of the army with the Nazis and its role as the instrument which enabled Hitler to implement his policies, were most evident during the war against Russia. It should therefore not surprise us that the army's criminal activities in the East remained taboo among the more traditional German historians for many years after the fall of the Third Reich.[7] Only more recently have some German scholars taken up this tragic episode and examined the wealth of material still stored in the archives of the Federal Republic. Although the so-called 'criminal orders' were already made public during the Nuremberg Trials,[8] it was only in the mid-1960s that their implications were subjected to a penetrating analysis. Since then such issues as the maltreatment of Russian prisoners of war, National Socialist indoctrination among the troops and the collaboration of the army with the Einsatzgruppen, the murder squads of the SS and the SD, have received close and comprehensive attention.[9]

The revelations concerning the army's participation in the mass killings carried out by the Einsatzgruppen demonstrated once more the great sensitivity of the German public to this issue. The weekly *Der Spiegel* wrote that this study had shown

the frightening extent of the army's integration in Hitler's extermination plans and policies . . . refuting the common thesis that the Wehrmacht had nothing to do with the murderous activities of the Einsatzgruppen in Russia . . . [and] correcting the much popularised view regarding the 'purity' of the Wehrmacht.[10]

In another article on this subject, a well-known German historian wrote that most Germans of the older generation remember the war as a long series of defensive battles and retreats, leading from the catastrophe of Stalingrad to the terror, flight and ultimate separation of East Germany. What is either forgotten or repressed, he claims, is the first stage of the war, and naturally not so much the rapid advance of German troops to the outskirts of Moscow and Leningrad, but rather the systematic extermination of so called 'Jewish-Bolshevism' and its biological basis, with the aim of creating a new '*Lebensraum*' for the German race. These actions, which were taking place directly behind the fighting troops, turned 'Operation Barbarossa' into the 'most terrible war of conquest, enslavement and extermination' of modern times.[11]

The works quoted above can, however, be criticised on two closely connected counts. The first is that historians have concentrated on the higher spheres of the army's command, be it the generals in the field, the staff officers in the rear, or the bureaucratic and administrative apparatus of the Wehrmacht's institutions. The second problem is that these works have tended to focus upon one single issue, whether it was the tactical aspects of the war, the maltreatment of POWs and civilians or the indoctrination of the soldiers. These two limitations have created both a factual and a methodological difficulty. For, as is admitted by these scholars, their knowledge regarding the situation as it really was among the officers and rank-and-file at the front is mostly based on speculation, conjecture, or reliance on the accounts of the generals. Manfred Messerschmidt writes, to quote just one example, that

> Among the troops a great deal actually looked different from the way it had been planned and imagined at the top. It had not come, perhaps, to a conversion of the theory into practice.[12]

However, the author himself is quick to admit in another passage in his study that he possesses no evidence with which to substantiate this speculation.

> In order to reach precise conclusions, it is necessary to undertake an exhaustive research concerning political instruction among the companies, its frequency and intensity, and the echo of conviction among the NCOs and men. But precisely here yawns a gap in the literature.[13]

This book is therefore an attempt to fill in some of the gaps in our knowledge, not only regarding the political indoctrination of the troops, but also concerning other issues related to the conduct of the German army in the East, as the next few pages will explain.

The basic hypothesis of this study is that the barbarisation of the troops on the Eastern Front was the result of three major factors: the conditions at the front; the social and educational background of the junior officers; and the political indoctrination of the troops. In order to examine these issues, as well as their ultimate consequences as manifested by the criminal activities of the army, it seemed necessary to limit the scope of the investigation to a small segment of the German army in the East. It was furthermore felt that this study should strive to achieve a view 'from below' of the soldiers, instead of examining the higher spheres of the military hierarchy as has been the case till now. The intention was thus to see how all these elements combined together to influence the conduct of the men at the front, right down to the lowest possible level. The methodological concept was consequently to investigate a selected and limited section of the army and thereby to enhance our knowledge regarding the actual life, education and behaviour of the troops, and at the same time to create a more complete picture of the various pressures exerted on the individual soldiers as they worked with and against each other.

As we have seen, one of the main arguments of the German generals has been that the soldiers at the front were far too preoccupied with fighting to find any time for either political education or criminal activities. In order to find out how far this was indeed the case, this study concentrates on three combat divisions which had spent most of the war at the front carrying out their 'professional duty'. The officers and soldiers who composed these formations were young men who belonged to a generation about which very little research has been done till now. Much of the research dealing with the Wehrmacht, as well as with the Reichswehr of the Weimar Republic and the Imperial Army of the Second Reich, has focused on the social background of the senior officers.[14] We thus have very little knowledge regarding the background of the junior officers of the Third Reich, those men who formed the backbone of the fighting formations at the front and carried the responsibility for both their achievements and their brutality. This study has attempted to enhance our knowledge on this issue by examining a sample of the officers who served in the divisions and pointing out their various characteristics.

This book is structured in the following manner. Chapter 1 analyses the conditions at the front, stressing in particular the heavy casualties, the difficult living conditions and the problems of morale and discipline among the troops. Chapter 2 investigates the social, educational and political background of a sample of the junior officers of the three divisions. The methodological difficulty concerning the fact that whereas in the other three chapters we discuss the divisions as a whole, that is both the rank-and-file and the officers, in Chapter 2 the investigation is limited to the officers, will be attended to in the appropriate place. Chapter 3 describes and analyses the extent, intensity and possible influence of the political education of the troops. Here too we will devote some space to a more general discussion concerning the efficacy of indoctrination, or the relationship between ideology and action. The last chapter is an account of the final consequences of the aforementioned issues–the criminal activities of these formations at the front. Chapter 4 also attempts to point out the fundamental difference between the barbarisation of the German army in the East and the brutal behaviour of other armies in other wars.

For the individual soldier on the Eastern Front there was no clear-cut division between one aspect of his life and another. In this study, however, it was necessary to make an artificial distinction between the various issues. The intention is nevertheless to prove the opposite. It was the combination of all these factors which turned this conflict into such a terrible war. Although we shall examine here only a very limited number of men and formations, we may perhaps have the advantage of understanding how the process of barbarisation actually took place. Under the circumstances described in this book it can be said to have been almost inevitable. For the men who were educated in Hitler's Germany, indoctrinated in the Wehrmacht of the Third Reich and sent into a war of unimaginable ferocity, barbarism was normality, humaneness long forgotten.

1 Life, Hardship and Death at the Front

INTRODUCTION

The aim of this chapter is to explore the conditions on the Eastern Front as experienced by the soldiers of the three divisions selected for this study. Following a brief survey of the military history of these formations, some of the more important issues relevant to the life of the combat soldier at the front are analysed. These include the rate of casualties and their impact on the manpower composition of the units; the physical and mental hardship experienced by the troops; and finally, the discipline and morale of the soldiers, with reference to records of courts-martial as well as to reports of unit commanders regarding the mental condition of their men.

This chapter is intended to set the chronological, geographical and military background for the main body of the book. In conclusion, however, it attempts to analyse how far the conditions at the front contributed to the barbarisation of the soldiers. Furthermore, it discusses some of the reasons for the remarkable resilience shown by the troops in the East and suggests that political indoctrination, examined in detail in Chapter 3, may have played an important role in this phenomenon.

THE MILITARY EVENTS

The 12th Infantry Division

The 12.I.D. was established in October 1934 in Mecklenburg (*Wehrkreis II*), and was composed of three infantry regiments, an artillery regiment and other supporting units. It was one of the thirty-five infantry divisions established before the outbreak of the war and belonged to the first 'wave' of conscription, which meant that over three-quarters of its original personnel were regular soldiers.[1]

The division took part in the Polish campaign, during which the former commander-in-chief of the army, von Fritsch, was killed while taking part in a battle in the divisional sector. The 12.I.D. was transferred to training bases near Bonn in October 1939.[2] It participated in the invasion of Belgium and France and succeeded in reaching the coast of Biscay in the Vendée before France finally surrendered.[3] In September 1940 the division was moved to the Netherlands, where it was stationed till 25 May 1941, when it was transfered to East Prussia.[4] On 22 June 1941 the 12.I.D. marched into Lithuania, crossed the Niemen river, captured Kaunas (Kovno) and reached the Dvina river by 7 July. In early August the division approached the area of Kholm, and following a series of heavy battles there and in the Valdai Hills, it reached the springs of the Volga south of Demyansk in mid-September.[5]

For the next fourteen months the 12.I.D. remained in what had become known as '*Festung Demjansk*'. In the course of the counter-offensive of the Red Army in the winter of 1941/2, the Russians cut off and encircled the II. Corps, numbering some 96 000 soldiers, among whom were also the men of the 12.I.D. In late August 1942 contact was re-established with the corps, but the situation remained precarious till the enclave was evacuated in February 1943.[6] Following a short rest along the Lovat river, south of Lake Ilmen and Staraya Russa, the 12.I.D. was sent south to the area of Vitebsk, where it took part in heavy defensive battles during December 1943 till mid-February 1944. The division was then transferred to Mogilev, where it was still stationed when the great summer offensive of the Red Army erupted on 22 June 1944 and virtually destroyed Army Group Centre, including the 12.I.D., whose survivors were sent to reorganise in West Prussia.[7]

In mid-September 1944 the newly established 12.I.D. was rushed to hold back the American forces converging on the city of Aachen. The exhausted formation, renamed 12th Volks-Grenadier-Division in October 1944, took part in the Ardennes Offensive and then retreated across the Rhine in March 1945. The division finally surrendered to the Americans as part of the forces in the 'Ruhr Pocket', near the area of Siegen.[8]

The Grossdeutschland Division

The establishment of the 'Infantry Regiment Grossdeutschland', based on elements of the Guards Regiment of Berlin, was officially announced on 12 June 1939.[9] The new motorised regiment did not take part in the Polish campaign. During the invasion of France it fought as part of Guderian's XIX Panzer Corps and ended the war in Lyon on 19 June 1940.[10] The GD Regiment was then transferred to Colmar, in Alsace, where it remained till the spring of the following year.[11] In early April 1941 it was moved to the Yugoslav border and entered Belgrade on 13 April.[12]

Having been moved again to Brest-Litovsk and attached to Guderian's Panzer Group 2, the GD Regiment entered the Soviet Union on 25 June 1941 and participated in the encirclement of Minsk.[13] On 11 July the regiment stormed across the Dniepr and fought along the road from Smolensk to Roslavl. During the first half of August the GD sustained heavy casualties in defensive battles near the town of Yelnya.[14] Following a short rest, the regiment participated in Guderian's drive into the Ukraine, but by early October it was back in the central sector, fighting in costly forest battles in Briansk and Karachev.[15] The GD took part in Guderian's last desperate attempt to capture the town of Tula, and following the Russian counter-offensive it retreated to the Oka river. In its last battle that winter, on 20 February 1942, the GD, reduced to one weak rifle battalion, failed to achieve its objective. Only three officers and some thirty NCOs and men returned from the battlefield. On 8 April the survivors of the regiment were sent to reorganise in Gomel.[16]

The establishment of the new Grossdeutschland Division began on 1 April and lasted till 23 May 1942. This was a powerful motorised formation, consisting of two infantry regiments, an artillery regiment, Panzer, assault-gun, motorcycle, anti-tank, anti-aircraft and engineer battalions, as well as numerous support units. The division recruited only young volunteers from all corners of the Reich.[17] By late June 1942 the GD Division went into action as part of the German summer offensive in the Ukraine. Having fought its way as far as the Donets river, it was pulled out of the front and sent to the enclave of Rzhev on the central sector.[18] The heavy and bloody battles there lasted till the end of 1942, and it was only on 11 January 1943 that the GD was allowed a period of rest in Smolensk.[19]

It was a brief rest, as only a few days later the division was rushed south to try and stem the Russian offensive directed at Belogrod and Kharkov. By mid-February the GD was compelled to evacuate these cities and retreated to Poltava.[20] Having been equipped there with new 'Tiger' tanks, the division took part in the successful German counter-offensive of March 1943, and was then allowed a somewhat longer rest in Poltava.[21] This time the tank elements of the GD were significantly reinforced, numbering three battalions, of which one was equipped with the powerful 'Tigers'. In late June the division was renamed 'Panzer-Grenadier-Division-Grossdeutschland', and soon afterwards it received under its command a new brigade of 200 'Panther' tanks, directly from the assembly lines. Between 5 and 18 July the GD took part in the Battle of Kursk, but having failed to reach its objectives it was transferred to face the Russian counter-offensive in Karachev.[22]

Throughout the latter part of July, August and September the GD fought a series of rearguard battles in Orel, Akhtyrka and Kharkov, and on 29 September 1943 it re-crossed the Dniepr in Kremenchug, covering the retreat of the 8. Army.[23] During the winter of 1943/4 the division tried to contain the Red Army, but following the Russian offensive of March 1944 the whole German line disintegrated and by early April the GD was already in Rumanian territory near the town of Yassi.[24]

In late July 1944 the GD was transferred to the other extreme of the Eastern Front, all the way to Gumbinnen in East Prussia. The division failed in its attempt to re-establish contact with the now isolated Army Group North and, following a major Russian offensive, found itself trapped inside the coastal city of Memel. In late November the GD was shipped out of the besieged city and transported to Rastenburg.[25] The plan to use this short rest period to establish a new 'Panzer-Korps-Grossdeutschland' by joining the GD with the Brandenburg Division never materialised. By 12 January 1945 the GD was rushed to the south in the face of a major Russian offensive across the Narev river, but by the end of the month it had retreated from Ortelsburg all the way to Brandenburg, where it remained till mid-March. Another offensive of the Red Army forced the few remaining GD soldiers to evacuate their positions in the Balga-Kahlholz and cross over to Pillau on the Samland Peninsula. On 12 April the remnants of the division were attacked once more, and only some 800 men succeeded in escaping to the thin strip of land of Frische Nehrung. These few survivors were taken by ship to Danish territory on 30 April 1945, and consequently sent to

Ostfriesland in Germany, where they became British prisoners of war.[26]

The 18th Panzer Division

The establishment of the 18.Pz.Div. began on 25 October 1940, as part of a general strengthening of the Panzer arm following the French campaign. The division was composed of two infantry regiments taken from two first 'wave' infantry divisions recruited in Dresden (*Wehrkreis IV*), a Panzer and an artillery regiment as well as other support units.[27] The 18.Pz.Div. invaded the Soviet Union as part of Guderian's Panzer Group 2 and took part in capturing the city of Minsk. By 12 July 1941 the division crossed the Dniepr and assisted in the encirclement of Smolensk. During the last week of July the division fought together with the GD on the road to Roslavl, where it lost most of its tanks.[28]

Following a much-needed rest period, the 18.Pz.Div. joined Guderian's Panzer Group in its drive to the Ukraine. By early October, however, it was already fighting Russian forces trapped in the Briansk pocket, and as of the second week of November it began advancing east of Orel, suffering badly from the atrocious weather and impassable roads. In its last attack that year, on 29 November, some of its units reached the Don.[29] This was to be the easternmost point of the division's advance. The Russian counter-offensive forced the 18.Pz.Div. back to the Susha river, from which it was ordered to move to Zhisdra in order to re-establish contact with another German formation trapped in the town of Sukhinichi. Having achieved its objective, the 18.Pz.Div. remained in the area of Zhisdra during the whole of 1942, taking part in some heavy defensive battles and sustaining severe casualties.[30]

In February 1943 the 18.Pz.Div. was moved to Orel, where it succeeded in containing a Russian offensive and prepared for the last great German offensive in the East, operation '*Zitadelle*'. Meanwhile, the division took part in a number of anti-partisan operations, described in greater detail in Chapter 4.[31] On 5 July 1943 the 18.Pz.Div. attacked the northern perimeter of the Kursk enclave, but having failed in achieving its objectives was quickly moved to halt the Russian counter-offensive around Orel. This, however, could no longer be carried out, and during August and September the division retreated all the way to the Dniepr, continuously engaged in fierce defensive battles and losing most of its units in the process. On 18 October 1943 the remnants of the 18.Pz.Div. were finally disbanded.[32]

MANPOWER AND CASUALTIES

In the previous section we have referred a number of times to the fact that the divisions sustained heavy casualties. It is now time to examine more closely what the impact of the fighting on the Eastern Front on the manpower composition of the divisions in question really was. In this section we shall therefore first present the relevant data in two types of tables: one which shows the growing gap between the numbers of troops as initially planned by the OKH for each of the formations, and the actual number of soldiers on the battlefield; another which demonstrates the enormous casualties sustained by the divisions. Each set of tables is followed by a short discussion on the significance of those figures and a few examples meant to demonstrate the effects of these data on the actual situation in the units at the front.

The 12th Infantry Division

Tables 1.1 and 1.2, presenting the known data regarding the manpower and casualties of the 12.I.D., enable us to draw two immediate conclusions. It is first of all quite clear that the number of soldiers serving in the division, and particularly that of the combatants, rapidly fell much below the figure stipulated by OKH. At the lowest point for which figures are available, the number of combatant soldiers fell to as few as 4993 men, that is, 33 per cent of the establishment (*Soll*) figure. It should further be emphasised that the situation was probably much worse during the first half of 1944 since the division was virtually decimated in a series of defensive battles, but unfortunately we have no figures for this period. The second conclusions, derived from Table 1.2, is that the division lost 16 112 men, of whom 527 were officers, between the beginning of the war in Russia and 16 October 1943. In other words, during less than two years of fighting the 12.I.D. lost over 118 per cent of its initial number of combat soldiers, and over 156 per cent of its combat officers. It should again be pointed out that the heaviest casualties

TABLE 1.1 *12. Infantry Division – manpower*

	Planned establishment manpower			Actual total manpower			Actual combat manpower		
	Officers	Other ranks	Total	Officers	Other ranks	Total	Officers	Other ranks	Total
1.9.1939 (total)	534	17 200	17 734						
1.9.1939 (combat)	465	14 646	15 111				231		
9.5.1940						16 677	182	9725	9907
22.6.1941							336	14 073	14 409
10.12.1941						15 106	287	11 351	11 638
1.10.1942			14 982			13 046			
1.3.1943							171	4822	4993
21.6.1943							203	7915	8118
16.9.1944 (West)						14 800			6600
16.9.1944 (infantry)									1800

were sustained by the division after this period. We can therefore say that during the fighting in Russia the 12.I.D. lost more men than it originally had among its ranks when it first invaded the Soviet Union, and perhaps as many as twice the number of officers who commanded its units on 22 June 1941. It would probably be safe to assume that as many as 30 000 men and 700 officers passed through the ranks of the division during the Russian campaign.[33]

The impact of the chronic lack of manpower and heavy losses on the state of those soldiers who survived can be illustrated with a few examples. Thus during November and December 1941 the II. Corps informed the 16. Army that its divisions, among them the 12.I.D., were so depleted that they could no longer hold a continuous line, let alone pull some of their units out of the front for a rest.[34] Consequently, the men of the 12.I.D. had to stand guard for five to six hours every night, with short intervals of some two hours of rest in between.[35] That the situation showed no signs of improvement was demonstrated in a report of the I.R.27, according to which its men had spent the previous six months in their positions without a single break, carrying out on average eight hours of guard duty every day and kept busy during most of their rest periods by either fighting or fortification work.[36] The rising casualties compelled the division to make use of its non-combat personnel as replacements. By April 1942

TABLE 1.2 *12. Infantry Division – casualties**

	Killed	Wounded	Missing	Sick	Total	Percentage of manpower on 22.6.1941	Shortage
1.9.–12.10.39	(11)	(10)			(21)		
9.5.–25.7.40	416	1091	24	418	2004		
	(22)	(33)			(55)		
22.6.–10.12.41	1005	3153	43		4201	29·2	
22.6.41–	1787	5692	77		7855	54·5	
24.4.42	(65)	(231)	(3)		(299)	(89·0)	
8.1.–8.2.42	270	700	17	1573	2560		
9.2.–20.3.42	303	886	20	924	2133		
10.4.42							4586 (52)
10.5.42							5769 (71)
22.6.41–	2205	6977	90		9272	64·3	
22.5.42					(341)	(101·5)	
22.6.41–					10 897	75·6	
1.8.42							3392 (50)
22.6.41–	2621	8500	331		11 452	79·5	
1.10.42							
9.3.43							2742 (42)
22.6.41–	**3464	**11 975			15 439	107·1	
30.4.43	(126)	(384)	(4)		(514)	(153.0)	
22.6.41–	**3571	**12 541			16 112	118·8	
16.10.43	(132)	(391)	(4)		(527)	(156·8)	
16.9.–21.10.44					1400		
(West: infantry)							

* Officer casualties given in brackets; total casualties include both officers and men, with officers' share in brackets. The same applies to percentages, but in shortages numbers are separate.
** Figure includes officers.
SOURCES for Tables 1.1 and 1.2 BA–MA RH26–12/6, 16, 22, 49, 52–4, 62, 69, 75, 78, 92, 130, 168, 252, 265. Mueller-Hillebrand, *Das Heer,* I. 70–1.

the 12.I.D. had altogether ten battalions at its disposal; in four of those battalions, 49 per cent had not been trained as infantry soldiers; in another, 44 per cent; in four other battalions, 23 per cent were not infantry soldiers; and only in one battalion all men had received proper training.[37] By that time the division was ordered to make do with no more than one officer for each company.[38] In fact, in July 1942 the situation had become even worse, so that of nine battalion commanders still available to the division, only four were actually serving with their units at the front. Consequently, eight company commanders were given the authority of sector, or battalion, commanders. The companies were thus left in the charge of very young and inexperienced platoon commanders, while most of the veteran NCOs had either been killed or made into officers themselves. Only a quarter of the men at the front were trained infantry soldiers.[39] The few replacements which did arrive were of inferior quality, having been thrown into battle after a very short period of basic training.[40] In times of crisis, as for example in October 1942, the division was forced to establish so-called '*Alarmeinheiten*', composed of soldiers from supply and service units. More often than not, casualties among those units were particularly high.[41] We can thus conclude that the heavy casualties and the ever-worsening shortage in manpower kept the units at the front in a state of permanent crisis which, as we shall see later on, had a severe effect on their physical and mental condition.

The Grossdeutschland Division

As can clearly be seen from Tables 1.3 and 1.4, the GD Division suffered extremely high casualties during the war. Between 23 May 1942, on which date the establishment of the division was completed, and late September 1943, the GD lost 17 712 men, of whom 583 were officers. In other words, within fourteen months of fighting the division lost over 98 per cent of its initial manpower of 18 000 men. If we add to this the figures known for the first four months of 1945, and excluding the unknown casualties sustained during late 1943 and the whole of 1944, we reach the astonishing total of 34 700 casualties, of whom 973 were officers; that is, over 192 per cent of the original establishment figure. These figures should enable us to estimate that between the establishment of the GD and the end of the war, the GD lost between two to three times the number of men it initially had, and between three and four times the number of officers, presumably put at some 300 on establishment.[42]

When these figures are put into their historical context, they illustrate how grim and bitter the fighting at the front really was. Here we can quote only a few of the numerous stories found in the divisional files and chronicle. Thus, for example, during the battle of Rzhev in September 1942, the I.R.GD1 had 1397 casualties and the regiment commander was killed. The Second Company began the battle with 141 men and returned with 47, its commander having also been killed. The II/I.R.GD2 was almost completely wiped out and lost its commander. The II/I.R.GD1 lost its commander and all its staff in one direct hit.[43] In November 1942 the reconstituted

TABLE 1.3 *Grossdeutschland Division – manpower*

	Planned establishment manpower			Actual total manpower			Actual combat manpower		
	Officers	Other ranks	Total	Officers	Other ranks	Total	Officers	Other ranks	Total
9.5.40 (GD Rgt.)						3900			
22.6.41 (GD Rgt.)						6000			
23.5.42 (GD Div)			18 000	300?		18 000			
Dec. 1944			10 000						
29.3.45						4000			
30.4.45						800			

TABLE 1.4 *Grossdeutschland Division – casualties**

	Killed	Wounded	Missing	Sick	Total	Percentage of manpower on 23.5.42	Shortage
9.5.–19.6.40	221 (8)	830 (40)	57 (1)		1157 (49)	***[29·7]	
22.6.41– 6.1.42	864 (36)	3081 (89)			4070 (125)		
27.6.–31.7.42	392 (8)	1664 (99)			2163 (107)		
31.7.42							2077 (101)
1.8.42– 25.4.43	1534 (98)	5989 (157)	418 (6)		8202 (261)	45·6 (87·0?)	
1.4.–30.9.43	1277 (73)	5550 (138)	305 (4)		7347 (215)	40·8 (71·7?)	
27.6.42– 30.9.43	3203 (179)	13 203 (394)	723 (10)		17 712 (583)	98·4 (194·3?)	
15.1.–29.3.45					14 586 (390)		
29.3.–22.4.45					2402		
27.6.42– 22.4.45**					34 700 (973)	192·8 (324·3?)	

* Officer casualties given in brackets; total casualties include both officers and men, with officers' share in brackets. The same applies to percentages, but in shortages numbers are separate.

** This total excludes unknown and probably very high casualties for 1.10.43–14.1.45, as well as most of April 1945 for officer casualties.

*** Percentage of manpower on 9.5.40.

SOURCES for Tables 1.3 and 1.4 BA–MA RH26–1005/5, 7, 50–1, 60. Spaeter/ Schramm, *Grossdeutschland*, I. 66–76, 85–6, 194, 199–213, 385, 429; III. 11–24, 381–404.

II/I.R.GD2 lost its commander, adjutant, as well as all company and platoon commanders in the course of one single Russian artillery barrage which lasted only twenty minutes.[44] In December 1942 the commander of the Grenadier Regiment (I.R.GD1) and all his staff were surrounded by Russian tanks and killed, including many of their men.[45] By January 1943 the manpower situation was so severe that the Second Fusilier (I.R.GD2) Company had one officer, two NCOs and eight men left; the Thirteenth Grenadier Company had one officer, one NCO and sixteen men.[46] The Grenadier Regiment had only thirty-five officers to staff eighteen companies, four battalions and the regimental staff post, which meant that only two companies had more than one officer and all platoons were led by NCOs or privates.[47]

Notwithstanding the fact that the GD Division, being an elite formation, received more replacements than the other two divisions, the manpower situation remained extremely severe, and the rate at which junior officers were being wounded or killed was very high indeed. Thus, between 26 July and 5 September 1943 the Sixth Grenadier Company had had ten commanders, of whom two were NCOs. Between 6 October and 16 November the company had three commanders, and during 8–9 March 1944 the company had three different commanders, of whom one was an NCO.[48] In September 1943, during its retreat to the Dniepr, the average size of a GD company was twenty men; average, because the Seventh Grenadier Company numbered only five men and was led by a corporal and the Thirteenth Grenadier Company had only eight soldiers left. The whole Second Grenadier Battalion numbered three officers and twenty-two men, and the Third Grenadier Battalion three officers and twenty-nine men.[49] In May 1944 the average strength of most GD battalions was sixty to seventy men, and the replacements sent to the division in June consisted mainly of boys aged 15–16 as well as First World War veterans.[50] By August 1944 most battalions had only one officer left, and during the siege of Memel battalions were reduced to the equivalent strength of weak companies.[51] During the Russian breakthrough to Brandenburg, the Third Grenadier Battalion, for instance, had forty to fifty men left.[52] By the end of March 1945 the 4000 survivors of the GD in Pillau had no vehicles or heavy weapons at all and had to fill their ranks with soldiers of every description found roaming in the peninsula.[53] It was no surprise, therefore, that when the Russians attacked, most of the remaining companies either fled or put down their weapons and surrendered.[54]

The 18th Panzer Division

The 18.Pz.Div. suffered from a particularly severe shortage of manpower, as we can see in Table 1.5. Thus a formation which numbered over 17 000 men, including 400 officers, at the beginning of the war in Russia, was reduced to about 2500–3500 and some 100 officers by summer 1943. In the course of two years of fighting the division lost the equivalent of its initial strength on 22 June 1941 and almost twice as many officers, not including the thousands of sick soldiers who predominated in its casualty lists especially during the first winter (see Table 1.6).[55]

The 18.Pz.Div. had sustained heavy casualties already in the first stages of the war in Russia. By 9 July 1941 the divisional diary noted

TABLE 1.5 *18. Panzer Division – manpower*

	Planned establishment manpower			Actual total manpower			Actual combat manpower		
	Officers	*Other ranks*	*Total*	*Officers*	*Other ranks*	*Total*	*Officers*	*Other ranks*	*Total*
15.3.41				401	14 615	15 016			
22.6.41				400	16 744	17 174*			
25.8.41				340	11 005	11 345			
30.9.41						15 334	293	9323	9616
1.11.41							227	9081	9308
1.1.42							221	8005	8226
25.1.42						10 459			5443
31.1.42									7165
									4775[+]
28.2.42									10 650
									7813[+]
28.3.42									6847
									4850[+]
26.3.43						7547	153	4281	4434
30.4.43				188	6716	6904	124	3782	3906
11.7.43							157	5275	5432
21.7.43							30	1347	1404*
1.8.43							113	3643	3756
11.8.43							107	3322	3429
25.8.43									2409

[+] Actual number of fighting men within combat units.
* Figure includes clerks not counted with officers and other ranks.

TABLE 1.6 *18. Panzer Division – casualties**

	Killed	Wounded	Missing	Sick	Total	Percentage of manpower on 22.6.41	Shortage
22.6.–10.7.41	457	1488	198	136	2279	13·3	
	(46)	(70)		(7)	(123)	(31·0)	
22.6.–27.7.41	755	2221	377		3353	19·5	
	(63)	(76)	(14)		(153)	(38·3)	
28.7.41							3200 (153)+
25.8.–5.9.41	69	224			293		
11.–31.10.41	166	592			758		
	(10)	(21)		(11)	(42)		
31.10.41							1066 (111)
1.11.–5.12.41	107	383	25		515		
					(35)		
22.6.–31.12.41	1009	5834	480		7323	42·6	
	(64)×	(202)	(9)		(275)	(68·8)	
15.2.42							2138 (136)
1.1.–31.3.42	353	1432	40	4962	6787		
	(14)	(33)	(1)	(72)	(120)		
22.6.41–	1362	7266	520	4962	14 110	82·2	
31.3.42	(78)	(235)	(10)	(72)	(395)	(98·8)	
1.7.–31.7.43	466	2040	756	81	3343		
	(40)	(96)	(6)	(3)	(145)		
1.8.–1.9.43	182	792	183	93	1250		
1.9.–1.10.43	215	691	127	148	1181		
4.7.–30.9.43	(55)	(153)	(10)		(218)		
22.6.41–	3277	11 583	2151	?	17 001	99·1	
30.9.43	(195)	(467)	(33)	?	(695)	(173·8)	

* Officer casualties given in brackets; total casualties, percentages and shortages all differentiate between officers and men.
+ Actual number of fighting men within combat units.
× Note that this figure (64) is considerably lower than the addition of earlier figures; it should, however, be taken as more precise because of the greater reliability of its source.
SOURCES for Tables 1.5 and 1.6   BA–MA RH27–18/3, 26, 63, 69, 133, 144, 169, 174, 178, 196, Paul, *18. Pz. Div.,* pp. 14–15.

that 'The troops look exhausted. The high officer casualties are noticeable. Fighting strength is greatly reduced.' There were still eighty-three operational tanks, or 39 per cent of the initial number.[56] On 14 July the supply column of the Panzer Regiment was ambushed and destroyed.[57] By late July the Rifle Brigade of the division, composed of two regiments, was reorganised as a single regiment of two battalions, consisting of no more than 600 men.[58] The Motorcycle Battalion lost the equivalent of three companies (351 men) and most of its group and platoon leaders. Replacements were composed of either inexperienced officers or freshly promoted NCOs, while NCO positions were occupied by privates.[59] At this stage there were only twelve tanks left of the original 212.[60] As early as 11 July the divisional commander warned that these heavy casualties and losses in equipment could not be allowed to continue 'if we do not intend to win ourselves to death [wenn wir uns nicht totsiegen wollen]'.[61]

Although the division had been re-equipped during August, by November 1941 it had already again lost all its tanks, and on the eve of the Russian counter-offensive it had only 50 per cent of its initial combat strength and 25 per cent of its vehicles.[62] The divisional Chaplain wrote in his diary:

> This is no longer the old division. All around are new faces. When one asks after somebody, the same reply is always given: dead or wounded. Most of the rifle company commanders are new, most of the old ones are gone.[63]

When the 18.Pz.Div. was attacked in July 1942, it sustained 1406 casualties within the first four days of fighting alone. The divisional Chaplain wrote in his diary on 9 July: 'This has been going on now for four days, without sleep, mostly without food, with no rest.' On the next day he added:

> The number of the dead is increasing, the number of the wounded is frightful. In my black book there is already one black cross after another, my whole community is either dead or wounded . . . Then last night we carried the dead out of the trenches and from no-man's-land . . . Our cemetery in Bukan has grown tremendously. At first there were only a few graves, now there are already over four hundred, all in a few days. And how many more will die later in the first-aid stations in the rear or be buried in other cemeteries? One regiment has brought its sacrifice. The colonel's face has thinned terribly during these last few days–sleepless nights, turbulent hours . . . He stands silently in front of the long rows of graves: 'There lies my old guard. In reality we should also be there. Then it would all be over.'[64]

Captain Amman, a battalion commander who had received the much-coveted German Cross in Gold was, according to the Chaplain, 'crying and running across the battlefield, looking for his destroyed battalion'.[65]

Following the failure of the Battle of Kursk and the Russian counter-offensive in Orel, the 18.Pz.Div. was virtually destroyed. What manpower replacements it received were either taken from disbanded supply units or were elderly recruits, all very poorly trained.[66] By mid-September 1943 the division was composed of four battalions, each numbering about 130 men.[67] Between 1 July and 30 September 1943 the division lost 1 regiment commander, 10 battalion commanders, 83 company commanders, 85 (officer) platoon leaders and ordinance officers and 15 other officers. Seen according to rank, the division lost 3 majors, 20 captains, 51 lieutenants and 135 second lieutenants. As a percentage of the number of officers in the units on 1 July 1943, this meant that the two infantry regiments lost 105 and 130 per cent, the Reconnaissance Battalion 125 per cent of their officers respectively.[68] We can thus say that the survivors of the 18.Pz.Div. at the time of its disbandment had very little in common with those men who drove across the Russian frontier just over two years earlier.

PHYSICAL HARDSHIP

Marching

The vast spaces of European Russia and the extent of Germany's strategic objectives compelled the army to cover enormous distances. The long weeks and months of forced marches played an important role in wearing out the troops and their equipment. By the time the soldiers reached their distant objectives, they were already weary from endless months of walking. Some of the combat elements of the 12.I.D., for instance, had marched on foot 560 miles (900 km) between 22 June and 28 July 1941, which meant an average of over 15 miles a day, not taking into account distances covered during actual combat.[69] Similarly, between the beginning of the summer offensive on 28 June and 4 July 1942, the GD division had advanced through 186 miles (300 km), and by 14 July it had crossed a further 261 miles (420 km). At this stage most of its vehicles had run out of petrol and the troops were advancing on foot.[70] Less than two years later the men of the GD retreated through hundreds of miles of mud in the face of the Red Army's offensive in the Ukraine in March 1944, marching in a single month all the way from the Dniepr to the Prut river.[71] The 18.Pz.Div. began establishing columns of Russian 'Panje-Wagons' as early as September 1941, and during the retreat of December 1941 the troops had to leave most of their vehicles behind and advance on foot in the ice and snow.[72] From then on, most of the soldiers of this Panzer division had to rely on their own feet for transportation.

Rest and Sleep

The direct result of the heavy casualties sustained by the divisions was that the surviving soldiers had to stand guard more often and for longer hours and consequently had less time for sleep and rest. By August 1942 one of the regiments of the 12.I.D. warned that its defensive system was nearing complete collapse and stressed that 'it must be taken into account that human ability has its limits'.[73] One of the battalion doctors reported that following a 48-hour stretch in the front-line positions, where no rest at all was possible, the troops were allowed 20 hours in the rear trenches, which were at best covered by tent-sheets and consequently were muddy, exposed, and offered no opportunity for drying the men's clothes or changing their boots.[74] In October 1942 the 12.I.D. reported that

> The consistent heavy strain on each individual defender of the front-line caused by the lack of manpower has created a burden which is approaching the limits of endurance.[75]

It was much the same situation among the troops of the other two divisions. During the Battle of Kharkov in early 1943, for instance, we read that the men of the GD Division had

> no rest, always out in the cold and snow . . . The division has been engaged ceaselessly since it was detrained . . . and has had to fight and march without pause, beyond the limits of human ability.[76]

Living Conditions

Even when the men at the front were allowed to rest for a while from the fighting, their accommodation facilities often turned out to be extremely miserable. As early as 28 October 1941 the commander of the II. Corps reported that

> The health of men and horses is deteriorating owing to the wretched housing facilities . . . The dug-outs are collapsing, building materials and work forces are lacking . . . The men have been lying for weeks in the rain and standing in knee-deep mud. It is impossible to change the wet clothing.[77]

In January 1942 the divisional doctor of the 12.I.D. described the same positions as consisting of dark, wet, cold and crowded bunkers. The men could not take off their boots, and heating the bunkers with fires had caused numerous respiratory infections.[78] Similarly, the Quartermaster of the 18.Pz.Div., who seems to have enjoyed better 'housing' than most of the front-line troops, wrote that during the winter of 1941/2

> the condition of the accommodation facilities [was] impossible by German standards. Five, six or even more men lived in each Panje-hut – small, wretched, miserable, bug-ridden and infested with lice, often only with . . . mud floors – while in the adjoining rooms squatted the Russian family with numerous small children and all their livestock.[79]

In February 1942 the commander of the 18.Pz.Div. reported that 'owing to the continuous great demand of guard duty and patrols and, furthermore, as a result of the wretched accommodation facilities, a significant deterioration in the physical and mental resistance power [of the troops] can be observed'.[80] And yet it was clearly better to have any sort of housing than none at all. When that happened, as it did to the men of the 18.Pz.Div. in winter 1941/2, the situation became critical:

> The morale of the troops was low owing to the almost inhuman strain and dropped even further as a result of the complete lack of any accommodation. In spite of the great cold of 42°C below zero, the troops often had to spend day and night in the open.[81]

Clothing

The lack of proper winter clothes greatly added to the suffering of the soldiers. The men of the 12.I.D. were still wearing the same clothes with which they had crossed the frontier when the bitter Russian winter began. The division advised its troops to wrap their bodies with newspapers under their uniforms – but paper was also lacking.[82] The constant freezing and thawing caused boots and gloves to soak up water and then freeze into hard and inflexible lumps of ice.[83] Only Russian felt boots proved to be of any use against the cold, and those could be acquired only by looting the civilian population and the POWs. Indeed, the 12.I.D. specifically ordered its men to 'remove ruthlessly from the civilian population their felt boots',[84] and by late January 1942 the Luftwaffe was complaining that it was no longer possible to distinguish between German soldiers and Russian civilians.[85]

Among the troops of the other two divisions the situation was not much better. In December 1941 the 18.Pz.Div., for instance, instructed its men to protect their bodies from the cold by anything they could lay their hands on, including 'paper, tent sheets . . . straw, hay'.[86] The divisional commander was far from pleased by the appearance of his men who had been compelled to improvise in such a manner:

> The picture that one confronts behind the front is far from gratifying at times. There are soldiers who both by their exterior as well as by their bearing can no longer be distinguished from Panje horses.[87]

Food

The difficulties of supplying the troops at the front with food, caused by the great distances involved and the atrocious roads and extreme weather conditions, further sapped the strength and morale of the soldiers. The commander of the II. Corps, for example, emphasised in October 1941 that the effects of the difficult terrain

> are manifested in the supply of the men and horses . . . Some of the troops have been eating only cold food for many days, as the field kitchens and Panje-wagons could not get through and the number of food carriers did not suffice.[88]

The divisional doctor of the 12.I.D. stressed that there was a lack of meat, potatoes and pulses, as well as of sugar and sweets, necessary against the cold. Furthermore, the food often arrived in the trenches filthy and cold.[89] Whether reports on cannibalism among Russian soldiers also reflected on the situation among the Germans is impossible to say;[90] we do know, however, that during the fighting in the Demyansk Pocket the rations of the 12.I.D. were cut by a third, the main meal of the day consisting of 36 grams of dried vegetables and 60 grams of horse-meat with bones.[91] A German soldier captured by the Russians reported that some men had been tried for eating the oats supplied to the horses.[92]

The 18.Pz.Div. reported on similar difficulties with its food supplies. In February 1942 its rations were cut by a third, and for a time even bread rations, usually set at 600 grams per day and comprising the main component in all meals, were cut down to 300 grams.[93] When the situation improved somewhat towards May 1942, this was achieved in part by cutting down the rations of the men in the rear.[94]

Health

All the factors mentioned above naturally combined together in weakening the troops at the front and increasing their susceptibility to illnesses and epidemics. The commander of the II. Corps did not mince words when he wrote in October 1941: 'I have seen the soldiers and spoken with them. They are hollow-eyed, pale, and many are ill. The incidence of frostbite is high'.[95] The divisional doctor of the 12.I.D. reported that as the troops could not wash or change their clothes they were infested with lice and suffered from frequent skin infections. The severe cold, reaching down to 44°C below zero, caused inflammations of the respiratory organs and the bladder as well as some cases of dysentery; frostbite was very common.[96] The I.R.27 claimed that serious skin irritations, numerous cases of diarrhoea and endless hours of guard duty combined to cause loss of weight and exhaustion to such an extent that some guards had fainted while on duty. There were also cases of kidney inflammations, rheumatism and nervous disorders; most of these complaints could not be treated and the men remained at the front.[97] By summer 1942 there were also some outbreaks of epidemics, particularly Spotted Fever, which was rampant among the civilians.[98]

The 18.Pz.Div. also suffered badly from the cold. By November

1941 it was losing more men as a result of frostbite than from enemy action.[99] By February 1942 there was a general deterioration in health and frequent outbreaks of Spotted Fever were reported, which had infected 221 men by April, of whom 26 had died.[100] This situation lasted till the division was disbanded, as a medical report for September 1943 clearly illustrates:

> The general health of the division reflects the almost ceaseless military action since early July. This is expressed in an increase in skin infections, cases of vermin and frequent cases of digestive and intestine illnesses.[101]

Battle Fatigue

When the great physical and mental strain caused by over-exertion and wretched living conditions was combined with actual combat, an increasing number of soldiers became subject to 'battle fatigue' or 'shell shock', a phenomenon which manifested itself in extreme physical exhaustion together with an almost complete lack of will, nervous disorders and mental instability. In January 1942 the divisional doctor of the 12.I.D. pointed out that the troops had become 'increasingly apathetic'.[102] In April the I.R. 27 stressed that 'The men are greatly over-strained', as a result of which there were increasing cases of 'friction, breakdowns and failures . . . caused by over-fatigue and over-strain of the nerves'.[103] In the GD Division there is at least one known case of an officer who completely broke down. Captain Gruss, 'an addict to strong coffee and a heavy chain-smoker, and therefore extremely nervous', was in such a state that he was dismissed from his post in December 1942, following which, we read, 'nobody wants to have anything to do with him'.[104] In early 1943 the operations officer of the GD reported that 'the fatigue within the division has become so severe that the feeling of indifference is spreading and cannot be opposed by any measures'.[105]

A report of the doctor of the Motorcycle Battalion belonging to the 18.Pz.Div. may serve to illustrate in the most striking manner the effects of prolonged fighting on the troops, following only five weeks of war:

> A complete state of exhaustion is to be observed . . . among all men of the battalion . . . first and foremost as a result of a far too

great mental and nervous strain. The troops have been under a powerful barrage of heavy artillery for six days without pause near Krasny and for four days south of Osarovka. The enemy . . . was repelled in hand-to-hand fighting . . . the men could not shut their eyes day and night . . . Many of the men, still with the troops now, had been burried alive by artillery shells . . . The men are completely indifferent and apathetic, partly suffering from fits of crying, and are not to be cheered up by this or that phrase. Food is being eaten only in disproportionately small quantities.[106]

DISCIPLINE AND MORALE

In this section we shall examine the discipline and morale of the troops. Each of the three divisions will be analysed separately, first according to the available courts-martial records and then by considering other reports found in the divisional files referring to the conduct and morale of the troops during the war. It should also be pointed out here that there are a number of inherent problems concerning the courts-martial records used in this section. First of all, the number of cases actually dealt with did not depend only on the number of the offences, but also on the possibility of bringing the offenders to trial. In periods of heavy fighting this was, of course, very difficult indeed. Second, we must also keep in mind that the definitions of the offences may well have changed depending on the period and location. Thus, for example, looting of boots in France may have been considered to be 'theft', whereas in Russia it would not be thought of as an offence at all; rape in France would be defined as a 'moral offence', whereas in Russia, if considered at all, it might appear as a racial offence, health hazard or even as 'collaboration with partisans'.

The 12th Infantry Division

As we can see in Table 1.7, there was a marked deterioration in discipline among the troops of the 12.I.D. following the Polish campaign. The number of offences increased from seventeen in September 1939 to sixty-three in the November. The most common were absence-without-leave, theft, violations of military regulations and traffic offences, and a large number of the cases had been caused by drunkenness. During the first half of 1940 discipline generally

TABLE 1.7 *12. Infantry Division – courts-martial**

	A	B	C	D	E	F	G	H	I	J	K	L	M	N	O	P
September 1939														17		
October 1939														32		
November 1939														63		
December 1939														48		
1.1.–31.3.1940														58		
1.4.–30.6.1940														48	42	5
1.7.–30.9.1940		3					10			23	9	4	5	54	12	5
1.10.–31.12.1940														91		
1.1.–31.3.1941	1	30			3		8	1	9	75	9			136	25	
1.4.–15.12.1941	3	3	1	4	3	32	8	6	16	101	8		87	272	50	3
16.12.41–28.2.43	3	8	7	26	1	66	9	5	4	173	3		64	369	53	11
1.3.–30.6.1943		3		2		6	3		1	12	2		9	38	5	2
1.9.39–30.6.43														1226	183	26
1.7.41–30.6.43	6	14	8	32	3	103	17	6	20	223	8		120	560	91	16
(1.7.–15.12.1941	3	3	1	4	2	31	5	1	15	38	3		47	153	33	3)

* A–Desertion; B–Absence without Leave; C–Cowardice; D–Self-mutilation; E–Incitement to Disaffection; F–Neglect of Duty while on Guard; G–Insubordination; H–Abuse of Rank; I–Plundering; J–Theft; K–Moral Offences; L–Drunkenness; M–Other Offences; N–Total; O–Over one year's imprisonment; P–Capital Punishment.
SOURCES BA–MA RH26–12/99, 108, 131, 139, 151, 235.

improved, both because of severe and summary punishment and owing to the fact that the division was again stationed in Germany. However, during the French campaign and the occupation of France and the Netherlands there was a marked increase in offences. Plundering and insubordination were added to the most common charges, as well as cases of 'moral offences' which denoted acts of rape and sodomy. The division reacted with vigour: ten men were sentenced to death and at least seventy-nine to more than one year's imprisonment.

During the war in Russia there was some change in the nature of the offences. For the first time we hear of cases of cowardice, self-mutilation and numerous charges of neglect of duty while on guard. The nature of this bitter war dictated to some extent the type of offences committed by the troops. The large number of men charged with neglect of duty while on guard was probably caused by the lack of manpower discussed earlier. The low numbers of deserters, cases of plundering and 'moral offences' do not seem to be credible; that there were many more acts of brutality than is reflected in the courts-martial records will be demonstrated in Chapter 4. The divisional court-martial tried to explain the drop in the number of cases of absence-without-leave as being a result of the conditions in Russia: 'The soldiers have less inclination to remain temporarily among the civilian population. This is also the reason that there have not yet been any cases of moral offences'. The same report admitted, however, that it was almost exclusively concerned with cases of theft by soldiers from the army itself, and not from the population. We can therefore surmise that looting the Russian civilians was not called 'plundering' and not prosecuted, and that raping Russian women was not considered to be a 'moral offence'. We shall have another opportunity to raise the subject of the army's attitude towards the Russian female population in Chapter 4. As for desertions, there was a marked reluctance among commanders to admit this phenomenon, and among the soldiers there was fear of severe punishment and fear of the partisans' and Red Army's treatment of deserters. It should also be noted that large-scale desertions took place much later than the dates for which we have these data.

To sum up the most outstanding figures presented in Table 1.7 we should point out that between 1 July 1941 and 30 June 1943 sixteen men had been sentenced to death and ninety-one received prison terms of over one year. The average number of cases per month between 1 September 1939 and 31 March 1941 was 28·8; the average between 1 July 1941 and 30 June 1943 was lower, 23·3. This, of course, had much to do with the difficulty of bringing the men to trial and also, perhaps, with the reluctance of some commanders to part with their men owing to the growing lack of manpower.[107]

As we have seen, death sentences were not particularly numerous, but on the other hand their execution was given great publicity and served to warn the troops against committing such offences as desertion, cowardice in the face of the enemy, and self-mutilation. Thus, for instance, the 12.I.D. sentenced three soldiers to death in early October 1941 having charged them with desertion.[108] In December 1941 and May 1942 the 16. Army, among whose formations the 12.I.D. was fighting, issued similar reports of death sentences.[109] The division also carried out a death sentence on a soldier charged with shooting himself.[110] A Russian soldier captured by the Germans described in his interrogation how seven German soldiers had tried to desert to the Red Army; four of those men were shot by their own officers while crossing the lines.[111] The division also warned its men that soldiers who had been executed or had committed suicide would not be buried with those men who had been killed in battle and that their graves would be marked differently.[112] A German soldier captured by the Russians said in his interrogation that many of his comrades were afraid of deserting because they had been warned that their families would suffer for their actions. He added that apart from fearing maltreatment by the Russians, they were afraid of being shot by either side while crossing the lines.[113] Death sentences were a permanent and important aspect of enforcing discipline among German troops. In May 1943 the 12.I.D. announced that it had executed another seven soldiers charged with self-mutilation.[114]

Other manifestations of the growing problem of morale owing to the great physical and mental strain of the war were treated by the division with more understanding. The two most common offences, theft and neglect of duty while on guard, were excused by the divisional court-martial as resulting from the long 'periods of serious shortages in supplies of food and tobacco' and the 'thinly held front-line' which caused 'a constant strain of guard duty'.[115] Similarly, the units emphasised the psychological effect of their men's lack of contact with their families. On 1 August 1942, 7701 soldiers of a total of 12 480 in the 12.I.D. (62 per cent) had not been on leave since the invasion of Russia more than a year earlier. Of the remaining 38 per cent, only 8·8 per cent had been on leave, the rest being replacements.[116] One of the regiments pointed out that 'the meagre prospects that even the married men have of going on leave in the foreseeable future could . . . have a detrimental effect' on the men's morale.[117]

Another serious problem with which the division had to cope was that because of the heavy casualties increasing numbers of ill-trained young recruits were being sent to man its units. In early August 1942 the 12.I.D. reported that the replacements it received had been given hardly any training and could not be used in offensive action.[118] Their morale was just as poor; they were said to have 'gained no self-confidence and failed in the attack'.[119] Furthermore:

> recruit replacements since early 1942 had not been acclimatised in their new units by training and could not be gradually introduced to battle experience. The good will they had brought with them had not proved sufficient in overcoming the feeling of isolation on the confused battlefield and the terror of the tanks.[120]

The Grossdeutschland Division

The data collected from the court-martial records of the GD Division and presented in Table 1.8 are, unfortunately, rather incomplete. It should therefore be pointed out that only the sum of the offences can be considered as a relatively reliable figure. Nevertheless, some conclusions can be drawn from this table. The average number of offences per month was 35·7, significantly higher than the 12.I.D. (23·3). This can probably be explained by the fact that the GD was often under a much greater strain at the front and that the combat discipline required from the troops was also probably somewhat stricter. We can also note that theft was the most common offence in the GD too, and that notwithstanding the missing data, we do possess records of seven executions.[121]

Problems of discipline and morale among the troops of the GD seem to have been closely connected with a sense of isolation and a growing need for some sort of rationalisation which would provide reasons for all this bitter fighting so far from home. The divisional chronicle states that in November 1941 the men were already asking themselves whether 'they had been forgotten there, in the supreme leadership or at home'.[122] 'The feeling of having been left in the

TABLE 1.8 *Grossdeutschland Division – courts-martial**

	A	B	C	D	E	F	G	H	I	J	K	L	M	N	O	P
27.6.–18.8.1942		2								19				95	2	1
19.8.–21.8.1942														15		
22.8.–31.10.1942														98		
1.11.–30.11.1942														58		
1.12.–31.12.1942	5													23		6
1.1.–31.1.1943														?		
1.2.–28.2.1943														29		
1.3.–31.3.1943	9													38		
1.4.–30.9.1943	3	10	2	1			7	1	10	27	5		78	144		
27.6.42–30.9.43	17	12	2	2			7	1	10	46	5			500	2	7

* A–Desertion; B–Absence without Leave; C–Cowardice; D–Self-mutilation; E–Incitement to Disaffection; F–Neglect of Duty while on Guard; G–Insubordination; H–Abuse of Rank; I–Plundering; J–Theft; K–Moral Offences; L–Drunkenness; M–Other Offences; N–Total; O–Over one year's imprisonment; P–Capital Punishment.
SOURCES BA–MA RH26–1005/5, 60–1, 75

lurch', it adds, 'paralyses the combat morale of the troops. The resistance strength of the soldiers, thousands of miles away from home in a foreign land, threatens to break.'[123] In December 1941 a young recruit wrote in his diary:

> When will they at last pull us out of the line . . .? What is all this for? . . . When will we ever get back home? . . . With an empty belly almost everyone is suffering from dysentery! We feel weak and as miserable as dogs. Add to this the terrible cold. The frostbite in my feet is growing ever larger and more infected with abscess every day . . . And there are the Bolsheviks! . . . We cannot halt them.[124]

Nevertheless it must be stressed that the GD Division went on fighting till the bitter end, in spite of repeated complaints of this kind. It was only in April 1945 that the division finally broke down. Coming under a heavy Russian artillery barrage, the Sixth Grenadier Company climbed out of its trenches and began walking to the rear. 'My attempts to keep the company together with threats failed', later wrote the battalion commander. 'The men would rather be shot down than stay in their positions.' He never saw the company again.[125]

The 18th Panzer Division

As in the case of the GD Division, the available data on courts-martial in the 18.Pz.Div. presented in Table 1.9 only allow us to point out that theft seems to have figured prominently among the most common offences, as well as neglect of duty while on guard, insubordination and absence-without-leave, probably for similar reasons to those ascribed to the other two formations. The average number of offences per month was thirty-two, slightly lower than among the troops of the GD.[126]

Problems of discipline and morale among the troops of the 18.Pz.Div. seem to have been more serious than in either of the two other divisions. As early as 26 June 1941 the commander of the Panzer Corps in charge of the 18.Pz.Div. noted that there had been 'occurrences of panic' in which 'whole battalions had turned around on their tracks and fled to the rear' and, moreover, 'it was the officers themselves who had given the signal' for the retreat.[127] In mid-August 1941 three soldiers who had fled from their positions were

TABLE 1.9 *18. Panzer Division – courts-martial**

	A	B	C	D	E	F	G	H	I	J	K	L	M	N	O	P
(1.1.–31.3.1941)														285)		
1.1.–31.12.1941		38				18	26			109				426		
1.1.–31.12.1942														459		
1.1.–18.10.1943														194		
1.1.41–18.10.43														1079		

* A–Desertion; B–Absence without Leave; C–Cowardice; D–Self-mutilation; E–Incitement to Disaffection; F–Neglect of Duty while on Guard; G–Insubordination; H–Abuse of Rank; I–Plundering; J–Theft; K–Moral Offences; L–Drunkenness; M–Other Offences; N–Total; O–Over one year's imprisonment; P–Capital Punishment.

SOURCES BA–MA RH27–18/76, 172, 178, 194, 207.

tried by the divisional court-martial; one was sentenced to death, the other two to a ten-year prison term.[128] Men caught asleep in their positions that winter were sentenced to between three and five years' imprisonment.[129] Throughout the winter of 1941/2 there were numerous reports of soldiers who had left their posts and were wandering aimlessly in the rear.[130] The division expressed its concern in its situation reports, as can be seen in the following example, dated 10 December 1941:

> One should not fool oneself . . . concerning the fact that owing to the long time in action and the extended service of the older men this entails, their yearning to return to the homeland and to their professions has greatly increased.[131]

Indeed, by March 1942 the Panzer Corps emphasised that 'The discipline of the troops has deteriorated during the winter' and warned that 'only the most severe punishment can be expected'.[132]

During the Battle of Kursk, one of the battalions of the 18.Pz.Div. left its positions and fled to the rear.[133] From this day, till the disbandment of the division, cases of panic and desertion steadily multiplied, and it is possible that this situation figured quite prominently among the reasons for disbanding the division. This crisis is clearly reflected in an order issued by the divisional commander in July 1943:

> It has happened that companies, on hearing the cry 'enemy tanks', spring on their vehicles . . . and drive away to the rear in wild confusion . . . I expect from every officer, NCO and soldier, who has retained his soldierly honour, to do everything he can to curb such outbreaks of panic . . . I expect officers to make ruthless use of all means at their disposal against men who cause panic or leave their comrades in the lurch and, if necessary, not to refrain from using their weapons.[134]

CONCLUSION

The long years of bitter fighting in the East, the tremendous casualties, physical hardship and mental strain experienced by the troops, all certainly played an important role in brutalising the individual soldier and blunting his sensitivity to moral and ethical issues. The question remains, however, whether we should be satisfied with this explanation for the conduct of the German army in Russia. In order to deal with this problem more fully, we shall first have to examine the nature, extent and possible efficacy of the political indoctrination of the troops, as well as the susceptibility of their junior officers to Nazi ideology. Only then, and after we have sketched the main outlines of the process of barbarisation itself, will we be able to consider the relative weight that the conditions at the front had in brutalising the troops.

Another question, related both to the conduct of the troops at the front and to their ideological convictions, concerns the remarkable resilience and stubborn determination manifested by most of the units we have surveyed. How are we to explain the relative scarcity of evidence regarding breakup and collapse, let alone mutinies, among the troops? One explanation offered by Edward A. Shils and Morris Janowitz sees the main cause for 'the high degree of stability of the German Army in World War II' not in 'the National Socialist convictions of its members', but rather in 'the steady satisfaction of certain *primary* personality demands afforded by the social organisation of the army', that is, the loyalty of the individual to his 'primary group', the men of his unit with whom he was in constant physical touch.[135] There is no doubt that this factor did indeed play an important part in the tenacity shown by German troops. Whether this theory invalidates the ideological component of the soldiers' mental make-up is another question, which will also be dealt with in the following two chapters. Here we would only like to point out some of the inherent weaknesses of the evidence provided by Shils and Janowitz. The authors rely mainly on interviews with German POWs, who may be seen as somewhat biased and often represent an exception to the combat soldiers still fighting at the front; they centre their discussion on the Western Front, which was very different from the Eastern Front, in that the fighting was of a much shorter duration, the ideological concepts underlying it were far less clear and rigid, and the fear of the enemy was of a fundamentally very different calibre from that of the 'Bolsheviks'. Furthermore, this theory does not take into account the tremendous casualties sustained by the formations at the front: it is difficult to speak of a more or less stable 'primary group' in divisions which suffered between 200 and 300 per cent casualties within the space of about three years of fighting. The rate of manpower mobility in units actually involved in fighting, and particularly among the officers and the NCOs who, as the authors rightly point out, were the backbone of the group, was even higher. Thus, although the group loyalty certainly had a part to play in the cohesion and determination of combat units, it does not seem to constitute a sufficient explanation for this phenomenon.

Another way of presenting the psychology of the German soldiers' stubborn resistance at the front is that typical of divisional chronicles, and adopted by quite a number of military historians. Here, too, the ideological component is played down, though more for apologetic reasons. The central theme of this argument is that 'war is hell', a battle is 'a struggle for survival', and that man, any man, necessarily 'becomes an animal' under such conditions. The chronicle of the GD Division provides us with numerous examples of this mixture of romanticism and nihilism, as the following quotes may demonstrate:

> It is something like a battle of knights. Behind us the artillery . . . Above us . . . Stukas . . . It smells of fire, gun-powder, oil and Russians . . . Man becomes an animal. He must destroy in order to live. There is nothing heroic on this battlefield.[136]

> The battle returns here to its most original, animal-like basis; [it] is no assault with Hurra cries over a field of flowers.[137]

> It is only the courage of the desperate, the will to defend and hold on to what has already been conquered, the fear to fall alive in the hands of the enemy, the instinct of survival, that cause the men of the East to make this sacrifice.[138]

> Here too it was fear, an instinct of self-preservation and the threat of a Bolshevist massacre, which often dictated the will to fight to the last bullet . . . combined with the bravery of some and the example set by the commanders . . . Questioning the sense of this bloody conflict becomes impossible on the battlefield, where it is a struggle of life and death.[139]

These arguments cannot easily be dismissed. The soldiers at the front did indeed fight for their own and their comrades' lives; they often did not surrender because they feared the Russians, and they rarely deserted also because they feared punishment at the hands of their own superiors. It is possible that many of them felt that to remain in the trenches and fight on offered them the best chance of surviving. Nevertheless, the question remains as to why the German soldier on the Eastern Front did not break, when so many armies have collapsed in the face of much less unfavourable odds. Put differently, the question is whether it was possible to fight for years on end in a foreign and hostile land, with the imminent danger of death lurking behind every tree and hill and to endure the most terrible physical and mental hardship, without believing that all this was necessary for the achievement of some 'higher cause', however confused and nonsensical, let alone inhuman, it may seem to us today.

Some insight into the sort of reasoning that the soldiers needed at the front, a mixture of nihilism and idealism, pessimism and optimism, cynicism and naïveté, is to be found in the memoirs of a veteran of the GD Division, a Frenchman who volunteered to serve Hitler's Reich and who seems to have felt a touch of nostalgia for those days of glory even while he was writing these pages, many years after the war had finally ended. Here he tells us how his company commander used to instil new energy and determination into the worn-out men. First comes the 'war is hell' explanation: 'You're nothing more than animals on the defensive . . . life is a war, and war is life. Liberty doesn't exist.' Then there is the cynical approach: 'The system in which we more or less believe is every bit as good as the slogans on the other side.' After this comes an appeal to loyalty: 'We must carry out our orders for the sake of our country, our comrades, and our families.' Now, at last, it is time to talk of hope and ideals: 'We are trying . . . to change the face of the world, hoping to revive the ancient virtues buried under the layers of filth bequeathed to us by our forebears.' Then it is again important to stress the danger of losing this war: 'If we should lose tomorrow those of us still alive . . . will be judged without mercy . . . accused of an infinity of murder . . . spared nothing . . . never forgiven for having survived.' Therefore, the ultimate conclusion is that everything is justified if it is a means to achieve victory: 'I would burn and destroy entire villages if by so doing I could prevent even one of us from dying of hunger.' And finally, the company shall win because it is united in spirit and body, in discipline and ideology: 'We shall daily oppose our perfect cohesion to the indiscipline and disorder of our enemies. Our group must be as one, and our thoughts must be identical.'

Were talks of this kind an essential element in maintaining the fighting spirit and morale of the German troops in the East? Guy Sajer, the author of the book quoted above, certainly thought so. He writes that the company commander 'made a deep impression on us. His obvious and passionate sincerity affected even the most hesitant

. . . we loved him and felt we had a true leader, as well as a friend on whom we could count.'[140] Who those enthusiastic junior officers were, what their social and educational background was, and how susceptible they were to National Socialism will be the subject of the next chapter. That there was indeed an intensive effort of political indoctrination among the troops, and that this ideological commitment played an important part in the barbarisation of the troops, will be discussed in the last two chapters of this book.

2 The Officers: Backbone of the Army

INTRODUCTION

This chapter examines the biographies of the officers of the three divisions selected for our study. The junior officers were the backbone of the German army, and served as the connecting link between the high command of the Wehrmacht and the political leadership of the Reich on the one hand, and the rank-and-file on the other. They transmitted the orders of the generals to the troops and at the same time acted as their educators and instructors in both military and ideological matters; they also reported to their superiors on the conduct, reliability and morale of the soldiers. It is therefore of crucial importance to enhance our knowledge regarding this relatively unknown stratum of the military hierarchy.

Following a brief exposition of the sample, the chapter examines the officers by dividing them into a number of categories. It first analyses the aristocratic officers; then it compares regular and reserve officers; finally it investigates the characteristics of those officers who were members of the Nazi party. The chapter then proceeds to consider those men according to their education, social status and rate of promotion. In conclusion, the potential loyalty of the officers to the regime and their willingness to implement its ideological tenets and to carry out its policies are considered in the light of our findings concerning their background.

THE SAMPLE

The German army invaded the Soviet Union with 19 Panzer, 14 motorised and 112 infantry divisions. The total army and Waffen-SS strength in Europe and Africa stood at 208 divisions, or 3 800 000 men, of whom 3 300 000 marched into Russia on 22 June 1941.[1] This was a very different army from the 100 000-man Reichswehr of the Weimar Republic. It is well worth considering that on 1 May 1933 there were only 3858 troop-officers in the Reichswehr, whereas by 1 September 1939 their number had risen to 89 075, reaching a peak of 246 453 officers on 1 September 1943. By that time, however, the professional officer corps had greatly changed its character, and five-sixths of the officers were reservists. Officer casualties were also extremely high, and reached the figure of 203 886 between the beginning of the war and 31 January 1945.[2]

As it is the intention of this chapter to examine the younger generation of combat officers who had not served in the First World War and had spent much of their youth under the National Socialist regime, all three formations selected for our study were composed of either first 'wave' conscripts or young volunteers. All in all, there were twenty-six first 'wave' infantry divisions in the force that invaded the Soviet Union. It should therefore be remembered that the officers of divisions which belonged to later 'waves' of conscription were probably quite different from those described here, since they were mostly older men belonging by and large to the reserve.[3]

By carefully examining all surviving files of these divisions, it was possible to identify a total of 1954 combat and staff officers.[4] This basic list made it possible to find the personal files of 201 officers, most of whom were regulars who had survived the war, as the files of most reserve officers and of those killed before 1945 were destroyed during the last months of the war.[5] The record cards of a further 341 officers were then found in the card-file catalogue of another archive.[6] After eliminating a number of doubtful identifications, it was finally possible to arrive at a sample list of 531 officers. This list was then processed by the Berlin Document Centre, and 155 officers turned out to have been party members, of whom ten had also been members of the SS.[7] All the available data on these 531 officers were then fed into a computer. The results of this data analysis form the basis of the following sections of this chapter.

It may be useful at this point to say a few words about the methodological difficulty which this chapter raises. As the reader may have already noticed, all other three chapters in this book deal with the divisions as a whole, without differentiating between the officers and the rank-and-file. It can therefore be claimed that this chapter does not conform to the general thematic of the book. There is, of course, much to be said for this argument as far as methodology is concerned. One solution to the problem would have been to eliminate this part of our study altogether; this, it seems, would have been methodologically correct, but would at the same time greatly hamper our understanding of the main issue discussed in the book, namely, how was the process of barbarisation brought about and who were the people who carried it out? Another way of overcoming this difficulty was to study a sample of officers and rank-and-file; this, however, was impossible on technical grounds, as even personal files of officers were exceptionally difficult to come by. Finally, it might be suggested that the study cover only the officers discussed in this book; but this too would not have been possible, as the divisional files do not enable one to distinguish between the activities of officers and men at the front, but usually speak of the units as a whole. It thus seemed that the best solution was to include this study as it stands, and make use of it in explaining the main issues discussed in the book. As we have said, the officers formed an extremely important link between the higher authorities of the Reich and the simple soldier. An officer corps which identified with the regime and its *weltanschauung* would ensure that the army would execute the plans of the Führer. It remains to be seen how susceptible these junior officers actually were to National Socialism. If we could show that they were, this would enable us to move on to a discussion of the ideological instruction of the troops, which was carried out by and large by those very officers.

Regarding the question of how representative this sample is, a few further comments should be made here. As we saw in Chapter 1, the three divisions selected for this study fought during most of the war in all major sectors of the Eastern Front, either as infantry, motorised or Panzer formations. Their experience was probably shared by a much larger number of combat divisions in Russia during the war, and their manpower composition was similar to that of other first 'wave' front-line formations. As to the officers of those divisions, there were about 1000 of them in all three formations when they marched into Russia (counting those of the GD Division in spring 1942). It can be estimated that between 2000 and 2500 officers passed through these divisions by the end of the war (or late 1943 for the 18.Pz.Div.). We can therefore say that our sample represents about a quarter of the overall number of officers who had actually served in the selected divisions. As some of the officers calculated as having passed through the divisions were not combat officers, whereas in our sample all were either combat officers or on staffs of combat units, we can say that they represent between a quarter and a third of the overall number of combat officers. Naturally, compared with the tremendous number of officers in the German army during the war, this sample is very small indeed. Regarding the young combat unit commanders of the Eastern Front, however, we may be able to claim that this study could serve us in drawing some more general conclusions.[8]

One last word on the biases that are built into this sample owing to the nature of the archival material. As we have already noted, far more personal files of regular officers who had survived the war are available than of reserve officers killed in the fighting. On the other hand, many of the names on the initial list were taken from casualty reports, a fact which may have biased the sample in the opposite direction. Furthermore, concerning some of the categories examined in the following sections, there was a great deal of missing data, and this will be pointed out in the relevant places.[9] All these qualifications notwithstanding, this analysis is perhaps the only method by which we can achieve a more profound understanding of the type of officer who commanded combat units on the Eastern Front during the Second World War.

DATA ANALYSIS

Aristocratic Officers

In 1860, 65 per cent of the officers in the Prussian army were aristocrats. By 1913 the proportion declined to 30 per cent, and following the First World War and the revolution only 21·7 per cent of the officers were nobles. In von Seeckt's professional 100 000-man Reichswehr there was a marked tendency to increase once more the number of aristocratic officers. By 1932, 23·8 per cent of the officers were nobles, while among the lieutenants the proportion had already reached 27·1 per cent, and as many as 52 per cent of the generals were aristocrats. Figures for the Nazi period and the Second World War are scarce, but the general opinion is that the numbers of aristocratic officers greatly declined owing to the massive and rapid enlargement of the army. By 1944/5 only 19 per cent of the generals were nobles.[10]

This decline in the number of aristocratic officers was also reflected in our three divisions, as can be seen from Table 2.1. It should be noted, however, that there was a distinct difference between the

TABLE 2.1 *Aristocratic officers – numbers*

	% of officers in division	% of nobles in sample
12. Infantry Division	20·3	50·6
Grossdeutschland Division	10·7	27·2
18. Panzer Division	14·6	22·2
Mean	15·2	
Total		100·0

SOURCES   Personal files in BA-Zentralnachweisstelle, Deutsche Dienststelle and Berlin Document Centre.

formations: the 12.I.D., a traditional regular infantry formation, retained a relatively high percentage of nobles; the GD Division, on the other hand, was an elite formation, initially recruiting only volunteers and, as was the case with the 18.Pz.Div., in need of a large number of specialists and technicians to maintain its motorised elements. The number of aristocrats in these two formations was consequently much lower.[11]

If we now break down the aristocratic officers into various age groups (Table 2.2), we find that in spite of the rather small numbers involved, the noble officers were clearly much better represented among the older men. Thus over 34 per cent of the officers born before 1900 were aristocrats; or, put differently, over 40 per cent of all aristocratic officers in the sample were born before 1910, as opposed to just under 24 per cent of the non-aristocratic officers. As will be shown later, this finding corresponded with the better representation of nobles among the senior officers.

TABLE 2.2 *Aristocratic and non-aristocratic officers – numbers in age groups*

	Aristocrats: % of total officers in age group	Aristocrats: % of total nobles in sample	Non-aristocrats: % of total non-nobles in sample
Pre 1900	34·1	18·5	6·4
1900–09	18·8	22·2	17·3
1910–14	9·9	17·3	28·5
1915–19	12·8	23·5	28·9
1920–25	15·0	18·5	18·9
Total		100·0	100·0

SOURCES   Personal files in BA-Zentralnachweisstelle, Deutsche Dienststelle and Berlin Document Centre.

TABLE 2.3 *Aristocratic and non-aristocratic officers – profession*

	Aristocrats: % of total officers in profession	Aristocrats: % of total nobles in sample	Non-aristocrats: % of total non-nobles in sample
Manual workers	5·0	3·5	7·8
Lower middle class	6·2	14·3	25·1
Middle class	0·0	0·0	17·7
Upper middle class	5·7	14·3	27·2
Land owners	35·3	21·4	4·5
Officer families	63·2	42·9	2·9
Students	2·7	3·6	14·8
Total		100·0	100·0

SOURCES Personal files in BA-Zentralnachweisstelle, Deutsche Dienststelle and Berlin Document Centre.

Another important distinction between aristocratic and non-aristocratic officers can be made by examining their social status, in this case according to their own or their fathers' professions. As can be seen in Table 2.3, almost 43 per cent of the nobles were sons of officers, as opposed to under 3 per cent of the non-aristocrats. In other words, although the nobles constitute only 15·3 per cent of the overall number of officers in the sample, they form over 63 per cent of all officers whose fathers too had been commissioned. As to education, we can see that the situation was reversed, and the aristocrats constitute only 2·7 per cent of the total number of officers who had been attending schools or universities when they joined up. Generally speaking, there can be no doubt that whereas the non-aristocratic officers were best represented among the middle classes, as well as among the students who would eventually, we may presume, join the middle classes, the aristocrats predominated in the officer class and among the land-owners. As the numbers involved in this breakdown are rather small, and the professions of just over 65 per cent of the nobles are unknown to us, it would be advisable to consider only the more outstanding conclusions of this analysis as reliable. Thus, taking into account that dividing the middle classes into lower, middle and upper strata leaves room for overlapping categories, we should therefore say that there was about the same number of nobles in each of the three middle-class categories, rather than that none of them belonged to the middle stratum of this category.

Although a further discussion of the officers' social status and of the categories used in this analysis will appear in a later section, one more point should be made here. In 1930, 54 per cent of the officers in the Reichswehr came from officer families, and in 1926 over 84 per cent were registered as having no civilian profession, that is, they were professional soldiers. Compared to the fact that in our sample only 7 per cent of the total number of officers came from officer families and, furthermore, that over 7 per cent came from families of manual workers and 24 per cent from the lower middle class, we can certainly say that the officer corps had been undergoing a significant change as far as its social structure was concerned.[12]

The number of aristocratic officers who were members of the Nazi party was significantly lower than that of their non-aristocratic comrades. Whereas over 31 per cent of the non-aristocrats were party members, only 18·5 per cent of the nobles had joined the NSDAP. Of a total of 155 party members in our sample, over 90 per cent were non-aristocrats. This tendency corresponds, of course, with the fact that such a high proportion of the aristocrats came from officer families where, although there was certainly no love lost for the Weimar Republic, the Nazi upstarts were also far from popular. It is also possible that the fact that the noble officers were generally older made them less susceptible to Nazi influence than the younger generation.

Finally, let us examine the rate of promotion among the aristocratic officers. As we can see in Table 2.4, far fewer nobles

TABLE 2.4 *Aristocratic and non-aristocratic officers – last rank reached*

	Aristocrats: % of total nobles in sample	Non-aristocrats: % of total non-nobles in sample
Second lieutenant	21·0	30·3
Lieutenant	25·9	32·8
Captain	13·6	15·6
Major	16·0	14·2
Lieutenant Colonel	2·5	3·8
Colonel	9·9	2·4
Major general	3·7	0·7
Lieutenant general	7·4	0·2
Total	100·0	100·0

SOURCES   Personal files in BA-Zentralnachweisstelle, Deutsche Dienststelle and Berlin Document Centre.

remained second lieutenants than their non-aristocratic comrades; on the other hand, whereas 7·4 per cent of the former reached the rank of lieutenant general, among the latter the percentage was as low as 0·2. Seen in absolute numbers, this meant that of 450 non-aristocrats in the sample only 3 became major generals and 2 lieutenant generals, as opposed to 3 and 6 respectively of the 81 aristocrats in the sample. These findings, which hold true also for the rank of colonel which was reached even by men who had joined the army after 1933, seem to indicate that not only was there no negative bias against the nobles in the army of the Third Reich, but that in fact, at least as regards promotion, they were doing better than the non-aristoctrats even in a period of mass conscription and bitter fighting.[13]

Regular and Reserve Officers

According to the plans of the OKH, the first 'wave' divisions were to consist of 78 per cent regular and only 22 per cent reserve soldiers. This ratio was never completely achieved, and the heavy casualties during the war reduced the proportion of regular troops even further. By 1 September 1943, for instance, over 83 per cent of the 246 453 officers serving in the army belonged to the reserve.[14] This situation was, of course, also reflected in the three divisions examined in this study, as can be seen in Table 2.5. Whereas the GD Division succeeded in retaining the most favourable ratio between regular and reserve officers, probably owing to the fact that it was an elite formation of volunteers, in the 18.Pz.Div. the ratio was reversed, so that there were in fact more reservists than regulars. This can be partly explained by the fact that as a Panzer formation this division needed a large number of technically trained officers, that is, men

TABLE 2.5 *Reserve officers – numbers*

	Reservists: % of total officers in division
12. Infantry Division	43·1
Grossdeutschland Division	24·3
18. Panzer Division	56·1
Mean	41·2

SOURCES　Personal files in BA-Zentralnachweisstelle, Deutsche Dienststelle and Berlin Document Centre.

who had already received some higher education following their regular service. Generally speaking, we can see that on the one hand there were more reserve officers than had been initially stipulated by the OKH, but, on the other hand, there were fewer than the overall ratio of September 1943, probably because these were combat formations which received a higher proportion of regular officers than other, less-favoured units.

It is well worth pointing out that the average age of both regular and reserve officers was very young indeed. Calculated on the basis of the age which these men would have reached by 1945, we find that both regular and reserve officers would have been about 32·5 years old. If we consider only the junior officers, that is second lieutenants, lieutenants and captains, we find that the vast majority of the officers in our sample were born between 1912 and 1917 or, put differently, that these men were 18 years old between 1930 and 1935. We should thus keep in mind that the commanders of the combat units at the front were still teenagers during the collapse of the Weimar Republic and the Nazi seizure of power, a crucial fact in our understanding of their mentality and background (see Table 2.6).

An important difference between regular and reserve officers was their rate of promotion. In Table 2.7 we compare the promotion of

TABLE 2.6 *Junior officers – average age by 1945*

	Reserve officers	*Regular officers*
12. Infantry Division	32·6	28·9
Grossdeutschland Division	31·3	28·5
18. Panzer Division	31·8	28·4

SOURCES Personal files in BA-Zentralnachweisstelle, Deutsche Dienststelle and Berlin Document Centre.

TABLE 2.7 *Reserve and regular officers – promotion (% of total promotions from first officer rank)*

	Reserve officers	*Regular officers*
Second lieutenant	100·0	100·0
Lieutenant	72·3	41·2
Captain	19·2	21·7
Major	8·5	25·5
Lieutenant colonel	0·0	6·1
Colonel	0·0	5·5

SOURCES Personal files in BA-Zentralnachweisstelle, Deutsche Dienststelle and Berlin Document Centre.

165 regular and 47 reserve second lieutenants who had been promoted at least once. Whereas over 72 per cent of the reservists reached only the rank of lieutenant, and the highest rank reached by them was major, a much higher proportion of the regulars succeeded in achieving the more senior ranks. This goes some way in explaining the faster promotion rate of the aristocratic officers, as most of them were regulars (75·3 per cent), and will also assist us in our discussion of the National Socialist officers in the sample.[15]

National Socialist Officers

One of the most striking findings in our sample is that of a total of 531 officers 155, or 29·2 per cent, were members of the Nazi party. Distributed among the divisions, they constituted 30·2, 25·2 and 34·1 per cent of the officers of the 12.I.D., GD Division and 18.Pz.Div. respectively. The significance of this figure can be understood when it is seen in the more general context of the support rendered to the NSDAP in Germany as a whole. Theodor Geiger has estimated that in 1925 there were in Germany some nine million '*Erwerbstätige*' who belonged to the middle classes.[16] Tim Mason has defined the '*Erwerbstätige*' as 'all persons who performed, part-time or full-time, productive work of any kind, except housework, whether they were employed, self-employed, or the so-called "family assistants" '.[17] Now David Schoenbaum has pointed out that in 1935, 1·5 million party members came from occupations similar to those of most of the officers in our sample, also corresponding to Geiger's middle classes.[18] This is to say that the party members belonging to the middle classes formed some 16 per cent of the total working population of those same social groups. The officers of our sample, belonging as they did by and large to the middle classes, were therefore relatively far better represented among the party members than their civilian counterparts, as over 29 per cent of them were registered Nazis. Keeping in mind the average age of the officers, we should take note of Schoenbaum's remark that 'Compared with the membership of 30 January 1933, the 18–21-year-old group had grown significantly, in all probability a by-product of the enormous growth of the Hitler Youth, which had mushroomed from 108 000 members at the end of 1932 to nearly 3 600 00 at the end of 1934.'[19]

Party membership is, of course, only an indication of the officers' political sympathies. Just as it is quite certain that not all party members were active Nazis, so too it can be argued that some of the officers who did not carry membership cards were in fact enthusiastic supporters of the regime. Nevertheless, the fact that almost a third of the officers were officially Nazis should be kept in mind in later discussions regarding both National Socialist indoctrination and policies.[20]

An important aspect of the biographical background of the National Socialist officers in our sample is their relatively high level of education. Although we have the educational histories of only thirty-seven party members, it is still striking that almost 60 per cent of them had either received the humanistic graduation degree of *Abitur* or had had some university education, as opposed to only 27 per cent among the non-party members (see Table 2.8). These were obviously very different men from the earlier members of the party, as for instance can be seen in Peter Merkl's study of the Abel Sample, according to which only 12·4 per cent had completed their *Abitur* or studied at a university.[21] In fact, they would seem much closer to Helmut Krausnick's list of Einsatzgruppen commanders, of whom almost 35 per cent had a doctoral degree, a fact which also corresponds with the findings of other historians regarding the enormous degree of support in German universities for the Nazis even before they came to power.[22]

The social status of the National Socialist officers was also relatively higher than that of the non-party members, as we can see in Table 2.9. In this case we have information on the professions of 119 party members and 152 non-members (or, in some cases, information

TABLE 2.8 *NS and non-NS officers – educational histories*

	NS officers: % of total in sample	Non-NS officers: % of total in sample
Less than 12 years	0·0	1·3
12 years, unknown degree	5·4	23·8
12 years, no *Abitur*	21·6	25·6
12 years vocational	0·0	11·3
Abitur	24·3	20·6
Over 12 years vocational	13·5	10·6
University	35·2	6·8
Total	100·0	100·0

SOURCES Personal files in BA-Zentralnachweisstelle, Deutsche Dienststelle and Berlin Document Centre.

TABLE 2.9 *NS and non-NS officers – profession*

	NS officers: % of total in sample	Non-NS officers: % of total in sample
Manual workers	6·7	7·9
Lower middle class	16·8	28·6
Middle class	15·1	17·5
Upper middle class	32·8	20·4
Land owners	8·4	4·6
Officer familes	0·8	11·8
Students	19·4	9·2
Total	100·0	100·0

SOURCES   Personal files in BA-Zentralnachweisstelle, Deutsche Dienststelle and Berlin Document Centre.

on their fathers' occupations). The National Socialist officers were much better represented among the upper middle class, the land-owners (unfortunately a rather vague category, as we do not know what sort of farmers they were), and among the students. We can also see once more that it was rare for sons of officers to join the party.

Our findings regarding the educational and social background of the National Socialist officers seem to indicate that these men constituted a social and intellectual elite within the officer corps, excluding the aristocratic officers who predominated in the officer families.[23] Was there also any correspondence between membership of the party and rate of promotion? Before we approach this question, two factors which determined to a large degree the rate of an officer's promotion should be examined. First it is important to point out that almost 66 per cent of the National Socialist officers were reservists, as opposed to just under 28 per cent among non-party members. In fact, party members, though they were a third of the overall number of officers in the sample, constitute a half of the 206 reservists, and only just over 16 per of the 325 regulars.

As to the question of age, as we can see in Table 2.10, reserve National Socialist officers were generally much older than reserve non-party members: whereas almost 61 per cent of the former were born before 1915, just under 35 per cent of the latter belonged to that age group. Among the regular officers, however, the trend is reversed, so that the older the age group, the less party members belong to it. As regards the reserve officers, their ages certainly

TABLE 2.10 *NS and non-NS reserve and regular officers – age groups*

	NS reservists: % of total in sample	Non-NS reservists: % of total in sample	NS regulars: % of total in sample	Non-NS regulars: % of total in sample
Pre 1900	9·8	4·8	7·5	9·2
1900–09	26·5	16·3	11·3	16·9
1910–14	34·3	18·3	24·5	27·6
1915–19	18·6	40·4	26·4	27·2
1920–25	10·8	20·2	30·3	19·1
Total	100·0	100·0	100·0	100·0

SOURCES   Personal files in BA-Zentralnachweisstelle, Deutsche Dienststelle and Berlin Document Centre.

correspond to our earlier findings concerning educational histories. As we saw, almost three-quarters of the party members had either completed their *Abitur* or taken university courses, as opposed to just over a third among the non-party members. This would go some way in explaining their relatively higher age and predominance among the reserve officers. Seen differently it can be argued that those officers who had been to institutions of higher education were either persuaded or compelled to join the party.[24]

A much smaller number of the party members belonged to the regular officer corps, and most of them were very young. Regarding this phenomenon, we should keep in mind that on 1 May 1933 the party rolls were closed to new applications, and were opened once more only in May 1938. Thus those who had joined the party before May 1933 were in all probability already in the reserve when the war broke out, whereas those who joined after 1938 belonged to the youngest age groups. Although even among the younger officers many had not joined the party this can be partially explained by the fact that when the party rolls were finally reopened there was a great deal of opposition within the party machinery to a further dilution of the 'Old Fighters', and consequently measures were undertaken to hinder massive applications to the NSDAP.[25] Furthermore, those who had joined the party later in the war had less of a chance of becoming officers. As we shall see, the best years for receiving commissions and being promoted were the mid-1930s, during which the party rolls were closed. It is also possible that the younger officers, who had come to maturity under the National Socialist regime and spent their early years in the Hitler Youth and the

Arbeitsdienst, felt less of a need to join the army. This does not mean, however, that they did not support the regime, by which they had been indoctrinated during most of their formative years. For many of them, particularly for the less opportunistic among them, it may have seemed unnecessary to show their loyalty to the regime and to Hitler by joining the party. They went directly to the army and executed Hitler's policies as officers sworn to personal loyalty to the Führer.[26]

The typical National Socialist officer can therefore be described as belonging to the reserve, somewhat older and with a relatively higher educational level than his non-party member comrades. Moreover, this officer would have often belonged to the age group born between 1900 and 1919, and particularly that of 1910–14; those were indeed the age groups which joined the party in the greatest numbers in 1933, and consequently had time to complete their regular service and continue their education before they were called again to the army as reserve officers at the outbreak of the war.

Now we can return to the question of promotion of National Socialist officers. Table 2.11 illustrates that even when we break down these officers to reserve and regular, there still seems to have been a slower rate of promotion among party members as opposed to their non-party member comrades. Part of this trend can probably be explained by the age structure of the party members. Whereas the National Socialist reserve officers were older, and therefore stood less of a chance of being promoted than the non-party member reservists, the regular National Socialists were younger than the

TABLE 2.11 *NS and non-NS reserve and regular officers – promotion*

	NS reservists: % of total in sample	Non-NS reservists: % of total in sample	NS regulars: % of total in sample	Non-NS regulars: % of total in sample
S. lieutenant	71·5	65·1	38·5	21·7
Lieutenant	22·2	24·1	35·9	30·0
Captain	6·3	6·0	15·4	16·7
Major	0·0	4·8	7·7	21·6
Lt. colonel	0·0	0·0	2·5	5·0
Colonel	0·0	0·0	0·0	5·0
Total	100·0	100·0	100·0	100·0
(Absolute Nr)	(63)	(83)	(39)	(180)

SOURCES   Personal files in BA-Zentralnachweisstelle, Deutsche Dienststelle and Berlin Document Centre.

average and consequently had less time to rise in the ranks before the war ended. Again we should mention that only a few of the party members belonged to those officers who had been commissioned between 1936 and 1939, the most favourable years for promotion.[27]

Our findings regarding the promotion of National Socialist officers make it clear that there was no positive bias towards party members; that is, if there were some young men who thought that membership of the NSDAP would help them further their military careers, they must have been bitterly disappointed. Indeed, all our explanations for the slow promotion of party members notwithstanding, there still seems to be room for asking whether there was not any negative bias against National Socialist officers within the army. No direct evidence for this could be found in the divisional files. On the contrary, as we shall see in Chapter 3, the divisions encouraged the instruction of National Socialist ideology among the troops by the officers. Furthermore, as Chapter 4 will demonstrate, there was no opposition among the officers to the execution of brutal Nazi policies by the troops. No definite answer can therefore be given to this question. We can nevertheless say that probably at least some of the National Socialist officers joined the party not for opportunistic reasons but rather as an act of ideological commitment.

Education

Studies dealing with the educational requirements for officer aspirants in the German army tend to leave the Second World War out of consideration. It is generally claimed that the statistical data are incomplete and that in any case the war is not typical of the overall trends.[28] Nevertheless, it is precisely this period which interests us here. Much of the discussion will therefore have to rely only on our own sample analysis.

The restricted number of officers in the Reichswehr of the Weimar Republic enabled the army's command to select its officer aspirants with great care. General Hans von Seeckt demanded a school certificate acceptable for entrance into a university from his officers; indeed, by 1926, 92 per cent of the officers came from the so-called '*sozial erwünschte Kreise*', a higher percentage than that achieved by the Imperial Army.[29] The mass recruitment begun in 1935, however, and the heavy casualties during the war, brought about a general lowering of social and educational standards.[30] How were these changes reflected in our sample?

TABLE 2.12 *Officers – education*

	% of total known in sample
Less than 12 years	1·0
12 years, unknown degree	20·3
12 years, no *Abitur*	24·9
12 years vocational	9·1
Abitur	21·3
Over 12 years vocational	11·2
University	12·2
Total	100·0

SOURCES   Personal files in BA-Zentralnachweisstelle, Deutsche Dienststelle and Berlin Document Centre.

Table 2.12 examines the educational histories of 197 officers in our sample. As can immediately be seen, the vast majority of these men had spent at least twelve years in school and over 33 per cent of them received the *Abitur* or continued their studies at a university. Compared to the Imperial Army of 1912, in which over 65 per cent of the officers were '*Abiturienten*', and, of course, to the Reichswehr where over 90 per cent had received the *Abitur*,[31] this is certainly not a very impressive figure. The enlistment of police officers, retired regular and reserve officers and NCOs of the Imperial Army, as well as Austrian officers, is thought to have reduced the number of '*Abiturienten*' to 50 per cent by 1939, and even lower during the war.[32] The effects of this process on the officers in our sample are illustrated more clearly in Table 2.13, which analyses the changes in

TABLE 2.13 *Officers – education (% of total known in each age group by educational history)*

	Pre-1900	1900–9	1910–14	1915–19	1920–5
Less than 12 years	0·0	0·0	3·5	0·0	0·0
12 years, unknown degree	0·0	19·3	21·1	24·6	15·6
12 years, no *Abitur*	0·0	32·3	19·2	29·8	21·7
12 years vocational	0·0	12·9	10·5	5·3	9·8
Abitur	100·0	9·7	12·3	17·5	41·2
Over 12 years vocational	0·0	16·1	12·3	14·0	3·9
University	0·0	9·7	21·1	8·8	7·8
Total	100·0	100·0	100·0	100·0	100·0
(Absolute numbers)	(1)	(31)	(57)	(57)	(51)

SOURCES   Personal files in BA-Zentralnachweisstelle, Deutsche Dienststelle and Berlin Document Centre.

the educational level of the officers according to their age groups. Here we find that whereas among those conscripted in the 1930s the number of 'Abiturienten' is low and the number of officers with vocational training is high, among the youngest age group the situation is reversed, and the number of Abitur holders is exceptionally high. This trend confirms what we have said earlier; that is, during the mid and late 1930s the massive enlargement of the officer corps compelled the army to lower its educational standards and commission officers who would have otherwise not been taken. By the late 1930s this manpower reserve had been exhausted, and at the same time a new generation of young school graduates could be enlisted.[33] If there was a growing tendency to commission ordinary soldiers and NCOs without any regard for their social and educational background, as Hitler intended during the war, this does not seem to be reflected in our sample. One of the reasons is in all probability to be found in the reluctance of commanders to pursue this policy; as we saw in Chapter 1, unit commanders preferred to suffer from a lack of officers and to have their places filled by NCOs, than to actually commission those NCOs themselves. Another reason would be that those NCOs who had been commissioned may well have been older and therefore will appear in the sample as belonging to the older age groups. We should also point out that if there was any significant change during the last stage of the war, it would probably not be reflected in our sample, as figures become rather sketchy for 1944/5.

One more interesting question may be raised concerning the educational standards of the army during the war, namely, how were they influenced by the recruitment of increasing numbers of reserve officers? As we can see from Table 2.14, and contrary to what is commonly thought, almost 80 per cent of the reservists had either received the Abitur or had had some university education, as opposed to only 26·5 per cent of the regulars. As we have already seen, many of these young reserve officers were also party members. Thus we can say that the recruitment of reserve officers during the war in fact pushed the educational standards upwards in spite of the fact that there was indeed a general decline of educational qualifications.

Regarding both the social context and the character of education in Germany during the 1930s, two general and essential points should be made here. It must first of all be emphasised that notwithstanding the decline in the educational level of the officers, these men still constituted the crème de la crème of their society at the time, as the following figures may serve to illustrate. In 1931/2 there were 11

TABLE 2.14 *Reserve and regular officers – education (% of total known in sample by educational history)*

	Reserve officers	Regular officers
Less than 12 years	0·0	1·2
12 years, unknown degree	9·7	22·4
12 years, no *Abitur*	9·7	27·7
12 years vocational	3·2	10·2
Abitur	29·0	19·9
Over 12 years vocational	6·5	12·0
University	41·9	6·6
Total	100·0	100·0
(Absolute numbers)	(31)	(166)

SOURCES   Personal files in BA-Zentralnachweisstelle, Deutsche Dienststelle and Berlin Document Centre.

pupils per 100 inhabitants in Germany studying in elementary schools (*Volksschule*); 0·4 and 1·2 pupils per 100 inhabitants were studying in the two different types of secondary schools, *Mittelschule* and *Höhere Schule* respectively. Of a population of over 66 million, only 71 850 students took part in the Winter Semester of 1936 in either universities or other institutions of higher education, and by the Summer Semester of 1939 the number had dropped further to 56 477.[34] Thus we may say that the officers still represented a minority, as relatively well-educated young men.

As to the content of the education these officers had received prior to their military service, it should be kept in mind that as early as November 1934 there were already close to six million children and youths enrolled in the Hitler Youth (HJ), and by December 1936 the 'Law of the *Hitlerjugend*' made membership in this organisation compulsory, and defined its goal as the education of German youth 'physically, spiritually and morally in the spirit of National Socialism'.[35] Similarly, the '*Reichsarbeitsdienstgesetz*' (RAD), which came into effect on 26 June 1935, ordered all German youths to take part in this 'service of honour to the German Volk' which would educate them 'in the spirit of National Socialism'. The RAD was to be carried out for half a year between the ages of 18 and 25, while the HJ enrolled children and youths between the ages of 10 and 18.[36]

Soon after the Nazi seizure of power, German youth was subjected to a large-scale process of political indoctrination. All those born after 1910 were liable to do service in the HJ and the RAD and, indeed, most of the officers in our sample belonged to those age groups. Furthermore, the population at large was confronted with an intensive attempt by the regime to 'co-ordinate' it into supporting National Socialism and its so-called *Weltanschauung*. All the means at the disposal of the Nazis were directed towards this goal; only few, often older, people, or those who still had access to information from outside, could withstand this ceaseless barrage of propaganda and indoctrination. For ten years the emotional and ideological character of a whole generation of young Germans was moulded by the propaganda machine of Goebbels and his numerous collaborators in the media, the arts and the professions, by the politicians at local, regional and national level, and, not least, by the army.[37] It was this generation which supplied the cannon-fodder for the Eastern Front, and it was the better educated and indoctrinated among them who led their troops into battle as junior combat officers.

Profession – Social Class

Several attempts have been made to divide German society into various classes according to professions. Theodor Geiger had shown that in 1925, of a total of 35 853 730 gainfully employed persons, 0·8 per cent were 'capitalists', 24·4 per cent belonged to the 'middle class' and 74·8 per cent came from the proletariat. He then proceeded to sub-divide these categories by making finer distinctions, between 'capitalists', 'medium and small employers', 'self-employed workers', 'skilled workers' and 'semi-skilled workers'.[38] More recently, Volker Berghahn has demonstrated that in 1933, 28·9 per cent of the population were employed in agriculture, 40·4 in industry and handicraft and another 18·5 in commerce and banking. He too then provides us with a more elaborate categorisation into six groups – 'civil servants', 'salaried employees', 'professionals', 'farmers', 'self-employed' and 'workers'.[39]

In this study it was not possible to use a highly sophisticated system of classification. Of the 531 officers in the sample we know the professions of 271 men or their fathers.[40] There were altogether 124 professions recorded in the files, and we have classified them in the following manner: 'manual workers' – all those who probably worked with their hands and did not own their place of work; 'lower middle class' – those who worked with their hands but owned a small business, as well as very junior civil servants; 'middle class' – civil servants of the higher echelons, technicians, teachers, police officers

TABLE 2.15 *Officers – social class*

	% of total known in sample (own or father's profession)
Manual workers	7·4
Lower middle class	24·1
Middle class	15·7
Upper middle class	25·8
Land owners	6·3
Officer families	7·0
Students	13·7
Total	100·0
(Absolute number)	(271)

SOURCES   Personal files in BA-Zentralnachweisstelle, Deutsche Dienststelle and Berlin Document Centre.

and so forth, that is wage-earners with 'respectable' occupations who did not receive exceptionally high salaries; 'upper middle class' – the highest-ranking civil servants, as well as men with academic titles, employers in large businesses and church men; 'agriculture' – owners of all types of agricultural property, ranging from small farms to large estates, as the documents do not allow further distinctions; 'officer' – those whose father was an officer; 'student' – those who were still studying either in a secondary school or at a university when they were drafted to the army.

Examining Table 2.15 it is immediately clear that the great majority of the officers in our sample came from the middle classes. Owing to the small numbers involved and the difficulties in precise distinctions, it would be safer to group some categories together, so that we can say that almost 40 per cent belonged to the 'lower middle class' and 'middle class', whereas 41·5 per cent came from the 'middle class' and 'upper middle class'; the middle classes as a whole formed 65·6 per cent of the sample.[41] A comparison with the Reichswehr of the Weimar Republic indicates that there were indeed some major changes in the social origins of the officers. In 1930 over 54 per cent of the officers came from officer families, whereas in our sample only 7 per cent belonged to that category.[12] Similarly, while in the sample 7·4 per cent were 'manual workers', that is, came from working-class families, in 1930 only 4·8 per cent of the officers were registered as lower-ranking civil servants, and workers were not even mentioned.[43] Nevertheless, it must be emphasised that most of the officers in the sample stemmed from those social strata which

TABLE 2.16 *Officers – social class (% of total known in each age group by own or father's profession)*

	Pre-1900	1900–09	1910–14	1915–19	1920–25
Manual workers	0·0	3·3	16·2	4·8	5·2
Lower middle class	13·3	24·6	21·6	28·6	24·2
Middle class	26·7	14·8	14·9	17·5	13·8
Upper middle class	46·7	37·7	23·0	19·0	19·0
Land owners	13·3	9·8	4·1	6·3	3·4
Officer families	0·0	8·2	6·8	4·8	10·3
Students	0·0	1·6	13·4	19·0	24·1
Total	100·0	100·0	100·0	100·0	100·0
(Absolute numbers)	(58)	(63)	(74)	(61)	(15)

SOURCES   Personal files in BA-Zentralnachweisstelle, Deutsche Dienststelle and Berlin Document Centre.

constituted not more than a quarter of the total population of Germany. If we add to this what we have already seen regarding the officers' educational histories, we can say that notwithstanding a marked decline in the elitist status of the officers during the Third Reich, they still came mainly from the higher echelons of German society.[44]

If we now proceed to break down the data into various age groups (Table 2.16), we can observe more closely the changes in the social qualifications of the officers during this period. Thus it is quite striking that among those officers who belonged to the 1910–14 age group, over 16 per cent came from a working-class background, three times as many as in any other age group. This was probably a result of the large-scale commissioning of NCOs during the 1930s caused by the enormous and rapid enlargement of the army. By the late 1930s this process was halted, both because the reserve of NCOs had exhaused itself to such a degree that the army expressed its profound worry regarding the weakening of this important element of its structure, and because there was always much reluctance in the officer corps to promote NCOs from the ranks.[45] By that time it had become possible to conscript a younger generation of officer aspirants, though it was still necessary to lower the social qualifications, as can be seen from the consistent drop in the number of officers from the upper middle class and the landed gentry (or farmers), as well as the growing number of men from the lower middle class (particularly in the age group of 1915–19). We can also see the larger number of school-leavers, an indication of the growing

TABLE 2.17 *Officers – social class and promotion*

	Time gap between enlistment and commission (in years)
Manual workers	8·42
Lower middle class	4·67
Middle class	2·96
Upper middle class	2·48
Land owners	5·33
Officer families	2·84
Students	3·57

SOURCES   Personal files in BA-Zentralnachweisstelle, Deutsche Dienststelle and Berlin Document Centre.

number of reserve officers. As to the sudden rise in the number of men from officer families among the youngest age group, this may be connected both with the reluctance of the army to give way on this issue of selecting its officers from its own traditional social strata, and with the fact that whereas the age group of 1915–19 suffered heavily from the war and was consequently much smaller, during the 1920s there was a rise in the number of children, many of whom were born to the officers of the First World War.[46]

There can be little doubt that there was a direct connection between promotion and social status, as can be seen quite clearly in Table 2.17. It was the men who had joined the army as officer aspirants, that is, those who belonged to the higher echelons of the middle class as well as to the officer families, who maintained the fastest rate of promotion, as opposed to those who 'came up from the ranks'. The students, on the other hand, were promoted relatively slowly because many of them belonged to the reserve. The slow promotion of officers from an agricultural background, notwithstanding the difficulty of defining this category and the small numbers involved, probably had to do with the fact that those were older officers who had joined the army when promotion was generally much slower, either during the Weimar Republic or the Second Reich. The very slow promotion of officers from the working class is obviously a result of their being former NCOs who had spent many years in that capacity in the 100 000-man army and were then commissioned during the mid-1930s.

Promotion

Promotion of officers during the 1930s and the Second World War

TABLE 2.18 *Officers – promotion (% in each rank by date of commission)*

	Before 1935	1935–39	1940	1941	1942	1943 and after
S. lieutenant	0·0	10·7	16·1	40·0	71·1	86·2
Lieutenant	0·0	9·3	42·8	48·0	27·1	13·8
Captain	0·0	24·0	30·4	10·7	1·8	0·0
Major	18·8	50·7	7·1	1·3	0·0	0·0
Lt. colonel	37·5	4·0	1·8	0·0	0·0	0·0
Colonel	43·7	1·3	1·8	0·0	0·0	0·0
Total	100·0	100·0	100·0	100·0	100·0	100·0
(Absolute Nr)	(16)	(75)	(56)	(75)	(114)	(29)

SOURCES   Personal files in BA-Zentralnachweisstelle, Deutsche Dienststelle and Berlin Document Centre.

was greatly accelerated. In 1942 the army calculated the rate of promotion of officers as follows: to lieutenant–3 years and 6 months; to captain–6 years and 2 months; to major–12 years and 1 month; to lieutenant colonel–19 years and 1 month; and to colonel–26 years. Compared with the First World War, officers were being promoted to those ranks listed above three, ten, eleven and six years earlier respectively. Lacking sufficient data, we may only assume that promotion was further speeded up during 1942–5.[47]

Turning now to our sample, we can clearly see (Table 2.18) that among these combat officers promotion was even faster than the rate calculated by the army in 1942. In fact, over half of the men who had been commissioned between 1935 and 1939 reached the rank of major within ten years at the most. Moreover, many of them must have taken much less than ten years, both because our records for 1944/5 are scarce and since many of them must have been commissioned after 1935. Thus those men who received their first officer rank during the mid and late 1930s doubtlessly had the best chance of promotion during the war. Nevertheless, even those commissioned in 1940 still had a fair chance of reaching the middle ranks, and as late as 1942 over a quarter of the men commissioned in that year were promoted at least once. Here again, lack of documentation for the last stages of the war may obscure an even faster rate of promotion.

What is the significance of our findings on the rapid promotion of officers regarding the more general questions raised in this study? It is first of all quite clear that a large number of officers in positions of some authority at the front were very young men. This means that the middle ranks of combat units on the Eastern Front, the officers who commanded companies, battalions and regiments, had joined the army after the great build-up of 1935 had already begun. It can thus be argued that these officers had only a very vague notion of the character and tradition of the old officer corps; they had spent the first years of their careers establishing an army of millions from the miniature Reichswehr of the Weimar Republic, and even before the job had been completed they found themselves in the midst of the war. Table 2.19 illustrates how young these officers really were. Over 94 per cent of the lieutenants were either 23 years old or younger when Hitler came to power, and of those over 32 per cent were 13 or even younger. Over 43 per cent of the captains and over 31 per cent of the majors of 1945 were only 18 years old or younger in 1933; over three-quarters of the men holding these ranks had not been older than 23 during the Nazi seizure of power. Even among the lieutenant colonels we find that most of them had been born after the turn of the century. It is the youth of the officers of the Third Reich which we must bear in mind when we discuss their potential susceptibility to the National Socialist ideology whose goals they were serving.

CONCLUSION

What is the significance of our findings in this analysis of a sample of junior officers with regard to the combat officers on the Eastern Front in general and the potential sympathy of those men to the Nazi regime, its *Weltanschauung* and its policies in Russia? Let us recapitulate the most important aspects of each of the six categories

TABLE 2.19 *Officers – age in 1945 (% in each age group by last known rank)*

	Lieutenant	Captain	Major	Lt colonel	Colonel
20–25	32·4	8·6	0·0	0·0	0·0
26–30	37·2	34·6	31·3	6·3	0·0
31–35	24·5	36·2	40·6	31·3	14·3
36–45	4·9	17·2	20·3	56·2	64·3
over 45	1·0	3·4	7·8	6·2	21·4
Total	100·0	100·0	100·0	100·0	100·0
(Absolute Nr)	(102)	(58)	(64)	(16)	(14)

SOURCES   Personal files in BA-Zentralnachweisstelle, Deutsche Dienststelle and Berlin Document Centre.

examined in this chapter, and at the same time see to what extent they assist us in answering the more general question posed above.

The number of aristocratic officers in the sample was relatively low, and they constituted about 15 per cent of the total. This corresponds more or less with what is known about the officer corps of the Third Reich on the whole, particularly if we take into account that these were combat formations which traditionally attracted more nobles than the less-prestigious service units. Moreover, a high proportion of the aristocrats were older, high-ranking officers, who stemmed mostly from officer families, the landed gentry and, to a much lesser extent, the middle classes. Educationally these men were below the average in the sample. All these findings correspond exceptionally well with the fact that only a very low percentage of the nobles were members of the Nazi party. It was the old aristocracy, the landed gentry, the officer families who showed less enthusiasm for the National Socialism than the broad mass of the disillusioned and partly impoverished middle classes. It was more a feeling of cold contempt which kept the older noble officers aloof from the Nazi upstarts, rather than any desire to protect the Republic. In fact, they did indeed collaborate with Hitler's regime and greatly assisted it in carrying out its barbarous plans. But they were not enthusiastic supporters of the Nazi *Weltanschauung*, if indeed they even took the time to contemplate its implications. Paradoxically, it was these representatives of so-called 'Prussian militarism' who had not been completely swept off their feet by the 'Brown Revolution', just as it was probably also the case among large sectors of the German working class. Thus it was these two classes which, potentially at least, opposed the Republic, from which the Nazis too could expect the least support, whereas the middle classes, which should have been the mainstay of Weimar, turned out to be enthusiastic followers of the Führer. Among the officer corps, and as is well reflected in our sample, both the aristocracy and the working class were weakly represented, the former because of the tremendous growth of the army and their diminishing numbers, the latter because, Nazi rhetoric notwithstanding, they still did not conform to the desirable social and educational criteria.[48]

On the other extreme we saw that almost a third of the officers in the sample were members of the Nazi party. Moreover, these officers belonged to the elite both of the officer corps and of German society as a whole. Almost three-fifths of the party members had either taken their *Abitur* or had been to a university, and a similarly high proportion of them belonged to the upper middle class. Only a few of the National Socialist officers came from the working class or from the officer families. Thus we could say that these men were indeed representative of the social groups which supported Hitler's regime and, furthermore, that their numbers among the officers of the sample were proportionately much higher than in the equivalent social strata in Germany as a whole. We should therefore keep in mind that contrary to the claims of former German generals, as well as some military historians, a high proportion of the German officers who commanded combat units at the front were, at least officially, committed to the Nazi party. The fact that, as we saw, their promotion was not faster than the usual rate can probably be related to the large number of reserve officers among them. It does indicate, however, that young officer aspirants could not expect to derive any career benefits from joining the NSDAP, and may well have decided to support Hitler's movement for ideological reasons.

The number of reserve officers indeed rose above that stipulated by the army command before the war, but on average it remained about 40 per cent of the total. Moreover, as far as age was concerned, there was no great difference between the regulars and the reservists, and both were very young. While regulars up to the rank of captain were on average less than 29 years old by the end of the war, the reservists were just over 31 years of age in 1945. The youth of these men is a further indication of their potential susceptibility to supporting the regime, particularly if we remember the enormous growth in the number of young followers of the party after the Nazi seizure of power.

As we saw, education too played an important role in bringing young people to the side of the Nazis. Indeed, though the educational level of the officers had certainly declined, the great majority of the officers in the sample had spent at least twelve years in school and a third of them had either received the *Abitur* or continued their studies at a university. Moreover, it was the recruitment of growing numbers of reserve officers, who were also very often party members, which raised the educational level of the mid-1930s. Thus we see that the general trend greatly favoured the Nazis: more and more young people, 'co-ordinated' and indoctrinated in educational institutions, were joining the junior officer corps and rapidly changing the character of the backbone of the German army along the lines preached by Himmler's Waffen-SS. The Prussian professionl officers were being replaced by the National Socialist political *Kämpfer*.

To age and education we should add our findings regarding the social background of the officers in the sample as a whole. The great majority of these men belonged to the middle classes, and compared with the Reichswehr of the Weimar Republic we can note a significant decline in the number of officers from officer families and from the landed gentry, together with a rise in the proportion of officers who stemmed from the lower middle class and even the working class. This lowering of the social qualifications should not prevent us from maintaining that the officers of the Third Reich were nevertheless representative of the upper strata of German society. This was probably because in a relatively modern army officers had to have the educational and technical qualifications which, by and large, only the middle classes could achieve. It is also possible that there was still a built-in bias within the military against the advancement of men from the ranks and, what often meant the same thing, from the lower classes. The most important aspect of this finding is, however, that again we see a marked correspondence between the social strata which supported Hitler's regime and those which provided the officers for his conquest of Europe. Those who brought the Führer to power or helped him to maintain his rule were also leading his armies to battle.

Not only did the junior officers belong to those very age groups and social strata particularly susceptible to National Socialist influence; owing to the rapid rate of promotion during the late 1930s and the Second World War, these young men achieved important command positions at the front and carried the responsibility for the military, as well as the criminal activities of companies, battalions and even regiments. These men, the backbone of the army, had grown up under the impact of the Great Depression and the social and political crisis which destroyed the Weimar Republic and brought the Nazis to power. They had come of age under Hitler's rule and absorbed the ceaseless propaganda and indoctrination of his regime in school, at the university, from the media and in the various youth and labour organisations. These young officers spent the most formative period of their lives under National Socialism, and those years must have left a lasting impression on their mentality. They maintained only a very loose connection with the traditional officer corps of old, and they can be viewed as potential supporters of the regime, as indeed a third of them indicated by officially joining the party. As we shall see in the following chapter, it was of supreme importance both to the regime and to the army that these men sympathise with the ideology and the policies of Hitler's Germany; for they were not only charged with implementing the military aspects of these policies, but also with instructing and educating the troops in the spirit of National Socialism, in their capacity as the newly created officers of the Third Reich and the executioners of its *Weltanschauung*.[49]

3 Indoctrination and the Need for a Cause

INTRODUCTION

The war against the Soviet Union was described by the leaders of the Third Reich as a '*Weltanschauungskrieg*', that is, a war of ideologies. In seeking the causes for the barbarisation of German troops on the Eastern Front it is therefore essential to examine the role played by political indoctrination among the combat elements of the army during the war. To what extent did National Socialist ideology motivate the individual soldier both in fighting the Red Army and in carrying out acts of brutality against POWs, partisans and civilians? Was there an essential difference between the war in the East and other fronts or other wars? In short, was this also an ideological, almost religious war from the point of view of the individuals at the front, and can this be seen as one of the major factors contributing to its ferocity and brutality?

These are very difficult issues indeed, and it would perhaps be impossible to end such a discussion with any definitive answers. Nevertheless, it seems that an attempt must be made to examine and analyse the numerous documents at our disposal relating to questions of ideology. It could be claimed, of course, that ultimately it is impossible to discover what was really motivating the soldiers, what was 'going on' in their minds, or how much attention they actually paid to ideological reasoning. In this chapter, however, we shall try to approach this issue in a somewhat more indirect fashion. First, we will examine the various forms of indoctrination and the intensity of these activities among the troops. Having established to the best of our ability how much indoctrination there actually was, we shall take a closer look at the content of the ideology as it was propagated among the soldiers, and point out the changes in emphasis and direction throughout the war. From here we shall move to the more problematic issue of the efficacy of this indoctrination or, put differently, to the possible impact of the ideology on the behaviour and conduct of the troops. We shall first examine those factors which may have enhanced the potential receptivity of the soldiers to National Socialist indoctrination; following that, we will present and anlyse the various indications found in the divisional files regarding the influence of the ideological instruction on the troops and the manner in which it was received by them.

By way of conclusion, some of the problems associated with identifying, gauging or 'measuring' belief will be discussed, and the problem of the relationship between ideology and action will be raised. Although it is probably impossible to reach a completely satisfactory conclusion to this problem, we shall attempt to show that such a relationship did exist and, by making use both of studies not directly connected with Nazi Germany and of further evidence from that period, we shall argue that, by and large, the German soldier on the Eastern Front felt that he was fighting for the cause of National Socialism and was motivated by an unquestioning belief in Hitler.

FORMS AND INTENSITY OF IDEOLOGICAL INSTRUCTION

Radio and Film

The Nazis were among the first political organisations to recognise the immense potential advantages which could be derived from the usage of radio receivers as a means for transmitting political propaganda. The army followed suit and made great efforts to provide its troops with large numbers of receivers. As can be seen from the divisional files, the radio was a popular means of entertainment, and thereby also played an important role in the indoctrination of the soldiers.[1] Thus, for instance, whereas in late 1939 the 12.I.D. still complained of a lack of twenty radio receivers, by January 1940 it could report that all companies and staffs were supplied with radios.[2] As the division penetrated deeper and deeper into the Soviet Union, its troops enjoyed the services of a 'radio-van' with a particularly powerful receiver which circulated among the units.[3] The GD Division was also given a large number of radios when it was established in spring 1942,[4] and the 18.Pz.Div. reported on the eve of the invasion of Russia that it had at least 134 receivers and that all its men could listen to radio broadcasts. By mid-1942 the number of radios in this formation was further increased.[5]

Numerous reports in the divisional files testify to the great popularity of films among the troops. This was recognised by the divisional commands very early on and used both as a means of entertainment and relaxation and as a further direct and indirect instrument of indoctrination.[6] When the 12.I.D. returned from Poland, its troops began regular visits to the cinema, both in their barracks and in civilian theatres.[7] During the occupation of France and the Netherlands the soldiers were also supplied with a 'film-van' which enabled each company to watch a film at least once a week, apart from visiting local cinemas.[8] Even in Soviet Russia, after the great summer advance came to a halt, similar 'film-vans' began circulating among the units.[9] In April 1943, for example, some 6800 men watched twenty-eight films, and the division pointed out that this was the most popular after-duty activity among the troops.[10] Similarly, the GD Division reported that in May 1943 alone, the divisional 'film-van' screened up to two daily shows while travelling among the various units.[11] The 18.Piz.Div., which took great care to supply its men with film entertainment while still training near Prague, adopted in Russia a policy of taking over local schools and turning them into cinemas, as well as making extensive use of its 'film-van' which, to quote but one example, screened two films a day to an estimated number of 1600 men during August 1943 alone.[12] We can therefore conclude that as far as the intensity and quantity of radio and film entertainment and propaganda were concerned, there is no doubt that even at the front the troops were as amply supplied with them as possible under the circumstances.

Written Propaganda

Newspapers, military news-sheets and various leaflets constituted a much more direct means of indoctrinating the troops, as they were often the only source of information for the soldier at the front. The impact of the ideologically oriented facts they provided can therefore hardly be overestimated.[13] The divisions were well aware both of the indoctrinational value of this sort of propaganda and of the great demand among the troops for news, and they consequently made a concerted effort to supply their units with large amounts of printed material. Thus the 12.I.D. was already fully supplied with daily newspapers in November 1939, and by January 1940 its troops were provided with at least two more military information-sheets.[14]

During the occupation of the Vendée, the division received a regular supply of German civilian newspapers, some 4000–5000 copies of each issue of the field-newspaper of the 4. Army, and transcripts of the official Wehrmacht Communiqué.[15] When the division was transferred to the command of the 6. Army it received daily some 2500–3000 copies of its field-newspaper *'Die Westfront'*.[16] During the occupation of the Netherlands the intelligence officer of the 12.I.D. reported that the supply of newspapers was 'more than sufficient'.[17] It should also be added that as of May 1940 every German division received some 180 copies of the bi-weekly news-sheet issued by the Propaganda Section of OKW entitled *'Mitteilungen für die Truppe'* (Information for the Troops).[18] At the same time, the officers were provided with another news-sheet, *'Nachrichten des Oberkommando der Wehrmacht'* (News from OKW), considered to be particularly popular.[19] There were also numerous other information-sheets issued by various commands in the occupation zones.[20] During the advance into the Soviet Union, the 12.I.D. provided its men with a daily information-sheet, as well as the field-newspaper of the 16. Army. When the advance came to a halt each company received some ten copies of the field-newspaper as well as copies of civilian papers, and as of spring 1942 the companies received as many as twenty copies of field-newspapers as well as a divisional news-sheet with excerpts from the Wehrmacht Communiqué.[21] Following the retreat from Demyansk the situation further improved, and the troops received a daily supply of some 2000 copies of the field-newspaper, 300 copies of the so-called 'German Newspapers of the East' (another compilation of news) and 800 divisional news-sheets every other day.[22] Throughout this period the men received a regular supply of the above-mentioned *'Mitteilungen für die Truppe'*, while the officers now had their own *'Mitteilungen für das Offizierkorps'*, a somewhat more informative, but at the same time more propagandistic, version of the former.[23]

The other two divisions were also provided with a multitude of written information, apart from printing their own news-sheets.[24] Thus, for example, in May 1943 alone the GD Division received 162 000 copies of front-newspapers; 41 901 copies of German, Austrian, Ukranian and Polish dailies; and 5364 copies of German illustrated newspapers. The division calculated that each unit received an average of 1400 newspapers per month, not including private subscriptions.[25] Similarly, the companies of the 18.Pz.Div. received a daily supply of 10–12 copies of newspapers as of spring

1942 at the latest, while during the whole of 1942 the division had been supplied with 412 000 copies of newspapers.[26] This supply continued throughout 1943 as well, and at the same time the number of civilian German newspapers was also significantly increased.[27]

Along with newspapers and information-sheets, the troops at the front were also supplied with a large number of leaflets and booklets whose main aim was to enhance the men's conviction in the historical, geographical, cultural and ideological necessity of the war and the inevitable ultimate '*Endsieg*' of their cause under the leadership of Adolf Hitler, who was repeatedly described as the greatest leader of all times.[28] As of December 1939 the 12.I.D. began receiving the '*Tornisterschrift*' (Knapsack-sheet), of which about one copy was given to every ten men. This OKW booklet dealt with such issues as treason, espionage, party–army relations, the economic situation and civilian morale.[29] Another brochure issued in 1940 was entitled 'Instruction Booklets for the Course on National Socialist *Weltanschauung* and National Socialist Goals' and its content can be gathered from its name.[30] Company commanders were given various booklets which were intended to serve them as the basis for company sessions, mostly dealing with political, ideological and economic issues and all written with a strong propagandistic bias.[31] During the occupation of the Netherlands the troops received yet another booklet entitled '*Solatenbriefe zur Berufsförderung*' which, among others, taught the Nazi view of European history, geography and politics.[32] These booklets, as well as special issues such as the immensely popular '*Was Uns Bewegt*' (What Drives Us On), were distributed among the soldiers throughout the war in Russia, and greatly assisted the company commanders, and later on the educational officers, in instilling their men with the Nazi *Weltanschauung* and persuading them that they were fighting for a just and inescapable cause.[33] This flood of leaflets and brochures was not unique to the 12.I.D. The GD Division reported that during May 1943 it received 4300 copies of the '*Tornisterschrift*', 5200 copies of the 'Soldier's Sheet for Leave and Off-Duty' as well as numerous other educational booklets.[34] The 18.Pz.Div. was supplied in 1942 with 16 700 'Leave and Off-Duty' sheets, 14 330 copies of the '*Tornisterschrift*', and 138 000 '*Soldatenbriefe*' which were said to be particularly popular. This massive supply continued in 1943, in spite of the rapid decline in the numerical strength of the division.[35]

For those of the soldiers and officers who could find the time and felt the need to read books during their rest periods, the divisions provided rather well-stocked libraries which they tried to enlarge whenever the opportunity presented itself. The 12.I.D., for instance, succeeded in establishing a fully fledged library system among its units by early 1940, so that each battalion owned its own library.[36] Whereas during the occupation of France the division was visited by 'library-vans', in late 1941 the 12.I.D. established a divisional library in Demyansk which served all its units, quite apart from the smaller regimental libraries and the 'library-van' which began circulating among the units during the following spring.[37] The GD Division established a similar library system and particularly emphasised the importance of fresh supplies of books.[38] Thus in September 1942 it received twenty boxes of books from the so-called '*Rosenberg Spende*', as well as 1000 books from the library of the OKW and twenty boxes from the 'Book-Club'. This supply was further enhanced in mid-1943 with 1600 volumes from the '*Rosenberg Spende*', 4000 from the OKW and a further 3700 from other sources.[39] It was the same regarding the 18.Pz.Div., which received a total of 16 140 books in 1942 alone.[40] We can therefore conclude that as far as reading material and written propaganda were concerned, the men of the three divisions here examined were extremely well provided for, and in fact would have had to make a special effort to avoid being influenced by the continuous stream of indoctrinational material directed at them throughout the war.

The Spoken Word

Probably the most effective propaganda and indoctrination was that conducted on a personal, face-to-face level. Political lectures by various party functionaries and academics were quite common as long as the divisions concerned were either in Germany or Western Europe. The 12.I.D. was visited frequently by lecturers arranged by the local party offices during its stay in Germany following the Polish campaign, as well as by professors from the universities of Bonn and Cologne.[41] Numerous lectures were delivered to NCOs and soldiers of the division also during its occupation of the Netherlands.[42] Similarly, the GD Division was visited by lecturers both during its establishment in Germany during the spring of 1942 and also at the front in September 1942,[43] while the 18.Pz.Div. reported on a series of lectures on the Soviet Union while it was training near Prague, and emphasised that a lecturer who visited its troops at the front in December 1942 had aroused great enthusiasm among the soldiers.[44]

It is quite clear, however, that the junior officers, assisted by the abundant propaganda material with which they were supplied, had a far greater influence upon the morale, *ésprit de corps* and ideological conviction of the troops than any outside functionaries. It was an old tradition in the German army that the company commander was solely responsible for the morale, discipline and instruction of the troops.[45] This did not mean, however, that the officers sheltered their men from the ideological penetration of the party. On the contrary, as we hope to have demonstrated in the previous chapter, these young men were particularly suited to serve as political instructors of the soldiers. Furthermore, the more senior commanders not only stressed the importance of the educational role of the junior officers, but also demanded time and again that this instruction should consist of a specific National Socialist content. Thus, as early as 18 December 1938, the Commander in Chief of the army, von Brauchitsch, issued the following order:

> The officer corps must not allow itself to be surpassed by anyone in the purity and conviction of its National Socialist Weltanschauung . . . It is obvious that the officer will behave according to the concepts of the Third Reich in every situation, even when such concepts are not clearly defined in legal provisions, orders or service regulations. He must be the leader of his subordinates also from the political point of view.[46]

Consequently, the commander of the 12.I.D. ordered on 8 July 1940:

> I order that twice a week, and when possible more often, the company commanders . . . will hold instruction courses [*Unterricht*] to their troops . . .; in particular they should discuss special occurrences in their own circles and current political issues. There is sufficient material for both issues.[47]

By October 1940 the underlying concept was further articulated:

> The company . . . commander is the central personality still retaining a direct influence upon the education, instruction and leading of the individual man . . . The troop-commander alone is responsible for the spirit and demeanour of his soldiers. Thereby the ideological education of the troops is also his task.[48]

The other two divisions, which of course received the same orders from the OKH, also emphasised the role of the officer as the educator of his men. The commander of the GD Division insisted that the scope of the officers' responsibilities 'ranges not only over pure leadership or training',[49] but that 'the company . . . commanders are the carriers of the "morale" [*Stimmung*] of their troops',[50] and that the officers should make extensive use of the company instruction sessions in influencing the conduct and mentality of the men.[51] Similarly, the commander of the 18.Pz.Div. demanded that his officers report to him on the company sessions they were conducting, as those constituted an important element in the '*Geistige Betreuung*' of the troops, a term which served as a euphemism for political indoctrination.[52]

The crisis on the Eastern Front in the first winter of 1941/2 brought both front-line commanders and staff officers in the rear to the conclusion that the traditional methods of propaganda among the troops were not sufficient and that only a further increase in the indoctrination of the soldiers would prevent them from breaking under the strain. On 15 July 1942 OKW issued an order establishing the position of a '*Bearbeiter für Wehrgeistige Führung*', that is an officer who was to supervise all educational matters within the intelligence sections of the formations at the front. Some divisions had already taken the initiative on this issue, and on 14 May 1943 the position of educational officers was officially sanctioned by the commander of the Replacement Army. This '*Offizier für Wehrgeistige Führung*' had by now become independent from the intelligence section, though he was still under the command of the combat officers. The next stage in this development was even more significant. On 22 December 1943 Hitler issued an order establishing a '*NS-Führungsstab*' in OKW which made for the creation of 'National Socialist Leadership Officers' (NSFO) in all military staffs down to divisional level. Thus ended a gradual process, begun almost ten years earlier, of an ideological and institutional penetration of the army by the Nazi party. It was only a matter of time before the NSFOs would be placed directly under the control of the party and thereby become fully fledged commissars, a final stage prevented only by the capitulation of the Third Reich.[53]

The developments described above, which affected most of the German formations at the front, were, of course, reflected in the three divisions dealt with in this study. The 18.Pz.Div., since it belonged to Army Group Centre which was the first to experiment with educational officers, nominated its own '*Betreuungsoffiziere*' as early as autumn 1942, and by October that year had already submitted a report stating that it had found the activities of these officers 'very valuable'.[54] The GD Division nominated educational officers on 24 May 1943 and ordered them to carry out all propaganda and 'political-educational' work among the troops.[55] The 12.I.D. issued the following order on 6 June 1943:

1. On the eve of the fifth year of the war the significance of a unified instruction . . . of the troops increases.
2. The commanders carry the basic responsibility for this work of instruction and education. For their advice and support they will nominate Educational Officers.[56]

Owing to the fact that as of late 1943 the files of the divisions become increasingly thinner, we have no direct information on the creation of NSFOs within these formations. The 18.Pz.Div. was in any case disbanded before the NSFOs were established, while concerning the GD Division it is hardly conceivable that this elite formation which was particularly favoured by Hitler did not carry out the order to introduce National Socialist commissars into its staff. As for the 12.I.D., though we have no knowledge as to when the NSFO was actually nominated, a document dated 20 February 1945 and signed by the divisional NSFO testifies to the fact that such an officer was indeed appointed, probably not later than the re-establishment of that formation in East Prussia following the Russian summer offensive of 1944.[57]

THE ENEMY AS 'UNTERMENSCHEN'

In the preceding pages we saw the various forms of indoctrination used by the army and the wide-ranging extent of radio, film and written propaganda supplied to the troops. Furthermore, we observed that the junior officers, amply provided with written material, conducted indoctrination sessions with their companies, assisted in the later stages of the war by educational officers and NSFOs. It is now time to examine the content of this continuous stream of propaganda and indoctrination material, and to establish whether it was essentially different from the more traditional patriotic and nationalistic rhetoric common in other European armies, as well as in the German army of the First World War.

The chronology and extent of the German generals' assimilation of Nazi ideology and policies have already been well documented. The senior officers believed that they could control Hitler once he came to power and exploit the mass popularity of the National Socialist movement to rally the German people to their own more traditional, albeit far from democratic, concepts of social organisation. Some, like Ludwig Beck, for instance (the Chief of Staff of the army, who later led the July 1944 Putsch), insisted in the early years of the regime on the so-called 'Two Pillar Theory', according to which the state would be based on the two most important institutions of the Reich–the Nazi party and the Wehrmacht–and these men believed that they could make use of what they saw as the 'positive' elements of Nazism. This dangerous underestimation of the dynamics of National Socialism doomed the army to an increasingly more rapid and fundamental '*Gleichschaltung*' from above and infiltration from below. While the participation of the army in the 'Night of the Long Knives' and the personal oath of loyalty to Hitler demonstrated the generals' willingness, or rather desire, to collaborate with the regime, the Fritsch-Blomberg affair of 1938 was one more sign of Hitler's determination to put the army under his strict control. While the vast growth of the army within the space of a few years brought to its ranks ever more young men who had already been indoctrinated by the Nazis in various civilian and party institutions, the crisis of 1941/2 on the Eastern Front gave the process of Nazification of the army a further impetus. At the top, Hitler became the commander of the army; at the front, there was a growing demand for an increase in the propaganda and indoctrination activity among the troops in the face of the first severe military setback of the war. The graver the situation at the front became, the greater was the willingness of commanders on all levels to make use of the Nazi *Weltanschauung* as a means of stiffening the morale of their men and persuading them of the greatness of the 'cause' for which they had been called upon to sacrifice so much. Indeed, the commanders were right; the soldiers needed some 'rationale' for their long years of suffering at the front, and it came in the form of the National Socialist 'cause' and transformed them into the Führer's *Kämpfer* who had been sent on a mission on behalf of the Germanic *Volk* to wage a racial struggle against the 'Jewish-Bolshevik *Untermenschen*' of the East.[58]

It has already been noted that Nazi propaganda was most successful where it 'could readily build upon already generally accepted values, ideological predispositions and dominant opinion'.[59]

In the case of the army this tendency was particularly evident. After all, the Nazis took much of their vocabulary of '*Kampf*', '*Kampfgemeinschaft*' and '*Frontkämpferbewusstsein*' from the trenches of the First World War, and then filtered them back into the army with some crucial additions such as racial concepts which, however, were also not completely unknown in pre-Nazi Germany. Indeed, the most striking indication of the growing influence of Nazi ideology in the army was the rapid change in the language used by the commanders. National Socialist terms seem to have rolled much more easily from their tongues the longer and more bitter the war became; and these terms were not just empty phrases–they signified a certain perception of reality, and they called for a certain mode of conduct. The easier it became to use them, the less inhibitions there were in implementing their contents.[60]

The blending of nationalistic and National Socialist propaganda is quite evident from the files of the 12.I.D. relating to recreation and indoctrination activities before the invasion of the Soviet Union. Thus lectures delivered to the troops on late-night radio broadcasts on the eve of the French campaign made use of traditional patriotic rhetoric, but at the same time attributed the unity and spiritual strength of the German Volk to 'what National Socialism has created in twenty years'.[61] Similarly, the films shown to the troops were intended both to encourage their admiration for the Reich's beauty and industrial efficiency, and at the same time to persuade the civilian population at home and the soldiers at the front of the invincibility of the Wehrmacht, whether in the offensive or the defensive. Such films as 'The Liberation of Danzig', 'The End of the Heroic Battle of Poland' and 'On the Soldiers of the Wetern Front', which we know were screened before the men of the 12.I.D.,[62] as well as the prestigious '*Blitzkrieg*' documentaries made before and after the French campaign such as 'Campaign in Poland', 'Baptism of Fire' and 'Victory in the West', which gained much popularity in Germany at the time,[63] purged of course of the more horrific aspects of war, greatly enhanced the belief in Hitler and 'his' army. Indeed, the SD report of 14 February 1940 stressed how well the film '*Feldzug in Polen*' was received by German viewers, whereas the film '*Im Trommelfeuer der Westfront*' (In the Artillery Barrage of the Western Front), based on documentaries of the First World War, was criticised by the public because it showed 'only the fear, death and misery of the war without dealing with the deeper meaning' and since 'the German soldiers appeared in it as old, bearded, worn-out and exhausted figures'.[64] This 'error' of presentation was not repeated in other productions of war films in the Third Reich, let alone in such Nazi 'masterpieces' as Leni Riefenstahl's 'Triumph of the Will'.[65]

The lectures delivered to the troops provided a mantle of academic respectability to the Nazi *Weltanschauung*. Whereas professors from the universities of Bonn and Cologne described their talks as dealing with 'historical, political [*raumpolitischen*], colonial-scientific and economic' themes,[66] the officers of the division were particularly impressed by those lectures which they graded as 'strongly racially [*völkisch*] oriented, filled with belief in the Führer and the future of Greater Germany'.[67] These pseudo-academic lectures were accompanied by pseudo-academic brochures, such as, to quote only one example, a booklet distributed among the men of the 12.I.D. and issued by the OKW in mid-1940, entitled *'England raubt die Welt'* (England Robs the World). The author, one Dr Hellmuth Rössler, describes how 'England' not only built a vast colonial empire and robbed its population of their wealth, but at the same time also 'robbed' their souls, while daring 'to label the peaceful *Anschluss* of the Austrian *Volksgenossen* to the Reich an act of German Terror!'.[68] This was the general tone of the lectures organised by the 12.I.D. in October 1940, which dealt with three major themes: general political and ideological issues; military spirit and politics and historical and scientific themes; and pure military issues.[69] For those who wished to do some more 'serious' reading, the divisional libraries offered a wide variety of books, ranging from Hitler's, Rosenberg's, Goebbels's and Chamberlain's works, to other less-well-known anti-Semitic tracts such as *'Der Judashof '*, *'Rothschild Siegt bei Waterloo'* and *'Stimmen zur Judenfrage'*.[70]

Newspapers constituted both a more direct and, quite probably, more influential means of indoctrination. Soldiers read newspapers because they wanted information, and the only newspapers to be had were either those controlled by Goebbels's Ministry of Propaganda or those issued by the military and supervised by the propaganda section of OKW. Much has already been written on the propaganistic character of the civilian newspapers during the Third Reich, and it is beyond the scope of this study to discuss them. We have demonstrated earlier that during most of the war the troops were provided with large numbers of these newspapers, and it can hardly be doubted that they played an important role in determining the views of the soldiers regarding the situation at home and abroad.[71] Nevertheless, it is just as important to examine the military news-sheets which were distributed among the units at the front throughout the war, even when supply difficulties hampered the delivery of civilian papers. Here we can clearly see the gradual infiltration of Nazi concepts into the military language and the increasing use made by the army of racial arguments as a justification for the war and its rapid deterioration into a barbarous life-or-death struggle. As early as 22 October 1939 the 'Information Sheet for the East Prussian Army' described the Jewish refugees encountered by German troops in Poland as 'the vermin of peoples' who 'whizzed to and fro like irksome flies over a carcass, still conducting business in this death and misery'. The Wehrmacht, of course, had nothing to do with 'this death and misery' for, as the paper asked rhetorically, 'have we beaten up even one single person, just because he was a Pole?'.[72] The widely distributed *'Mitteilungen für die Truppe'* issued by OKW also explained to its readers in August 1940 that 'Everything in the world which is Jewish is unified and identified by its hatred to Greater Germany'.[73] The *'Nachrichten des OKW'*, supplied to officers, maintained that 'a real peace in the world' could only be achieved following the 'decisive battle between the totalitarian, racially defined *Weltanschauung* and the aspirations of Jewish World-democracy'.[74] Whereas the German *Volk* was fortunate enough to be led by Hitler, who 'is opening the way for a great development of our people in the Greater German Reich' and in whose genius 'lies resolved the knowledge of the future',[75] the racial enemies of the Aryans were to pay a heavy price for their biological inferiority. Thus the *'Nachrichten des OKW'* brought to the knowledge of the young Wehrmacht officers the content of a speech made by Himmler in 1940, regarding the 'Future Tasks of the Germanic Race':

He began by saying that the cleansing of our own race by the Nuremberg Jewish Law as well as the building up of the economy and the Wehrmacht, and furthermore the unification of the German race by solving the Austrian, Bohemian-Moravian and Polish questions, demonstrate the new course of this policy. A war is not won by acquiring peoples of other races, but by acquiring land.

To be sure, Germany has had to incorporate 8 million people of alien races through its military victory, but all preparations have already been made in order to segregate the different races. All races, and particularly the Jews, will be sent to the *'General-gouvernement'* in the future. This means that some 500 000–

600 000 Jews will be transferred there and enclosed in a separate ghetto, including of course all Jews from the whole Greater German Reich.[76]

Even more important than the written propaganda was, as we have already pointed out, the direct and personal contact between the junior officers and their men, whether during the company sessions or on less-formal occasions during rest periods. The officers made use of the various newspapers, booklets, leaflets and brochures with which they were amply provided. The OKW supplied the commanders with a special booklet designated 'Nationalpolitischer Unterricht im Heere' (National-Political Instruction in the Army), specifically labelled as intended 'for the company commander, leaflet for instruction'. These booklets, issued throughout the war, were intended to assist the officers in indoctrinating their men, and ranged from subjects such as 'The English War' (May 1940) and 'The German Soldier in the Occupied Territory ' (July 1940), to 'The Great Germans till Adolf Hitler', 'The German Social State' (both February 1943) and 'The NSDAP and its Branches' (April 1943).[77] The young company commanders were to strengthen the belief of their troops both in the greatness of their Führer and in the profound historical significance of their bitter years of fighting. It is interesting to see how the Führer was portrayed as the last and the greatest of all 'Great Germans':

Only the Führer could do what had not been achieved for a thousand years, and establish the real Reich of the Germans, in which all authority lies in the hands of the leadership of the Reich and in which all German stock [*Stämme*] and lands can find their homeland. In the new Greater German Reich there is only one leadership of the Reich and one law of the Reich . . .

With his strong will and unwavering belief in the power and future of the German *Volk* the Führer brought together all the German stock into the German Reich and gave them a common idea. Now he could mobilise their concentrated strength for the struggle for the freedom and living space of the Germans.

He saw the increasingly threatening behaviour of the old enemies of the Reich. He therefore directed all his thoughts and efforts towards a National Socialist education of the *Volk*, the inner cohesion of the state, the armament and offensive capability of the Wehrmacht. He reacted with determination against all that could have threatened the inner unity of party and *Volk*. He knew that action had to be taken immediately, and answered punches with punches . . .

Adolf Hitler has said numerous times that all real greatness must first prove itself by bearing failures and retreats. He called upon us to view the example of Frederick the Great. When the German Eastern Armies fought an unparalleled battle during the winter of 1941/2 in the snow and ice of the Russian winter, he said: 'Any weakling can bear victories. Only the strong can stand firm in battles of destiny. But heaven gives the ultimate highest prize only to those who are capable of withstanding battles of destiny'. In the difficult winter of 1942/3 the strength of the Führer has been demonstrated once more, when following the unparalleled courageous battle of the 6. Army in Stalingrad he called upon the German *Volk* at the front and in the homeland to stand firm and to make the supreme effort.

The Führer has had a decisive influence on the history of the German *Volk*. He clearly sees the goal ahead: a strong German Reich as the Power of Order in Europe and the firm root of the German *Lebensraum*.

This goal will be achieved if the whole *Volk* remains loyal to him even in difficult times and as long as we soldiers do our duty.[78]

The divisional commanders clearly understood the importance of the instruction sessions performed by the company commanders. The commander of the 12.I.D., who ordered his officers to conduct a bi-weekly company session, issued soon afterwards a detailed booklet of instructions outlining all major themes to be discussed with the troops. These included, among others, the following subjects:

Theme 1: The German *Volk*
Main points: Clean race. Healthy and vigorous women. Many children. Reinforcements for soldiers . . .
Theme 2: The German Reich
Main points: The establishment of the Reich. Party and Wehrmacht as pillars of the state. Führer State . . .
Theme 3: The German *Lebensraum*
Main points: The aim of the war–ensuring the German *Lebensraum*, not subjugating neighbouring peoples . . .
Theme 4: National Socialism as a Foundation
Main points: (a) For a healthy and united *Volk*

(b) For a strong Reich . . .
(c) For ensuring the *Lebensraum*.[79]

The invasion of the Soviet Union brought about a fundamental change in the character of the indoctrination of the troops. The Nazi *Weltanschauung* was much better defined regarding the East, composed as it was of both racial and political enemies of the 'German National Socialist *Volk*'. Thus the Russians were seen from the start as 'Jewish-Bolshevik *Untermenschen*' and 'Mongol hordes'. Nazism strove to achieve a complete dehumanisation of the peoples of the East; the army followed suit at an increasing pace. The crisis of the first winter, and then the catastrophe of Stalingrad, only served to enhance the conviction of the officers that their appeals to the troops should consist of an even greater National Socialist content. The bitterness of the long and costly war, the ideological convictions of the opposing sides, as well as the traditional hatred towards the Slavs, dating long before Hitler appeared on the scene, made it easier for the military to adopt the Nazi view of the war. During the war in Russia the process of dehumanisation of the enemy was probably more successful than in any other war in modern history–the Russians, Slavs, Jews, Mongols, all had lost any relationship to the human race, and were nothing more than satanic monsters trying in vain to appear human, imposters whose identity had to be exposed and whose existence endangered everything which civilised men held dear. As the following passage from the '*Mitteilungen für die Truppe*' makes clear, there was only one thing to be done with these beasts–mercilessly wipe them out:

Anyone who has ever looked at the face of a red commissar knows what the Bolsheviks are like. Here there is no need for theoretical expressions. We would be insulting the animals if we were to describe these men, who are mostly Jewish, as beasts. They are the embodiment of the Satanic and insane hatred against the whole of noble humanity. The shape of these commissars reveals to us the rebellion of the *Untermenschen* against noble blood. The masses, whom they have sent to their deaths by making use of all means at their disposal such as ice-cold terror and insane incitement, would have brought an end to all meaningful life, had this eruption not been dammed at the last moment.[80]

One of the best indications of the penetration of Nazi ideology into the army and its influence upon the soldiers is the changing vocabulary of the front-line commanders. The orders issued by these officers were not controlled by Goebbels or the OKW, and therefore reflected to a much greater degree the actual mentality of the commanders, or at least what they thought to be useful rhetoric in exhorting their men to keep on fighting. At the same time, these orders may well have had a greater influence upon the soldiers, coming as they did not from the party functionaries in the rear but from respected officers who shared with the men much of their experiences at the front. There are abundant examples for orders with a strong ideological content among the files of the three divisions discussed here. Thus on the eve of the invasion of the Soviet Union the commander of the XXXXVII.Pz.Corps, one of whose formations was the 18.Pz.Div., issued the following order of the day:

> We are on the eve of a great event in the war. The Führer has called us again to battle. It is now our task to destroy the Red Army and thereby eradicate for ever Bolshevism, the deadly enemy of National Socialism.
> We have never forgotten that it was Bolshevism which had stabbed our army in the back during the [First] World War and which bears the guilt for all the misfortunes which our people have suffered after the war. We should always remember that![81]

Similarly, the commander of the 16. Army, to which the 12.I.D. belonged, stated as early as 24 August 1941:

> I am certain that we shall defeat and destroy the enemy . . . and create thereby the preconditions for the ultimate crushing of the Bolshevik system.[82]

Soon afterwards the troops were supplied with copies of von Reichenau's notorious order, which explained in much greater detail what 'crushing the Bolshevik system' actually implied:

> The essential goal of the campaign against the Jewish-Bolshevik system is the complete destruction of the sources of power and the eradication of the Asian influence on the European cultural sphere . . . The soldier in the East is not only a fighter by the rules of war, but also the carrier of an inexorable racial concept [*völkische Idee*] and the avenger of all bestialities inflicted upon the Germans . . .

For this reason the soldier must have complete understanding for the necessity of harsh, but just measures against [*Sühne am*] Jewish sub-humanity . . . Only in this manner will we do justice to our historical task, to liberate the German people for once and for all from the Asiatic–Jewish danger.[83]

Thus the Russians and Jews were not to be treated according to any accepted rules of military conduct, as they had lost their right to such a treatment both by their racial and cultural inferiority and by the historical role they had played against Germany. As an order of the commander of the II. Corps made clear in one appeal to the troops of the 12.I.D. on 20 December 1941, the conduct of Red Army soldiers was in any case so criminal that they deserved no mercy whatsoever at the hands of the Wehrmacht:

The battles of the last few months have shown you that the Russian soldier is a spineless tool in the hands of his commissars, and that therefore he is prepared to commit any vile act, be it murder or treachery . . . What would have happened had these Asiatic Mongol hordes succeeded to pour into Europe and particularly into Germany, laying the country waste, plundering, murdering, raping?[84]

Was the commander of the II. Corps aware of the parallel which could be drawn between his description of the Red Army's behaviour both on the field of battle and towards German civilians, and the criminal activities of his own soldiers? Was this an attempt to justify to himself, to his troops and to posterity the barbarous conduct of the German soldiers? As the war continued and the *Endsieg* seemed farther and farther away, it was no longer sufficient to emphasise the sub-human character of the enemy as a reason for 'eradicating' him. Now the commanders felt that they had to persuade their troops of the historical significance of this 'struggle for existence' and to strengthen even further their ideological commitment and belief in the Führer. Thus the commander of the 16. Army issued the following order at the beginning of 1943:

Greater Germany celebrates today the tenth anniversary of the victory of the National Socialist movement. This victory of 30 January 1933, fought for in tough battles, with a fanatic belief and an unshakable confidence in the Führer, had created the preconditions for the victory of arms in the struggle of the German people for a new and just order of existence [*Lebensordnung*], for freedom and for bread. United and strong in its belief in the justice of its cause and with an iron will for victory, National Socialist Greater Germany is now in the fourth year of its struggle for its *Lebensraum*. Many have sealed their love to Führer and Reich with death.[85]

Indeed, this was no time to show any doubts in the certainty of the ultimate victory, which was to be achieved because of the superiority of the German race, its leadership and its professionalism. Fanaticism was called for, where all rational analyses were bound to demonstrate how near the final catastrophe actually was. The men of the GD Division were told that there was only one way by which the could win the war:

> By our unshakable belief, that we are and will remain absolutely superior to the enemy even in the most critical situation owing to our morale, our toughness, our training and our leadership . . . The company . . . commanders are the carriers of the 'morale' [*Stimmung*]. If a company commander talks or indeed whines about the heavy battles and casualties of the past, the precarious situation of the position, the bad weather and the dwindling strength of the company, he can be sure that his men will weaken and cause him shame . . . He would therefore be unfit for the struggle in the East and should immediately be dismissed![86]

Thus the officers of the GD Division were ordered in April 1943 to increase even further the ideological indoctrination of their troops, which was to bring about the final victory when everything else had failed, and to persuade them to fight on for another two bloody years in spite of the fact that the war had already been lost for all practical purposes:

> The length of the war calls not only for extraordinary efforts regarding the military performance of the Wehrmacht, but also makes demands upon the power of resistance of each individual soldier. This mental power of resistance has to be repeatedly strengthened, particularly during rest periods. This will be achieved by:
> 1. The uniform orientation [*Ausrichtung*] of commanders and troops in questions of ideology [*Weltanschulichen Fragen*].

2. Strengthening of soldierly qualities: bravery, toughness, the will to fight and to obey.
3. The recognition of the historical significance of the war.
4. Creation of a confident view of the military and political situation even in the face of setbacks and the length of the war: education to steadfastness in crises [*Erziehung zur Krisenfestigkeit*].[87]

In September 1939 the German army did not go to war with the same enthusiasm that had characterised all European armies in August 1914. From one *Blitzkrieg* victory to another, however, the confidence of the generals and the troops in their superiority grew in leaps and bounds. The invasion of the Soviet Union was to have been just one more lightning victory, particularly as it was fought against the inferior races of the East. Gradually it became increasingly clear that the war could not be won with the old *Blitzkrieg* techniques. The soldiers at the front had not been prepared for the bitter resistance of the Russian *Untermenschen*, and their officers felt that only growing doses of ideological injections would stiffen their morale and keep them in their positions. The worse the military conditions became, the more stress was put on indoctrination. The obvious paradox was that whereas militarily the war could no longer be won, ideologically it was impossible to be defeated by the 'Jewish-Bolshevik hordes'. Thus all rational arguments had to be done away with, replaced by a fanatic belief in the Führer and the *Endsieg*. Indeed, the troops went on fighting against all odds for another two years after the catastrophe of Stalingrad, which spelt the final beginning of the end for the German army in Russia. Part of this stubborn determination of the German soldiers in the East can be explained by the efficacy of the indoctrination examined in the preceding pages. In the following section we shall investigate some of the factors which contributed to the success of that indoctrination and thereby to the extraordinary resilience of the troops of the East.

THE EFFICACY OF INDOCTRINATION

Contributing Factors

The general agreement which seems to have existed among the ranks of the German military in the East regarding what they perceived to be the aims of the war against the Soviet Union and the 'cause' for which they were fighting, was the result of a number of factors which should be pointed out briefly before we turn to examining the various indications found in the divisional files concerning this apparent ideological concensus. As we have already observed, ideological indoctrination is particularly effective when it makes use of existing ideas, prejudices, frustrations or beliefs. In the case of the German army of the Third Reich, it is not only that the Nazis made clever use of phrases and concepts which had been popularised in the military during and after the First World War and blended them with their own racial theories, thus emphasising that the '*Kampfgemeinschaft*' was not only a community of warriors, but also one of racially pure soldiers, and that the '*Frontkämpferbewusstsein*' was not just the state of mind of the combat soldier, but also and even more so of the Germanic, Aryan fighter sacrificing himself for the Master Race in a struggle against a world of *Untermenschen*. It is also the fact that the backbone of this newly founded army was the young junior officers who, as we have shown in the previous chapter, belonged to those social strata and age groups most susceptible to the Nazi *Weltanschauung*, and who were allowed, indeed ordered, to serve as the ideological instructors of their men. Furthermore, it would be wrong to stress only the affinity between the military language and the terms used by the Nazis. What has been called 'The Crisis of German Ideology' and 'The Politics of Cultural Despair[88] dates back even before the war of 1914–18. One of the most powerful and dangerous ideas which emerged from the pre-war period, and which may well have played an important role in preparing the mental and intellectual background for the Nazi *Weltanschauung*, was the concept of the racial differences between human beings, accompanied by a new and much more radical form of cultural and political anti-Semitism, combined with a general sense of superiority towards non-Germanic races, and particularly the Slavs.[89] This development was not manifested only in the writings of cranks, but in the surprising electoral success of anti-Semitic populist parties, among leading academic circles in German universities, and in racist opinions uttered by some of the political and military leaders of the Second Reich.[90]

Under the impact of the defeat, the revolution and the economic crisis, the first years of the Weimar Republic saw an upsurge of violent, radical right-wing and racist organisations, which looked back to the supposed comradeship of the soldiers in the trenches, the glorious days of the empire, and at the same time hoped to create some new, albeit vaguely defined, society. What united the various para-military groups was their deep hatred of the republic. Following the Great Depression of 1929 and the consequent massive unemployment, the numbers of the supporters of the republic dwindled even further and there seems to have been a general feeling that the system had failed and that what was needed was a new political and social order.[91] The army too was embittered and frustrated; as the Ulm Trial had shown, the junior officers, destined to become the senior commanders of the Second World War, were rapidly drifting away from Seeckt's concept of professional military '*Überparteilichkeit*' and moving closer to Nazism, or at least to what they thought it meant.[92] When Hitler came to power, all the resources of the new Reich were mobilised in an attempt to produce a massive and incessant stream of propaganda aimed at brainwashing the public into a 'blind belief' in the Führer and a complete and uncritical acceptance of the tenets of National Socialism.[93] Many of the professed goals of the new regime, such as ridding Germany of the 'shameful' peace treaty of 1919, re-arming the Wehrmacht, expanding the borders of the Reich and crushing the left, were shared by a majority of the population. Furthermore, as has recently been shown, the emergence of the '*Führer-Mythos*' was not just an act of propagandistic manipulation from above, but also a reflection of a deep popular need, quite apart from the less obvious and, perhaps, more restricted support for the party.[94] It is thus clear that the indoctrinational material supplied to the troops was anything but new, and in most cases was just a continution of a process of indoctrination which had begun many years before the soldiers joined the ranks.

Another factor that may well have contributed to the soldiers' receptivity to ideological indoctrination was the war itself. We have a significant amount of evidence, both among the divisional files and from other sources, that the troops at the front actually asked for, and were glad to receive, radio, film, written and verbal propaganda. This should not at all surprise us, particularly since much of this material was not seen as propaganda but rather as entertainment or information and news. It is obvious that the men at the front wanted to know what was happening in the war, and especially what the conditions were at home, where they had left their families. It is also clear that receiving newspapers, films and visiting lecturers made the individual feel somewhat less isolated and forgotten, a feeling which always threatened adversely to influence morale, as we have observed in the first chapter. It was also extremely important for the men to have their officers, platoon, company and battalion commanders come to their positions and discuss with them the 'greater' issues of the war, and there can hardly be any doubt that the more intimate relations between officers and men in the German army contributed a great deal to the morale and combat efficiency of its units. However, all the material delivered both to the men and to their officers was, as we have seen, heavily loaded with Nazi jargon and concepts, and was intended to enhance the soldiers' belief in the regime's *Weltanschauung*. Thus by expressing the natural desire to receive information on the political and military situation, and by welcoming the morale-lifting company sessions, the troops invited more and more propaganda. To say that soldiers in time of war are only interested in their own survival or, at the most, in their families at home, is, of course, partly true. But to be given information on the more general scene of the war and, even more so, on the situation in the rear, was a widespread demand among the troops in Russia, as we have seen in the documents of the divisions. Moreover, it seems that the individual soldier, far away from his homeland and his beloved, in an alien and hostile land, wanted something more than just information– he wanted to be told why all this was necessary, for what 'cause' he was risking his life. Thus company sessions were not only important for the morale of the troops because their commander sat and talked with them, but also because he told them that what they were doing was necessary, indeed crucial and of a historical significance. The company commanders read from their little booklets what the soldiers wanted to hear–that they were fighting for a cause which transcended their miserable and wretched existence at the front and made it all 'worth it'.[95]

A good example of the soldiers' interest in matters beyond their immediate existence at the front is a questionnaire distributed by the 18.Pz.Div. among its troops in an attempt to gauge their morale. It was found that the men were particularly worried about the following issues: (1) that their shops, businesses or farms would greatly suffer from their long absence; (2) that they would face severe educational and professional difficulties in returning to civilian life once the war was over; (3) that their families might break down. On this last point the report stressed that:

> owing to stories told by soldiers returning from leave and from
> medical treatment, there is increasing anxiety regarding the

morality of women and girls in the homeland. In many cases a serious fear concerning the men's marriages can be observed. The malicious phrase in the homeland – 'children by remote-control' – may serve as proof for the fact that among the soldiers who have not been home for over a year, a real deterioration in the concepts of morality can be seen.[96]

Thus it is only natural that the troops at the front did indeed want to know how long the war would last, what was was happening on other fronts and, especially, what the situation at home was like. But it is important to emphasise that if it was difficult for the German civilian population to receive any information from sources other than the official Nazi ones – and we know that a great many people were in fact listening to the broadcasts of the BBC notwithstanding the heavy penalties this involved[97] – for the men at the front the situation was even more difficult. Far from the Reich, spread along the vast Russian front, eager for information in their islolated positions, the only sources for news they had were the newspapers and official radio broadcasts. Whether they took it all at face value or not, it was difficult to contradict the official version without hearing any conflicting versions, and however critical the men might have been, the propaganistic content of the information they received must have had an effect on their perception of the situation.[98]

The only other source of information to which the German soldiers in the East were exposed was the countless propaganda leaflets rained on them by the Red Army. It seems, however, that the Wehrmacht troops had heard too much of the satanic qualities of the 'Bolshevik *Untermenschen*' to believe their promises of good treatment (as the low numbers of German deserters demonstrate), or for that matter their descriptions of the nature of the Nazi regime. On the other hand, the massive propaganda campaign of the Russians, as well as the strong ideological character of the Red Army, manifested in the institution of the commissars, did have a rather more oblique effect. One of the more paradoxical phenomena in the war is that whereas the Red Army, greatly impressed by the performance of the Wehrmacht, succeeded in gradually weakening the position of the commissars, the Germans, similarly impressed by their enemies, drew the opposite conclusion, and believing the commissars to be the driving force behind the Russian troops, gradually introduced their own commissars, the educational officers and later the NSFOs. Thus the ideology of the enemy only persuaded the Germans to further intensify their own indoctrination efforts and served the commanders to justify this propaganda by pointing at the Russians and demonstrating its positive influence upon their troops. The '*Mitteilungen für das Offizierkorps*' of March 1943 made this point quite clearly:

> The motivating motor of the Bolshevist enemy is a political idea [which] must be overcome by an even more powerful political dynamic.[99]

Similarly, as early as April 1942, the same news-sheet stated:

> It is known that day after day the arms of the Soviet Russian soldiers are steeled with Bolshevik ideas by thousands of political commissars . . . Thus the German Wehrmacht must confront its enemy not only with the superiority of its leadership and weapons; the German soldier must be clear in his mind . . . regarding the political and spiritual context within which [the war] is being fought . . . because political determination and military achievement are one and the same thing and both form an inseparable unity.[100]

Indications of Success

Up to now we have examined some of the factors which probably played an important role in enhancing the receptivity of the troops at the front to the propagandistic efforts of the regime and the higher echelons of the military, and even made for a demand among the junior officers and the rank-and-file for such indoctrinational material in the form of ideologically oriented information and personal contacts between officers and men. We shall now turn to analyse some of the indications found among the divisional files regarding the possible influence which this propaganda may have had on the troops. We should perhaps begin by providing some more evidence on the growing desire among the troops to be exposed to any sort of morale-lifting and ideological stiffening activity, which naturally enhanced the efficacy of their indoctrination.

The fact that the closer the soldiers were to the front and the more imminent the danger was, the more they needed some sort of spiritual encouragement, preferably in the form of someone who would repeat again and again that their dying would be in the service of a high and profound cause, was noted by the divisional priests and parsons. In the spring of 1942, for instance, the catholic priest of the

18.Pz.Div. observed, regarding the growing demand among the troops for religious booklets, that 'the soldier is not only interested in entertaining lectures, but also seeks serious writings'.[101] In October 1943 he again stressed that 'the high rate of participation of officers and men [in religious services] serves as proof for the strong religious need among the troops . . . The troops repeatedly ask for religious writings.[102] The same phenomenon was noted also by the Lutheran parson who wrote in late 1942 that he repeatedly sensed 'in personal conversations how absolutely necessary a firm religious basis is for the soldier'.[103] It was of the greatest importance for the parson to be as close as possible to the fighting, because this was where he was needed the most: 'the farther is the soldier from the front-line, the greater his indifference'.[104] In late 1943 he wrote 'I have repeatedly experienced how important it is for the parson to be . . . on the front-line with the fighting troops . . . the religious faith is still now as always one of the most important preconditions for battle.'[105]

The opinions of the divisional chaplains have been quoted not because it is our intention to show that many of the soldiers still retained their Christian faith, though there can certainly be no doubt that this was the case. Rather, it is our intention to demonstrate that the troops at the front were in great need of what the German army termed '*Geistige Betreuung*', literally translated as 'spiritual care' and in fact a euphemism for ideological indoctrination. The fact that the divisions had only one Catholic priest and one Lutheran parson, provided with very limited means, whereas National Socialist propaganda was continuously increasing throughout the war, meant that the soldier received much more Nazi than Christian care or indoctrination. Both the chaplains and the Nazis, as well as the military commanders, agreed that 'faith is still now as always one of the most important preconditions for battle'; they even agreed that it had to be a religious faith. But National Socialism, which was rapidly becoming more and more a fanatic religion the worse the objective situation at the front became, replaced Christianity as the driving force of the troops. In a sense, the war in the East was becoming a religious war, reminiscent of the Thirty Years War both in its brutality and in its fanaticism; but the two religions facing each other were Nazism and Bolshevism, and of the two it was the former which proved to be far more barbarous and nihilistic.

Indeed, neither the officers nor the soldiers were called upon to 'understand' the Nazi *Weltanschauung*; rather, it was repeatedly stressed that they must 'believe' in it. The '*Mitteilungen für die*

Truppe' of April 1941 described the ideal officer as possessing the following qualities: (i) always knows what the aims of the war are–the ultimate victory; (ii) is always optimistic; (iii) has absolute confidence in the just German cause and an ability to inspire his comrades to believe in that too; (iv) expresses himself in such a manner in all letters and conversations; (v) by such an attitude he will strengthen those who think likewise and shame those who suffer from an 'inferiority complex'.[106] As the *'Mitteilungen für das Offizierkorps'* stressed time and again, it was the task of the officer to give his men spiritual support, that is, to replace the chaplain. The arguments used in these leaflets were repetitious, based on a few dogmatic and axiomatic theses, while thinking or debating was considered to undermine morale. This was a war of ideologies, or of religions. The soldiers must become political fighters, because the *'Urkraft'* of the Russians is 'diabolically increased owing to the fact that they are pushed into action by the conscious, Jewish-Marxist intellingentsia drunk with hatred and a desire for destruction . . . They are driven forwards by a political idea.[107] Thus the German soldiers must become 'political' too, that is, a believer in his own nation's ideology, or political religion. Politics have replaced ideology, but ideology has been turned into a religion, a 'blind' faith about which no questions may be asked. And if the 'Bolsheviks' are driven forward by hatred, so must be the Germans too. Thus already in 1939 the instruction leaflet of OKW for company sessions stated that the war had two major aims: '1. Wiping out all after-effects of the Jewish influence . . . 2. The struggle against World Judaism [which] we fight the way one would fight a poisonous parasite . . . the plague of all peoples.'[108] OKH repeated these sentiments in an order to the officer corps in October 1942, which demanded that

> Every officer must be filled with the conviction that it is first of all the influence of the Jews which hinders the German people in realising its claims for living space and status in the world and forces our people for the second time to turn against a world of enemies with the blood of our best sons. Therefore the officer must have an unambiguous, completely uncompromising position regarding the Jewish question. There is no difference between so-called decent Jews and others.[109]

This was almost word-for-word an anticipation of Himmler's infamous speech in Posen, precisely one year later.[110]

The more hopeless the situation became, the greater was the need for a fanatic, religious-ideological belief. By 1945 the troops were supplied with so-called '*Kampfparolen*', such as the battle slogan issued by the NSFO of VII. Army Corps:

1. Asia has never defeated Europe. We will break the Asian flood this time too.
2. A rule of the Asiatic *Untermenschen* over the West is unnatural and goes against the sense of history.
3. Behind the flood of the red mob grins the face of the Jew. His desire for power will be broken, as his rule over Germany had been.[111]

Another slogan read:

The language of our weapons is directed by cold hatred and fanatic determination. The future does not belong to the destructive idea, to the red beast, but to the constructive idea of our *Weltanschauung*.[112]

The 4. Panzer Division devised a real credo, or catechism, which was quoted in the '*Mitteilungen für die Truppe*' of January 1945:

I Swear – remembering my oath to the flag, to front-comradeship to my division. I Am Determined – to give my whole strength, my blood and my life to my people in this decisive battle . . . I Believe – in Germany . . . I Believe – In the German people unified under National Socialism and in the victory of its just cause. I Believe – as a National Socialist Soldier in my Führer Adolf Hitler!'[113]

The opinion of some historians, as well as some military men, that soldiers at the front are not interested in ideology or in anything beyond their narrow sphere of activity, does not seem to be justified in the case of the Eastern Front. Major Lersner, who toured units of Army Group Centre in summer 1942, reported that 'the troops think much more than one often assumes'.[114] Indeed, the files of the three divisions examined in this study support his conclusion. The torrent of propaganda did not fall on deaf ears; on the contrary, the men at the front received it willingly, in some cases even enthusiastically.

Thus we find that the educational officer of one of the battalions of the 12.I.D. reported in June 1943:

> Platoon and company commanders, as well as other officers, discussed current political issues. In many bunkers radio-connections had been installed, so that music, news broadcasts and political speeches could be heard . . . The soldier is thankful for any change . . . The soldier shows an interest in instruction on political and other current issues, which comes to show that he is more preoccupied with them than one usually thinks.[115]

Another officer stressed that the troops were becoming increasingly worried about the situation at home and maintained that therefore 'political issues should be discussed more often'. On the other hand, he found that in spite of the recent setbacks in the war, the situation did not have 'a detrimental influence on the orientation of the troops and the confidence in our military superiority had not been shaken.'[116] In other words, the soldiers wanted to hear precisely what the propaganda was telling them – that in spite of all appearances to the contrary, the *Endsieg* was sure to come.

The commander of the 18.Pz.Div. had a similar impression of the usefulness of ideological indoctrination and the positive reactions to it among officers and men alike. In autumn 1942 he reported to his corps commander:

> The initiative [introduction of educational officers] was viewed quite positively by all officers and welcomed enthusiastically by some. The view that owing to the length of the war the mental energy of the men has to be particularly preserved and encouraged, and that this cannot be achieved to a sufficient degree by the conventional means of entertainment, was generally accepted . . . The soldiers listened to the lectures [of the educational officers] very attentively. In many cases there is an inner response and a need to be spoken to in such a manner.[117]

Moreover, the commander was well aware of the fact that the intention of this indoctrination was not to turn it into a political debate, but to instil the men with a faith in their ultimate victory and their leadership, just as religious sermons cannot become philosophical discussions on the existence of God. He thus added:

> This exchange of thoughts in a small group can certainly be more

fruitful than a lecture to a whole company; to be sure there is also some danger that a debate could begin which would demand versatility and firmness from the unit commander.

Thus it was of great importance that the officers who conducted this indoctrination had the confidence and respect of the men. For this the German army was particularly suitable; for, as we have already observed, it was the junior officers who had been most influenced by the Nazi *Weltanschauung* and who, at the same time, acted as their men's commanders on the battlefield. The divisional commander made this point very clearly:

> Doubtlessly this institution depends particularly on the personality of the officers nominated to carry out this work; they must have the confidence of the commanders and the unit leaders. Where this is the case, their work is *very* valuable. In the division this institution has till now proven itself and promises good results when it is further expanded.[118]

It seems, therefore, that the intensification of political indoctrination among the troops became a mutual interest of both the Nazi and military leadership in the rear and the commanders and troops at the front, particularly as the war in the East became increasingly bloodier and the ultimate victory seemed farther and farther away. The Nazis believed that only a fanatic ideological, almost religious, determination could bring about the *Endsieg*; the generals hoped that this growing propagandistic effort would stiffen the morale of the troops and keep them in the trenches; the junior officers were aware of the growing need among their men for 'spiritual care' and encouragement, however irrational and myth-ridden it might be, or perhaps just because it *was* based on 'belief' rather than on an empirical evaluation of the situation, and they themselves were well suited both for absorbing these myths and for disseminating them among their men. The soldiers welcomed any sign of attention and care from their officers, and were grateful when their commanders climbed down into their foxholes and explained to them in the traditional paternalistic manner that they were fighting and dying for *Volk*, Reich and Führer, that they were the spearhead of the expanding *Lebensraum* and that they were defending their homes and families from the menace of the Jewish-Bolshevik *Untermenschen* across the barbed wire and minefields.

If we accept the evidence propounded above which, contrary to what some contemporaries in the rear and quite a number of former generals and historians claimed after the war, demonstrates that not only was there a continuous stream of propaganda and indoctrination at the front, but that the soldiers actually wanted it and were thankful when it was intensified in the light of the deteriorating military situation, we should now ask what purpose was all this supposed to serve and whether it actually succeeded in its aims. Apart from the long-term aims of indoctrination, it seems clear that at the front it had two clearly defined goals. First, it was intended to enhance the determination and resilience of the troops and hinder any signs of breakup or rebellion; second, it was intended to increase the sympathy of the troops for the National Socialist policies and actions carried out in the East, and to persuade them of the necessity of taking part in these criminal activities. We have already elaborated both on the extremely brutal and costly nature of the war and on the extraordinary resilience demonstrated by the divisions, in the first chapter of this study. As is well known, the Wehrmacht as a whole continued fighting against increasingly unfavourable odds and ultimately in the face of a rapidly approaching catastrophe with remarkably few signs of breakdown or rebellion till the very last months of the war. This is particularly striking in the case of the Eastern Front which, as we have shown concerning the three divisions examined here and as is generally admitted regarding the war in Russia as a whole, was probably the most brutal and costly military confrontation in modern times. However we explain the fighting spirit and resistance power of the German troops in the East, we must take into account the effect that indoctrination had on their perception of the situation. German soldiers feared falling into Russian hands, for instance, more because of what they were told would happen to them by German propaganda than because of what was actually taking place at the front. In fact, two-thirds of the German POWs held by the Russians ultimately returned home, as opposed to only one-third of the Russian POWs, who seem to have been much more willing to go into captivity at the beginning of the war, and only later on, when they gradually found out what had happened to their comrades, generally did all they could to avoid capture. Similarly, the concept of '*Kampfgemeinschaft*' or, to use the sociological term, 'primary group', was not just 'created' by circumstances at the front, but rather served as an ideal propounded again and again by Nazi propagandists. Even more important, the belief of the troops that they were being led by a great Führer who would ultimately bring about a victorious end to the war, was also an indication of the success of the propaganda, which we will touch upon once more in our conclusion. As the Nazis and the generals well knew, soldiers who trust their leaders fight better than those who have lost that trust, and the belief in Hitler's genius was one of the greatest assets of the German army throughout the war. In any case, it is difficult to find another example of an army which fought so long under such terrible conditions and yet showed no significant signs of rebellion or breakup such as were observed, for example, among German and French troops towards the end of the First World War.[119] The Red Army, which fought under similarly difficult conditions, was indeed also exposed to its own propagandistic barrage which, as the Germans themselves believed at the time, significantly increased its fighting capability.

The success of the indoctrination in preventing outbreaks of mutinies was also demonstrated by the almost complete lack of opposition to either ideological instruction or the implementation of the policies it stipulated. Whereas we know that among some senior staff officers there was a general feeling of disgust with the barbarous actions of the SS, SD and also units of the Wehrmacht, which led some of them to join the opposition, the vast majority of the officers and troops at the front showed no sign of being prepared to reject these policies. As we have shown, the officers as well as the troops welcomed the intensification of the indoctrination.[120] Moreover, it is difficult to avoid anticipating the last chapter of this study and pointing at the marked correlation between the content of the indoctrination directed at the troops and their own criminal activities at the front. The troops were told over and over again, as we have tried to demonstrate, that the fighting in the East was no ordinary war, for it was against the Jewish-Bolshevik and Mongol population of Russia, the *Untermenschen* who threatened their own Reich. The fact that, as we shall show in Chapter 4, the soldiers often treated their enemies as sub-humans, cannot be divorced from this indoctrination, though it also had to do with the generally brutal nature of the war itself. Here the regime could certainly feel that its propagandistic efforts had been crowned with success, and that not only its 'Elite Corps', the SS, was carrying out its barbarous plans, but also the supposedly strictly 'professional' Wehrmacht.[121]

CONCLUSION

Victor Klemperer, a Jewish philologist who succeeded somehow in surviving all the twelve long years of Hitler's regime inside the Third Reich, published a few years after the war a fascinating book based on the diary which he had kept throughout that period. This is a study of the corruption of the German language by the infiltration into it of an increasing number of Nazi terms and concepts. Klemperer asserts that the most powerful instrument of propaganda in the Third Reich was not Hitler's and Goebbels's speeches, nor the leaflets, newspaper articles, posters and flags, nor any other measure which strove directly to influence thought or conscious emotions; rather, Nazism penetrated the flesh and blood of the multitude through the single word, the manners of speech, the construction of sentences, repeated in a mechanical and unthinking manner over and over again by the individual. With numerous examples Klemperer demonstrates how even the opposers and, moreover, the victims of Nazism subconsciously adopted the National Socialist forms of speech and expression. As regards the language of the army, the infiltration of the Nazi vocabularly was even greater for, as he points out, there was here a reciprocal relationship: first an influence of the military language on the Nazi vocabulary, and then a corruption of military forms of expression by the Nazis.[122]

Even before the Second World War ended, scholars from various disciplines began debating the question of whether ordinary Germans actually 'believed' the ideology, the so-called *Weltanschauung*, directed at them by the Nazi regime. It will probably never be possible to determine the precise extent of persuasion of the German public in the tenets of National Socialism, not only because the *Weltanschauung* was vague, unclear, and meant different things to different people, nor just because of the lack of evidence and the difficulties involved in gauging public opinion in a totalitarian regime, but first and foremost because there is no simple or precise method of establishing whether an individual 'believes' in something or not. The British anthropologist Evans-Pritchard wrote in his study of primitive religion that

> Statements about a people's religious beliefs must always be treated with the greatest caution, for we are here dealing with what neither European nor native can directly observe, with conceptions, images, words, which require for understanding a thorough

knowledge of a people's language and also an awareness of the entire system of ideas of which any particular belief is part, for it may be meaningless when divorced from the set of beliefs and practices to which it belongs.[123]

More recently, another anthropologist addressed himself to the same problem in a remarkable study of 'Belief, Language and Experience'. He first demonstrated how some of the greatest minds of modern times have grappled with the question of belief, finding it both a central and at the same time an extraordinarily difficult issue. Thus David Hume wrote in 1739 that 'This act of the mind has never yet been explain'd by any philosopher',[124] and added later that

this operation of the mind, which forms the belief of any matter of fact, seems hitherto to have been one of the greatest mysteries of philosophy.[125]

Bertrand Russell, too, admitted that 'Belief . . . is the central problem in the analysis of mind.'[126] Ludwig Wittgenstein wrote in 1953:

Believing is a state of mind. It has duration; and that independently of the duration of its expression in a sentence, for example. So it is a kind of disposition of the believing person. This is shown me in the case of someone else by his behaviour; and by his words. And under this head, by the expression 'I believe . . .' as well as by the simple assertion.[127]

Having surveyed these and other opinions on belief, Rodney Needham then concludes that

There is no point . . . in speaking of collective representations, or dogmas which are true of a culture as a whole, as 'beliefs' if it is not implied that the individual human beings who compose this social aggregate in question actually and severally believe them . . . In this case, we are not dealing with the overt organisation of society but with the recognition of an inner state which can pertain only to individual men.[128]

Thus it seems that the debate on whether the Germans believed in the Nazi *Weltanschauung* or not cannot be resolved; all too often it is influenced by the beliefs of the scholars writing on it. Two excellent recent studies by the historian Ian Kershaw have demonstrated once more how difficult it is to analyse this problem. While Kershaw has provided us with a great deal of evidence to show that there was a growing wave of dissatisfaction and even political dissent as regards the Nazi party, particularly concerning religious and economic issues, he has also pointed out the tremendous influence of what he calls the 'Hitler Myth' and the pseudo-religious character of the Führer-worship. In fact, it was only very late in the war that the 'Hitler Myth' gradually weakened, and only Hitler's suicide that ended it completely. Not only was there no contradiction between the two trends, but they supported each other, creating a mechanism similar to that which existed much earlier in European history, whereby rebelling peasants demanded to be allowed to inform the king, who obviously was on their side, of the injustice of his nobles. The 'Hitler Myth' served as a safety valve, and people felt that had the Führer known what the 'little Hitlers' were doing, he would surely put an end to their actions.[129] However, if people 'believed' in Hitler but expressed opposition to the party, or at least to specific actions carried out by party representatives, what does this tell us about their ideological convictions? Again, we must return to the point made earlier, that the Nazi *Weltanschauung*, that vague and ill-defined set of ideas, was most influential in areas where it harped on existing emotions, beliefs and prejudices. There is no doubt that it would have taken a great deal of brute force to compel Bavarian catholics to desert the church, or to persuade German miners that they were indeed part of an harmonious '*Volksgemeinschaft*'.[130] It was far less difficult to persuade those same people to fight against 'Bolshevism', to see the parliamentary system destroyed, or to persecute Jews – or at least to show extraordinary indifference to their persecution by the authorities.[131]

The Eastern Front, with its harsh climate, difficult geography and, especially, brutal fighting, formed a particularly fertile ground for the growth of 'beliefs' and myths, and seems to have enhanced the need of the troops to be provided with ideological credos and catechisms, irrational and pseudo-religious in character, not only in order to stiffen their determination in fighting the enemy, but also to drive away from their minds the growing realisation of the approaching defeat and the hopelessness of their situation. The tendency of soldiers to relapse into myths during long, costly wars, has been described with much force by Paul Fussel, writing on the Western Front of the First World War:

A world of such 'secrets', conversions, metaphors, and rebirths is a world of reinvigorated myth. In many ways it will seem to imply a throwback way across the nineteenth and eighteenth centuries to Renaissance and medieval modes of thought and feeling. That such a myth-ridden world could take shape in the midst of a war representing a triumph of modern industrialism, materialism, and mechanism is an anomaly worth considering. The result of inexpressible terror long and inexplicably endured is . . . a plethora of very un-modern superstitions, talismans, wonders, miracles, relics, legends and rumors.[132]

The German soldier on the Eastern Front of the Second World War was, however, much better prepared for such myths, superstitions and legends. He had been the target of years of anti-Bolshevik, anti-Slav and anti-Semitic indoctrination, specifically aimed at the irrational, and combined during the war with the vast, intimidating spaces of an unknown land inhabited by strange peoples speaking unintelligible tongues, seen both as *Untermenschen* and as possessing satanic powers which enabled them to face up to the indestructible Wehrmacht and inflect on it bloody defeats and endless retreats. Indeed, the situation at the front and the Nazi concept of propaganda complemented each other. Goebbels was the first to admit that to expect an officer returning from action to read Rosenberg's 'Mythos' was 'pure nonsense'; the soldier 'lives' the *Weltanschauung* at the front. As Manfred Messerschmidt has pointed out in his study of Nazi indoctrination, the party was not interested in a sophisticated educational programme which would allow soldiers to ask questions; instead, it wanted to deliver the '*Ideengut*', that is, to create and nourish a belief in some dogmas, and particularly to encourage the 'Führer Cult'. Not 'understanding' was desired, but an emotional 'instinct'.[133] Similarly, Ian Kershaw has stressed that 'The vagueness of the Nazi Weltanschauung was no hindrance. On the contrary: *Weltanschauung* meant for most Nazi sympathisers in 1933 nothing more precise than the engendering of a new spirit of sacrifice and struggle, necessary to combat the internal and external enemies of the German people in the interests of national unity and harmony'.[134] It seems that this feeling was also common among many soldiers, and particularly junior officers, during the war against the Soviet Union. The pseudo-religious credos given out to the troops during the last months of the war, as we saw in the preceding section, were a recognition on the part of the military and the propaganda authorities of the need of the troops for a religious faith both in a victory which their rational thoughts could no longer envision and in a Führer who had obviously led them to catastrophe; and at the same time these catechisms were the ultimate conclusion of an ideology which was never anything but a fanatic, 'blind' belief, whose whole strength was precisely its lack of any rational basis. Thus the war in the East was not just a 'war of ideologies', as Hitler had named it, but a religious war, in the sense that the troops chanted credos in which God, the Son and the Holy Spirit were replaced by the Führer, the *Volk* and the spirit of National Socialism.[135]

That there was a firm belief in the Führer among German troops, at least as strong as has been shown to have existed among the civilian population of the Third Reich, and that this belief played an important role in stiffening the morale of the soldiers, has been quite convincingly shown. Even in defeat this belief persisted, perhaps because it was the only thing that the soldiers could still believe in, as one of them admitted in a letter from Stalingrad, shortly before it fell to the Russians:

> The Führer has promised to get us out of here. This has been read to us, and we all firmly believed it. I still believe it today, because I simply must believe in something. If it isn't true, what is there left for me to believe in? . . . Let me go on believing, dear Grete; all my life – or eight years of it, at least – I have believed in the Führer and taken him at his word . . . If what we were promised is not true, then Germany will be lost, for no other promises can be kep after that.[136]

As polls among German POWs have shown, as late as January 1945 over 60 per cent of the prisoners expressed confidence in the Führer.[137] Goebbels wrote in his diary on 10 March 1945:

> All the [German] prisoners [in Allied hands] . . . have an almost mystical faith in Hitler. This is the reason why we are still on our feet and fighting.[138]

Two days later Goebbels added:

> The enemy also confirms that in general German troops in the West are showing an unbroken fighting spirit. Almost all prisoners, they say, are firmly convinced of a German victory. Hitler presents to them a sort of national myth.[139]

The dilemma presented by Ian Kershaw, whereby the German civilian population seems to have 'believed' in Hitler but become disenchanted with the party, posed a lesser problem for the soldier at the front. Here he had very little contact with the party, whereas Hitler was both his Führer and his supreme commander, and the '*Führerprinzip*' was a logical extension of the army command system. We certainly cannot say with confidence precisely how many soldiers believed in Hitler, what the relationship between this belief and their National Socialist convictions was, and how much these convictions were implanted in their minds by propaganda and indoctrination. As we have already admitted, there is no sure way to gauge belief. Yet if we return for a moment to Wittgenstein's assertion, according to which belief is demonstrated by an individual's behaviour, words, and the expression 'I believe', then we can say that a great number of German soldiers seem to have shared this sentiment, as was shown both by their determined fighting at the front, by their statements of belief even towards the end of the war and, as we shall demonstrate in the following and last chapter of this study, by their barbarous behaviour towards Russian POWs and civilians, very much in accordance with their Führer's *Weltanschauung*. In this context of the relationship between the Nazi indoctrination of the troops and their conduct at the front, it may be fitting to end with one more citation from David Hume, who asserted that belief is:

something felt by the mind, which distinguishes the ideas of the judgement from the fictions of the imagination. It gives them more force and influence; makes them appear of greater importance; infixes them in the mind; and renders them the governing principles of all actions.[140]

4 Barbarism and Criminality

INTRODUCTION

The barbarisation of warfare on the Eastern Front was the consequence of a number of interrelated factors, such as the brutality of the fighting itself, the harsh living conditions at the front, the susceptibility of the junior officers and probably of many of the soldiers to Nazi ideology, and the constant political indoctrination of the troops. The most direct cause for the criminal activities of the German army in the East and the resulting brutalising effect that they had on the individual soldier, however, were the so-called 'criminal orders'. This complex of commands, issued by the OKW and OKH on the eve of the invasion of Russia, determined to a large extent the brutal conduct of the troops at the front by providing them with a pseudo-legal and disciplinary framework. The 'criminal orders' were composed of four sets of instructions:

(1) Regulations concerning the activities of the *Einsatzgruppen* of the SS and SD, which enabled these murder squads to operate with relative freedom within the areas controlled by the army groups under the direct command of Reinhard Heydrich.
(2) The curtailment of military jurisdiction (*Die Einschränkung der Kriegsgerichtsbarkeit*), which stipulated that guerrillas, and civilians suspected of assisting them, were to be shot by the army, and that in case no guilty party could be found, collective measures were to be taken against the civilian population in the area.
(3) The Commissar Order, which called for the shooting of any Red Army political commissar captured by the troops.
(4) The 'Guidelines for the Conduct of the Troops in Russia', which ordered ruthless measures against 'Bolshevik agitators, guerrillas, saboteurs and Jews' and called for the complete elimination of any active or passive resistance.[1]

The 'criminal orders' were sent to all German formations on the eve of the invasion. The 12.I.D., for example, reported that it had received the orders of the Führer and OKW regarding the treatment of the Russian civilian population, the POWs 'and so forth', and had sent them to its units on 19 June 1941.[2] Similarly, Himmler's order regarding the activities of the SS and SD in the combat zones and Brauchitsch's endorsement of it were delivered to the division on 17 June.[3] Five days earlier the 12.I.D. received the 'Guidelines for the Conduct of the Troops in Russia' in sealed envelopes, with the instruction to distribute them among the battalions only after receiving their orders for the attack.[4]

This chapter examines three major aspects of the criminal activities of the divisions selected for our study, both from the point of view of the policies pursued and the orders issued by the commanders, and as they were manifested in the conduct of the troops. The first section deals with the maltreatment of Red Army POWs; the second section describes the war against the partisans and the consequent mass killings and evacuations of the Russian civilian population as well as the large-scale destruction of inhabited areas; and the last section concentrates on the exploitation of the population. Here we shall examine the official economic exploitation, the so-called 'wild requisitions' carried out by the troops, the conscription of labour both for work at the front and as forced labour in the Reich, the recruitment of 'volunteers' and, finally, the implementation of the 'scorched earth' policy and the devastation of wide-ranging areas from which the divisions retreated towards the end of the war.

THE MALTREATMENT OF RUSSIAN POWs

During the Second World War some 5 700 000 Russian soldiers fell into German hands, of whom about 3 300 000 died in captivity. In a recent study, the historian Christian Streit has argued convincingly that this terrible tragedy was both the result of the ideological concepts of the Nazi regime, which strove physically to eliminate the 'Bolshevik *Untermenschen*', and a consequence of Hitler's fear that the economic burden of caring for millions of prisoners would bring about unrest among the German population or even cause a collapse of the 'civilian morale'. Indeed, the trauma of 1918 was ever present in the minds of the Nazi leadership. However, Streit demonstrates that in late 1941 it was realised that the best way to avert just such a disaster would be to mobilise the Russian POWs and civilian population to the German war effort. Tim Mason's work has indicated that even before the outbreak of the war Germany's economic situation was such that if it wanted to continue its military build-up and keep its population relatively satisfied, it had to rely on foreign labour which became available as a consequence of its victorious campaigns. Paradoxically, the decision to use Russian labour brought about an improvement in the treatment of prisoners. The ruthless exploitation of these workers, however, ultimately led to yet another wave of mass deaths during 1943. Throughout this period the army collaborated with the regime in implementing these policies, both by making use of the POWs for its own purposes at the front and by sending them as forced labour to the Reich.[5]

Precise figures regarding the numbers of Russian soldiers who fell into the hands of the division examined here are unfortunately not available. The data found in the divisional files do indicate, however, that the numbers involved were very high, particularly during the first months of the war. The 16. Army, one of whose formations was the 12.I.D., reported on 24 August 1941 that it had captured 34 000 Red Army soldiers since the invasion of Russia. The 12.I.D. itself had taken 3159 POWs between 31 August and 8 October 1941 alone. By 20 December 1941 Army Group North claimed to have taken 438 950 prisoners since 22 June, whereas the 16. Army spoke of 212 971 POWs during the same period.[6] Army Group Centre, under whose command both the GD Regiment and the 18.Pz.Div. were, took 287 704 POWs between the beginning of the campaign and 8 July 1941. Panzer Group 2 reported 166 044 prisoners between 25 August and 18 October 1941, whereas the XXXXVII. Panzer Corps, commanding the 18.Pz.Div., spoke of 61 544 POWs between 30 September and 19 October 1941. The 18.Pz.Div. itself reported 5500 captured Red Army troops just for the five weeks between the start of the invasion and 28 July.[7]

The best-known aspects of the army's barbarous treatment of Russian POWs are those which were a direct consequence of the 'official' criminal orders issued by military commanders. Some historians have expressed doubts regarding the actual implementation of these orders by the units at the front. To quote just one rather recent example, an American historian writing on Nazi propaganda has claimed that 'As a general rule, the farther one travelled from Hitler's headquarters, the more humane were the Army directives regarding the treatment of the Russian population.'[8] It would be false, of course, to presume that all German units behaved in the same manner, and there were doubtlessly some whose conduct was more humane than that stipulated by the 'criminal orders'. The assumption that combat units behaved 'generally' better than the regime ordered them to is, however, based by and large on claims made in the numerous apologetic memoirs published after the war by former Wehrmacht generals. As we have already pointed out, a number of German historians have provided much evidence during the last few years that stands in stark contradiction to this assumption.[9] The files of the three divisions examined in this study support the thesis that most commanders at the front were quite eager to carry out the criminal directives of OKH and OKW. The most some of them were prepared to do was to try and keep their own and their troops' hands clean by leaving part of the dirty work to the 'expert' murderers of the *Einsatzgruppen*.[10]

On the eve of the invasion of the Soviet Union, the 18.Pz.Div. and the 12.I.D. ordered their troops to separate officers, NCOs and commissars from the rest of the POWs immediately upon capturing them and send them at once to the rear, where they were 'treated' by the SD. The 18.Pz.Div. added that Politruks, that is company commissars, were to be 'treated in the same manner'.[11] As we shall have occasion to show later on, even after it had been decided that the shooting of commissars should not be carried out at the front, some German soldiers continued this practice, as, for instance, a directive of the GD Division from September 1942 clearly indicates:

All Russian commissars – politruks – who fall alive into the hands of the troops are to be transferred immediately to the divisional intelligence section. Shooting by the troops after taking them prisoner is strictly forbidden.[12]

The shooting of commissars also served commanders at the front as an excuse for taking revenge. On 4 November 1941, for example, a regiment commander in the 18.Pz.Div. ordered the execution of three commissars in front of 450 POWs as punishment for the alleged atrocities committed in a previous battle against German troops.[13] Furthermore, the divisions also divided the POWs according to racial categories, and took care to point out who among their prisoners were of Jewish origin. This, of course, made the work of the *Einsatzgruppen* who regularly combed the POW camps much easier and facilitated the elimination of the racial enemies of the Reich.[14]

During the first months of the war in Russia, the German army executed a number of successful encirclement battles which cut off large formations of the Red Army from the main bulk of the Russian forces. This meant that technically many thousands of Russian troops found themselves behind the front. Nevertheless, on 13 September 1941 the OKH ordered that Russian soldiers who had been overrun by the German forces and had then reorganised behind the front were to be treated as partisans – that is, to be shot. It was left to the commanders on the spot to decide who belonged to this category.[15] Consequently this became the standard treatment of all Red Army soldiers found behind the front, regardless of whether they were 'organised' or not. Thus, for instance, the commander of the 12.I.D. instructed his officers on this issue:

> Prisoners behind the front-line: . . . Shoot as a general principle! Every soldier shoots any Russian who is found behind the front-line and has not been taken prisoner in battle.[16]

A high proportion of the deaths of Russian POWs during the early stages of the war occurred after they had already been organised in temporary camps and then sent to the rear. The German army made no special arrangements for transporting, feeding or clothing the enormous numbers of prisoners which it expected to capture in its battles of encirclement.[17] It may be pointed out here that during the fighting in France in 1940 things looked very different indeed. In a series of orders sent to the 12.I.D. before and during the French campaign the troops were instructed to maintain strict discipline among enemy POWs, but at the same time not to harm or abuse them in any way. Transportation, food, work and codes of behaviour were all set down so as to avoid chaos and to prevent unnecessary hardship. Furthermore, the German soldier was warned that unsoldierly conduct would entail severe punishment; plunder and rape could, as indeed they occasionally did, lead to a death sentence. Living off the land was strictly forbidden, and purchasing food was limited to the most essential items, which had to be paid for in cash. Soldiers were ordered not to intervene in the cultural life of the occupied population. Nevertheless, even here we see the first signs of a process of barbarisation deeply rooted in the ideological concepts of the Nazi regime, though restricted in this case to more specific groups. On 21 June 1940 the 12.I.D. received the following order:

Prisoners who are Germans belonging to the Reich [*Reichsdeutsche*] (including areas annexed to the Reich) and Czech citizens, since they also count as members of the German Reich, as long as they are so-called emigrants, are to be shot after their identity has been established. The execution should take place in POW camps.[18]

The 'so-called emigrants' were, of course, either the political or racial enemies of the Nazis, be they socialist, communist, other political dissidents, or Jews. In Russia on the other hand, the category of 'enemies of the Reich' was much more sweeping, and it included, apart from Jews and 'Bolsheviks', also the intelligentsia and the generally defined '*Untermenschen*', of the East. Hermann Goering was utterly serious when he declared that it would be only for the better if 'many scores of millions' of Russians died of starvation.[19]

Owing to the lack of any organised means of transportation for Russian POWs, many thousands of them died while marching on foot for hundreds of miles or packed into open or unheated goods trains in the midst of the fierce Russian winter.[20] This general policy of the German army in the East, described in detail by Christian Streit, was well reflected in the files of the divisions examined here. The 16. Army, for instance, instructed its formations on 31 July 1941 not to transport their prisoners in empty trains returning from the front for fear of their 'contaminating and soiling' the wagons.[21] The 18.Pz.Div. also warned its units on 17 August 1941 against allowing POWs to infest their vehicles with lice.[22] Even on the eve of the summer offensive of 1942 the GD Division instructed its commanders to organise the prisoners in march-columns, notwithstanding the vast distances which were to be covered by the advancing Wehrmacht.[23] Only in July 1942 did the 18.Pz.Div. admit that marching on foot was seriously sapping the strength of the prisoners, if not actually killing them outright.[24] By that time, however, thousands of them had already perished. Ironically, even people such as 'Gestapo Müller' complained about this situation, though for reasons of their own, as reported on 9 November 1941:

The commanders of concentration camps complain that from five to ten per cent of the Soviet Russians slated for execution arrive in the camps dead or half dead.[25]

Starvation among POWs was also a consequence both of a lack of any organisation and of a deliberate policy of 'elimination'. The 18.Pz.Div. simply ordered its troops five days before they marched into the Soviet Union to feed prisoners 'with the most primitive means'.[26] Soon afterwards both this formation and the 12.I.D. received directions from the OKH sent out to all German divisions regarding supplies for POWs. Whereas German soldiers were given a total of 24 203 calories per week, POWs who worked received 15 400 and those not involved in any 'work worth mentioning' only 14 280 calories per week.[27] On 21 October 1941 the OKH lowered the rations to non-working prisoners to a mere 10 407 calories per week,[28] and it is no wonder that many of them indeed died of starvation during the severe winter of 1941/2.

Winter caused heavy casualties among both German troops and Russian POWs also because of the lack of proper clothing. Not only did the Wehrmacht make no plans to supply clothes to prisoners; it was short of supplies even for its own troops. As Russian winter equipment was far superior to the German, the units at the front resorted to stripping POWs and civilians of whatever usable clothes they still possessed. The complaints of senior commanders regarding the 'appearance' of the troops, and of the Luftwaffe pilots who could not distinguish between German and Russian troops were only the less serious consequence of these actions.[29] So-called 'requisitions' of clothes and boots, both 'organised' and 'wild' – that is, on the soldiers' own initiative, particularly during the first winter in Russia[30] – added yet one more cause of the mass deaths of POWs, already weakened by forced marches and lack of food. Even when the divisions received clear orders to take better care of their prisoners, they clothed them by requisitioning the necessary items from the civilian population, as the 18.Pz.Div. did in September 1942.[31] A year later, when this division began relying increasingly on 'volunteers', it again stripped its POWs of their clothes, and especially their boots, and supplied them to the '*Hiwis*', while the prisoners had to make do with wooden clogs, obviously far from useful in the Russian winter.[32]

From what we have seen above, and because of the fact that many Red Army soldiers were captured wounded, it is clear that medical treatment was of paramount importance. The German army, however, refused the POWs any such care, and while various epidemics raged in the *Dulags* (transfer POW camps) in the rear, the condition of prisoners closer to the front was just as bad.[33] The army command ordered its fighting formations to allow only Russian doctors using Russian equipment to treat POWs.[34] These orders were repeated by the formations we have studied. The 18.Pz.Div., for example, stressed on 6 August 1941 that 'under no circumstances' were Russian prisoners to be 'treated, accommodated or transported' together with German wounded. Instead, 'they should, where possible, be treated by captured medical staff, accommodated in civilian houses and transported in Panje-wagons' to the POW camps.[35] Orders of a similar nature were also given by the II. Corps to the 12.I.D. on 21 August 1941.[36]

The mounting casualties and the resulting chronic lack of manpower in the Wehrmacht compelled combat formations to make increasing use of POWs both in their service units and, later on, even as fighting troops. These prisoners were euphemistically named *'Hilfswillige'* or *'Hiwis'*, that is, volunteers. Even if some of the POWs actually volunteered to serve in German units, whether out of hatred for Stalin's regime or for fear of the notorious *Dulags*, the high rate of desertion among them may serve as proof that they were quick to change their minds, particularly as it became clear that they were fighting on the losing side.[37] The ambiguity with which those *Hiwis* were viewed by the Germans is well reflected in an order of the 12.I.D. from 14 November 1941:

The Russian deserters and POWs designated as volunteers [*zu Hilfswilligen ernannten*] are to be treated with caution also after their appointment. It must be absolutely clear that the volunteers still remain POWs.[38]

This was the first mention of *Hiwis* in the files of the 12.I.D. By winter 1941/2 the divisions began making increasing use of POWs as *Hiwis*. In November 1941 the 18.Pz.Div. reported that most of its prisoners 'were kept by the troops for work duties'.[39] By March 1942 the 12.I.D. was including its *Hiwis* in the regular monthly situation reports.[40] Similarly, while preparing for the summer offensive of 1942, the GD division ordered its troops to make immediate use of POWs for building roads, collecting booty, burying corpses and assisting the service units of the division.[41]

In July 1942 the 18.Pz.Div. went a step further and established a 'work-company' of 533 POWs, guarded by twenty-one Germans.[42] A month later this unit was expanded into a 'POW-work-battalion' composed of three companies.[43] The GD Division also established POW companies for carrying out fortification works and clearing snow in September 1942.[44] Two months later this formation was ordered to reorganise its units by replacing German service personnel by *Hiwis* and transferring the former to combat duties.[45]

It should again be emphasised that as far as we can tell from the documents, Russian *Hiwis* were far from enthusiastic about their employment by the Wehrmacht. German commanders repeatedly warned their troops to beware of sabotage on the part of the 'volunteers', indicating thereby that they were less than certain about the loyalty of their indigenous recruits.[46] One of the reasons for the unreliability of the *Hiwis* was that they were often used for activities which the German soldiers were only to glad to avoid. Thus, for example, the 18.Pz.Div. received the following order on 2 November 1941:

> The Commander in Chief of the army has decided that in order to spare German blood, mines should be tracked and cleared by Russian POWs.[47]

Only nine days later the division could already report that it had established a POW engineer unit;[48] this was probably one order that everyone was quite willing to execute. In March 1942 a further POW mine-clearing unit was built, this time intended to deal with German mines as well.[49] The GD Division also began investigating the possibility of using POWs for the same purpose in June 1942,[50] while the 12.I.D. reported the establishment of a platoon of thirty-six Russian POWs for clearing minefields in early December 1942.[51] As the division itself admitted, these prisoners had received only 'superficial' training for carrying out this dangerous task.[52] We should therefore not be surprised to read in a report of the GD Division dated 11 January 1943 that 'Between the months of January and May a great number of the volunteers attached to the division have run away.'[53]

Maltreatment and indiscriminate shooting of Russian POWs was not only a result of specific orders from above, carried out in a disciplined manner by the troops at the front; nor was it only a consequence of the general brutal character of the fighting on both sides, though both these factors did indeed play a major role in the process of barbarisation. The files of the divisions indicate that 'wild', undisciplined and indiscriminate shooting of Russian soldiers who had put down their weapons and surrendered, began during the very first days of the campaign and was carried out by the troops in spite of their commanders' objections to such 'unmilitary' behaviour. These actions can only be traced back to two causes: the ceaseless and ruthless propaganda of the regime against the 'Jewish-Bolshevik *Untermenschen*' to which the soldiers had been exposed throughout their youth ever since the Nazis came to power in 1933, some elements of which had even deeper roots dating back to earlier periods in German history; and the 'criminal orders', which allowed for a very loose definition of the racial and political enemies of the Reich and specifically stressed that the war in the East should not be viewed as an ordinary military confrontation, but rather as a 'war of ideologies' between two *Weltanschauungen* and two racial groups which could never exist side by side nor reach any sort of compromise.

Indeed, intances of brutality among the troops reached such a level that many of the more senior commanders became increasingly worried that they would lead to a general breakdown of discipline and have a detrimental effect on their own authority. It is possible that in some cases commanders were using the argument of discipline when in fact they were trying to do away with some of the uglier aspects of the fighting for moral reasons as well, but this could not be openly stated because of the ideological character of the war dictated from above. By and large, however, it seems that the senior officers were much more concerned with questions of discipline than with morality. This is reflected in the numerous orders directed at the troops, in which it was repeated time and again that while 'undisciplined' and 'wild' shootings of prisoners were forbidden, organised and orderly executions were not only legitimate, but even necessary, as they were done according to the expressed wishes of the Führer.

The fact that orders from senior commanders regarding the brutal behaviour of their troops persisted throughout the war may serve as an indication that they failed to limit their men only to 'organised' barbarism. The often ambiguous wording of their commands may help us to understand why they failed in controlling their soldiers. As we have pointed out, it was those same officers who also served as the ideological instructors of the soldiers and who drummed into them the tenets of National Socialism. The official policy regarding the treatment of uniformed and civilian *Untermenschen* alike, explicitly stated in the orders, must have made it extremely difficult for the individual soldier to distinguish between 'disciplined' and 'wild' acts of brutality. As we shall see below, it was possible for the same commander to warn against indiscriminate shootings of POWs and to stress the importance of killing commissars. This fine differentiation between 'Untermenschen' who should be shot right away, and others who were to be treated 'decently' but at the same time also marched, worked and starved to death, failed to impress the troops. Having been told on the one hand that this was no ordinary war but a '*Weltanschauungskrieg*' in which there were '*keine Kameraden*', and on the other hand that 'the Russian soldier has a right for decent treatment', they seem to have adopted the former, more brutal definition of the war, which also corresponded much better with their indoctrination in civilian life and in the army, as well as with the wishes of their Führer and the general brutality of the fighting.

It should be pointed out, however, that we have very little direct evidence on acts of brutality by the troops. The diaries of the soldiers refrain from dwelling on them; the orders of the commanders often do not describe them in detail. Furthermore, as we have already said elsewhere, the standards of conduct and morality applied by the German army in the East were different from, for example, those applied in the West. Thus, while the divisional courts-martial hardly mention cases of plundering, the commanders complain repeatedly of 'wild requisitions', which, however, do not seem to have called for actual disciplinary measures as they did in France. Similarly, 'sexual offences' during the occupation of France were described as 'rape', whereas in Russia they were, at the most, 'racial offences' or 'fraternisation'. The fact that officers and men refrained from describing their brutality during and after the war should not surprise us. The documents that have been found indicate that they were much more widespread than the memoirs would like us to believe. They also make it clear that most of the officers reacted against the brutality of their men because they feared chaos among their troops and desperation among the Russians, and not because they opposed the ideology which they themselves were pumping into their soldiers.[54]

The best proof for the fact that acts of brutality and indiscriminate shootings began even before the brutalising effect of the war could come into play, is an order issued on 25 June 1941, three days after the beginning of the war in Russia, by the commander of the XXXXVIII. Panzer Corps, one of whose formations was the 18.Pz.Div.:

I have observed that senseless shootings of both POWs and civilians have taken place. A Russian soldier who has been taken prisoner while wearing a uniform and after he put up a brave fight, has the right for a decent treatment. We want to free the civilian population from the yoke of Bolshevism and we need their labour force . . . This instruction does not change anything regarding the Führer's order on the ruthless action to be taken against partisans and Bolshevik commissars.[55]

General Lemelsen's order, however, did not have the required effect and had to be repeated five days later:

In spite of my instructions of 25.6.41 . . . still more shootings of POWs and deserters have been observed, conducted in an irresponsible, senseless and criminal manner. This is murder! The German Wehrmacht is waging this war against Bolshevism, not against the united Russian peoples. We want to bring back peace, calm and order to this land which has suffered terribly for many years from the oppression of a Jewish and criminal group. The instruction of the Führer calls for ruthless action against Bolshevism (political commissars) and any kind of partisan! People who have been clearly identified as such should be taken aside and shot only by order of an officer . . . [descriptions] of the scenes of countless bodies of soldiers lying on the roads, having clearly been killed by a shot through the head at point blank range, without their weapons and with their hands raised, will quickly spread in the enemy's army.[56]

Not only does this order make it clear that POWs and civilians were being shot by German soldiers already during the first days of the war. We also find here the strange mixture of arguments for and against barbarism failing to produce a coherent whole and ultimately leading, as they indeed did, to further brutality. The general invokes the traditional concept of comradeship in arms; he stresses that they have come to liberate Russia from oppression; he warns that the enemy will retaliate in kind: 'The disorganised enemy hides in forests and fields and continues to fight from fear, while we lose countless comrades.'[57] But at the same time he legitimises murder and hatred. Red commissars should be shot, though in a disciplined manner, because they are Bolsheviks; partisans should share the same fate; and the Jews, it is clearly implied, are a major element in the 'criminal group' oppressing the Russians and should be done away with.

It should thus hardly surprise us that indiscriminate shootings of POWs continued unabated throughout the war, given further impetus both by the fierce resistance of the Russians, the growing casualties, the harsh weather conditions and, not least, the intensification of the Nazi indoctrination of the troops. In some cases the behaviour of German soldiers actually harmed their own war effort, since they seem to have continued shooting even those prisoners who had been organised to work alongside them. Thus, for instance, the 16. Army ordered its troops on 5 July 1941 that 'after the POWs have been organised into work-battalions they should not be attacked and shot'.[58] This order again failed to produce any positive results, as less than two weeks later the 12.I.D. had to repeat that 'the "doing in" [*Umlegen*] of Russians who have already been taken prisoners is unworthy of German soldiers'.[59] Similarly, the 18.Pz.Div. failed in persuading its troops that their brutal behaviour towards POWs was ultimately harming their own cause. In February 1942 the division pointed out to its men that

> Numerous interrogations of soldiers of the Red Army have repeatedly confirmed that they are more afraid of falling prisoner than of a possible death on the battlefield . . . Since November last year it has become known that only a few deserters have come over to us and that during battles fierce resistance was put up and only a few POWs were taken . . . The troops must be instructed that not all Russians are communists.[60]

At the same time, as we saw in the previous chapter, the German soldier was provided with an increasing flood of propaganda which said precisely the opposite, namely, that the Russians were indeed dispensable '*Untermenschen*', no matter whether they were communists, Jews, or simply Slavs. Consequently, in September 1942, the GD Division reported on similar incidents among its own troops:

> Many deserters brought wounded [from the battlefield] have claimed that they had received their injuries from the Germans hours after they had thrown down their weapons and had indicated their intention to desert by visibly raising their arms.[61]

This phenomenon was not limited to the divisions we have selected for this study. In December 1942 the OKH reported:

In spite of the orders issued on the treatment of POWs, OKH is continuing to receive reports testifying to the fact that the treatment of POWs still does not correspond with existing instructions.[62]

It should not be thought that 'existing instructions' on the treatment of POWs were particularly humane, as we have seen already from the 'official' maltreatment of prisoners. Nevertheless, the army did decide to halt the indiscriminate shooting of prisoners at the front and to make use of their labour force. That it failed in implementing this policy was connected to a large extent with the fact that its indoctrinational policies went in precisely the opposite direction, and that the 'criminal orders' issued on the eve of the invasion of Russia remained in force and legitimised in the most general terms the brutality of the troops. In a sense, ideological indoctrination proved so successful that even when the commanders wanted to avoid its ultimate conclusion, mostly for utilitarian reasons, the troops refused to go along with their instructions. Thus we find the GD Division repeating the same orders that we saw issued at the beginning of the campaign in April 1943:

[The troops] must understand what the ultimate result of the maltreatment or the shooting of POWs after they have given themselves up in battle would be . . . a stiffening of the enemy's resistance, because every Red Army soldier fears German captivity.[63]

FIGHTING PARTISANS AND MURDERING CIVILIANS

Though the orders concerning the treatment of POWs were somewhat modified after the first months of the war, the complex of the criminal orders provided the troops at the front with a blank cheque for the mass killing of civilians on the slightest suspicion of resistance to the army, and often without even that, as part of 'preventive' and 'collective' measures, as well as on political and racial grounds. Thus the ideology underlying the Russian campaign, together with the orders instructing its implementation and the frustration caused by the failure to 'pacify' the population, brought about a vicious circle of violence and murder and resulted in the destruction of wide-ranging areas in western Russia.[64] The three divisions examined in this study took part in these activities, and their files demonstrate the extent of the participation of German combat troops in these crimes, until recently attributed mainly to the rear echelon, the *Einsatzgruppen* and the SS. As we shall see below, the worsening situation at the front caused the troops to go even beyond the rules of conduct set down by the 'Barbarossa Directives', which in any case allowed for a very loose interpretation of civilian resistance.

The 12.I.D. issued its first order regarding the treatment of guerrillas on the day it marched into the Soviet Union, 22 June 1941. It allowed no flexibility in the reading of the instructions of OKH; guerrillas (*Freischärler*) were not to be treated as POWs but 'sentenced on the spot by an officer', that is, shot.[65] By 31 July 1941 the 16. Army instructed its formations that 'Partisan-Battalions' forming behind the front and not fulfilling precisely the laws of war regarding clothing, weapons and means of identification, were to be treated as guerrillas, whether they were soldiers or not. Civilians who rendered them any assistance were to be treated in the same manner.[66] The euphemism 'treated as guerrillas' always meant one thing only: death by shooting or hanging. This same order was also issued by the 18.Pz.Div. on 4 August 1941.[67] This meant, of course, that if a unit of guerrillas moved into a village and helped itself to the facilities there, the Germans saw that as collaboration with the partisans and retaliated by destroying the village and killing its inhabitants. Indeed, on 30 January 1942 the 12.I.D. reported that following an incident in which a few of its sledges had driven on mines in the vicinity of the village of Nov. Ladomiry, the whole male population of the village was shot and the houses burned down as a 'collective measure'.[68]

The units at the front were also ordered to strike against so-called 'suspected elements'. The II. Corps instructed its troops that 'As a protection from partisan groups, patrols should be sent into the depth of our area in order to enforce strict control on the villages and their inhabitants. Ruthless action is to be immediately taken against suspected elements!'[69] It is important to remember that according to the 'Guidelines for the Conduct of the Troops in Russia', 'suspected elements' included 'Bolshevik agitators, guerrillas, saboteurs and Jews', while 'ruthless action' (*rücksichtlos vorzugehen*) meant shooting or hanging.[70] The significance of this order was that the army did not only act against civilians who put up active or passive resistance, but also against the potential political and racial enemies of the Reich – Bolsheviks and Jews – whether they resisted or not. Already on 4 July 1941 the 12.I.D. reported on the execution of ten civilians in the village of Dukszty, accused of membership of the communist party or youth organisation and of belonging to the Jewish race.[71]

It is clear that the brutal behaviour of the army towards the civilian population only increased partisan activity.[72] In turn, the formations at the front further intensified their operations and caused even more hardship and destruction to the inhabitants of the occupied areas. In August 1941 the II. Corps, commanding among others the 12.I.D., ordered that 'partisans are to be publicly hanged and left to hang for some time', whereas communists and former Soviet bureaucrats 'about whom nothing can be proved' should be delivered to the prison camps, that is to the reliable hands of the *Einsatzgruppen*.[73] The 18.Pz.Div. issued similar orders.[74] Curfew regulations, which at first restricted movement only at night and called upon the troops to make 'ruthless use of firearms',[75] were extended in September 1941 to cover movements during the daytime as well. The 12.I.D. announced that anyone 'walking about' (*Herumlaufende*) was to be treated as a POW.[76] Shortly afterwards the division declared that mayors of villages would pay with their own and their families' lives for any partisan activity in their areas.[77] In October it was announced that 'tolerating partisans' would be punished by hanging.[78] The 18.Pz.Div. also ordered on 8 October 1941 that anti-partisan operations should include the taking of civilian hostages, the evacuation of civilians from areas of operations, the charging of village mayors with responsibility for denouncing all politically involved persons and aliens, and the establishment of patrols in the rear areas.[79] By this time the 12.I.D. had issued special passes for the population; those caught without such a pass were shot.[80] It was also recommended to the troops that any houses suspected of harbouring partisans should be burned down instead of risking entry into them. If the suspicion proved to be correct, 'The fire forces the partisans to jump out and shooting them down is then easy.'[81] The most that could happen, according to this technique, would be that a few innocent civilians would be burned alive.

Yet to the growing frustration of the Germans, partisan activity was on the increase.[82] In early November 1941 the 12.I.D. was compelled to pull one of its regiments out of the front on a 'mopping-up' operation in the rear areas.[83] A few weeks later more units were dispatched to assist in this operation. The instructions were to conduct collective measures against villages which had failed to report 'aliens', including shooting of the inhabitants, and to send all 'aliens' and 'suspected elements' to labour camps in the rear, where they could be 'treated' by the SD.[84] Public hangings were to be given even more publicity.[85] As we can read in the files of the division, its units hanged and shot civilians on such grounds as 'suspicion of partisan activity', 'feeding a Russian soldier', and 'possession of firearms' which were sometimes admitted to have been obsolete hunting rifles. In some cases Russian soldiers in uniform were taken prisoner and then 'shot as partisans'.[86] The supply column of the 12.I.D., for instance, shot or hanged sixteen civilians during November 1941 for the following reasons: six for having no passes; two for 'wandering about'; two for trying to escape; one for being an 'assistant's assistant of the partisans'; two for hiding arms; two soldiers for trying to escape; and only one single civilian for actually taking part in an attack on German troops.[87] By 24 November 1941 the II. Corps reported that its formations had succeeded in 'destroying' 198 such partisans since 11 November.[88] The 16. Army, which reported on a similar operation between 29 November and 5 December 1941, had killed 77 'partisans' in the combat zone and a further 265 in the rear. All in all, 387 civilians were killed within the space of six days, at a total cost of ten killed and eleven wounded Germans. The low number of German casualties may serve as an indication that most Russian dead were anything but guerrillas.[89]

With the stabilisation of the front-line the German army resorted to a more systematic method of 'controlling' the civilian population. On 7 December 1941 the 12.I.D. was ordered to evacuate all the civilians along a six-mile-deep stretch parallel to the front within nine days. The inhabitants were allowed to take some food and property, while their houses were either used by the troops for accommodation or burned down. Even in areas where civilians were allowed to remain, they had to leave all the houses used by the soldiers.[90] On 14 December the 12.I.D. reported that it had succeeded in evacuating 'only' 350 of a total of 2000 inhabitants living in the 'evacuation zone'.[91] A few weeks later the II. Corps had to admit that some of the civilians had been evacuated 'with entirely inadequate food supplies'.[92] Nevertheless the Corps ordered the creation of a further 'barred zone' in which civilian movement was strictly supervised.[93] Indeed, control was so rigid that the 12.I.D. reported a few days later that the supply of villages with essential items was 'made quite impossible'.[94] Not only were the regulations to remain unchanged throughout the winter, but they were enforced by special patrols and 'village-commanders' (*Orts Kommandaten*), thus knowingly allowing the population to starve and freeze during the harsh winter of 1941/2.

Civilians breaking these regulations were either shot on the spot or taken to internment camps in the rear, where they were 'treated' by the *Einsatzgruppen.*[95]

While these evacuation operations were taking place, the 12.I.D. continued its routine 'anti-partisan' activities and reported daily on the shooting and hanging of civilians.[96] From time to time large-scale operations against 'partisan areas' were launched, with particularly terrible consequences for the population. Between 19 November and 5 December, for instance, units of the II. Corps operating in the area of Polisto Lake killed 250 'partisans', destroyed fifteen 'camps' and burned down sixteen villages, taking away cattle and horses and destroying food supplies. The Germans suffered only six killed and eight wounded, all in a single partisan ambush beyond the area of operations.[97] Such 'purging operations' only caused a growing number of the civilians to join the partisans and encouraged the bloody vicious circle initiated by the Wehrmacht. The policy of the army, however, remained the same. On 31 January 1942 the commander of Army Group North issued the following order:

> The recent revival of partisan activities in the rear area . . . together with the battles at the front, demand that action be taken . . . with the greatest ruthlessness. Partisans are to be destroyed wherever they appear, as are their hiding places [that is the villages] if not needed by our troops for accommodation.[98]

The 'war against the partisans' on the central sector of the Eastern Front was conducted with the same ruthless measures, and was even less successful in 'pacifying' the population, owing to the geographical conditions which were much more favourable for guerrilla warfare. During 1942 the 18.Pz.Div. evacuated large areas along the front of their civilian population, established special anti-partisan units and executed all suspected collaborators.[99] Similarly, the GD Division ordered its troops to 'destroy' all captured partisans and, by order of a battalion commander, to kill all civilians suspected of helping the guerrillas.[100] These measures only intensified partisan activities, and the 18.Pz.Div. suffered increasing casualties and particularly complained of disruptions of its rear communications.[101] The policy, however, was not changed; on the contrary, the scale of such anti-partisan operations was increased even further in the following year.

In mid-May 1943 the 18.Pz.Div. was pulled out of the line and sent to the forest areas south of Briansk. It was given the code name '318. Infantry Division', and together with other German, Hungarian and Russian 'volunteer' units was ordered to 'purge' the forest of an estimated force of some 3000–3500 guerrillas.[102] The troops about to take part in this operation, code-named '*Zigeunerbaron*', were ordered to evacuate all the civilians unfit for military service and to allow them to take only food for fourteen days. The rest of the property was to be confiscated by the army. Men between the ages of 15 and 65 were to be treated as POWs. Red Army officers and commissars were to be taken to the intelligence section, while soldiers, party functionaries and Jews were to be used as guides or to clear minefields. All villages in the area were to be burned down.[103]

'*Bandenunternehmen Zigeunerbaron*' lasted two weeks, between 17 May and 2 June 1943: 1568 prisoners were taken, 869 deserted and 1584 people were killed; the units involved destroyed 207 'camps' and 2930 battle position, some of which were in fact civilian houses. Along with that, 15 812 civilians were driven out of the area and all their villages burned down.[104] As the Germans had made no provisions for resettlement, nor, for that matter, for food or shelter, it is probable that many of the evacuated civilians died. On the basis of the involvement of the *Einsatzgruppen* in such anti-partisan operations it is also possible that many of the evacuated Russians were later 'eliminated'.[105] Moreover, the operation seems to have been a failure, as only 700 partisans were either killed or captured. Nevertheless, the 18.Pz.Div. tried to present it as a great success by stating in its final report that

> It is quite clear that the operation will influence the civilian population of the adjacent areas in a favourable propagandistic direction.[106]

The effect of such operations on the Russian population may be described as anything but 'favourable' from the German point of view. The fear, disgust and hate which those barbarous actions aroused in the civilians and soldiers of the Red Army may partly account for the conduct of the Russians when they themselves reached German territory, as well as for the decision to retain German POWs as forced labour until the mid-1950s. Those who speak of the barbarous conduct of the Red Army in the eastern parts of Germany during the last months of the war, should be reminded of the scenes that revealed themselves to those soldiers as they advanced through areas once 'controlled', 'purged' and 'evacuated' by the retreating Wehrmacht.[107]

One last aspect of the 'war against the partisans' should be mentioned in this context. The euphemism 'agent', like the terms 'partisan', 'guerrilla' or 'bandit', served the troops at the front and their commanders, as well as the various SS and SD units operating behind them, in legitimising activities which often had very little to do with countering enemy espionage, but rather were based on ideological and racial concepts and orders; it was repeatedly used as a means of dispelling any possible doubts or reservations regarding the criminal maltreatment of women and children. It was thus convenient to label any movements of the civilian population, uprooted and homeless as a result of the fighting, as a security risk for the army. The 18.Pz.Div., for instance, ordered its troops to prevent any movement of civilians (that is, refugeees) to the East, if necessary by force of arms.[108] This policy was justified by the XXXXVII. Panzer Corps two weeks later, when it explained in early July 1941 that these civilians hampered the free flow of traffic and were 'especially' an 'espionage' hazard. Consequently, all men of military age were to be taken to POW camps and the rest sent back to where they had come from. High-ranking political commissars were to be sent to the Panzer Group headquarters; the rest were presumably shot or delivered to the SD.[109] By the end of July instructions regarding the movement of civilians in front-line areas were greatly simplified – they were all to be immediately shot.[110] Similarly, the 12.I.D. in the northern sector of the Eastern Front ordered on 11 July 1941 that 'Civilians coming from the rear and trying to cross the forward German line are to be stopped and shot on the spot for suspected espionage.[111] By August 1941 the 18.Pz.Div. began to include in its instructions all civilians found 'wandering about', 'who seem in any way suspicious'; they were to be 'treated' by the troops if stopped in the combat zone, and delivered to the *Einsatzgruppen* if found in the rear areas.[112] The 16. Army tried to stem the flow of refugees from Leningrad besieged by its formations by ordering in January 1942 the delivery of all civilians crossing the front-line to the military police or the SD, by whom they were most probably shot.[113]

This policy of labelling any civilian shot by the army for a variety of reasons as an 'agent' without even bothering to subject him or her to the most elementary interrogation, seems to have given the troops at the front a feeling that they could do almost anything they wished with the population. Indeed, by February 1942 some commanders began realising that this policy was endangering their own authority. The II. Corps found it necessary to forbid the shooting of 'agents' by soldiers and ordered that they should be delivered to the 16. Army for further interrogation. The 18.Pz.Div. admitted in June 1942 that 'bad mistakes' had been committed in the treatment and interrogation of 'agents' and instructed that they be given over to the Secret Field Police (GFP).[114] The GD Division also ordered its troops to report cases of 'partisans' and 'agents' to the GFP and not, as they had obviously done till then, to the SD.[115] However, as far as we know, these orders were more a manifestation of administrative rivalry than a sudden awakening of guilty consciences; the *Geheime-Feld-Polizei* was considered to be just as ruthless as the *Einsatzgruppen* in its treatment of civilians and, indeed, received from the SD high marks for its efficiency.[116]

As we have said above, the euphemism 'agent' was frequently used as a justification for the maltreatment of women and children. The phrasing of some of the orders makes it clear that in some cases the commanders were trying to prevent any sympathy on the part of the troops for the population, and particularly to dissuade them from fraternising with Russian women. In October 1941 the 12.I.D. warned its soldiers that 'the carrying of information is mostly done by youngsters in the ages of 11–14', and recommended that 'as the Russian is more afraid of the truncheon than of weapons, flogging is the most advisable measure' for interrogation; the Russians were liars, 'especially the women . . . a few powerful pats on the back will shorten' the process considerably. The fraternisation which was obviously taking place between the troops and the female population was also dangerous for racial reasons, as the division pointed out: 'Lately women have been repeatedly found in the barracks. Those are almost always Jewish females . . . always women whose Jewish origin cannot be seen.'[117]

These same arguments were used also by the 18.Pz.Div., which warned its men in November 1941 of a groups of 'agents' between the ages of 12 and 18, and went on to forbid the employment of Jews, notwithstanding their usefulness as interpreters.[118] The problem of relations between soldiers and women was clearly disturbing the senior officers of the division, as soon afterwards it elaborated further on this issue:

> Lately venereal diseases have been discovered for the first time as a result of contacts with the female Russian population. Instruction

to the troops should stress that intercourse with female civilians is not only unworthy of the German soldier, but also carries with it the danger of being exploited or harmed by a spy, of falling into the hands of a female partisan and of being terribly mutilated or infected with VD or other infectious diseases. Russian doctors have pointed out that from their own experience up to 90 per cent of the female population is infected with gonorrhoea and 50 per cent with syphilis.

Women caught with German soldiers were, according to this order, to be immediately delivered to the police on 'security' grounds.[119] Similar arguments were also used by the GD Division. In October 1942, for instance, the GD issued a leaflet for its troops dealing with enemy espionage, which emphasised that 'men of all ages, good-looking women and particularly young girls and lads and even children' were given some 'story' to tell, such as, for example, that they were looking for their family, while actually carrying out espionage activities.[120] Here too the GD Division was quick to stress the 'dangers' involved in contacts with Russian women, citing as evidence the rise in VD incidence among the troops and warning of the possibility of these women acting as 'agents'. The division resorted to a simple solution to the problem of fraternisation by evicting all the inhabitants of houses used for accommodation by the soldiers.[121] Nevertheless, this proved to be an insoluble problem, particularly because the German army employed growing numbers of women in the barracks in various service duties. Thus the XXXXVI. Panzer Corps found it necessary to raise this issue again in April 1943, reminding the men of the 18.Pz.Div. that 'the Russian woman is prepared to make unscrupulous use of her physical advantages and of our soldiers' confidence for purposes of espionage in the interest of the war'. The troops were called upon to exercise 'strict self-control' and were warned that anyone caught while having sexual relations with a Russian woman would be suspected of working for the enemy's intelligence services and could expect severe punishment.[122]

That this image of the child–woman perfidious spy, created by the German army, was not only used to prevent fraternisation but also to justify and legitimise brutality, can be seen from the following intelligence report, dealing with the interrogation of fifteen 'agents' by the II. Corps between December 1941 and March 1942. Twelve of those 'spies' were between 15 and 17 years old, one was a child, one 24 years old, and one a woman, the child's mother. About the methods used in interrogating the prisoners we can learn from this description concerning two boys, aged 15 and 16, who, we are told,

> in spite of their youth and a certain stupidity, gave the impression of being two fanatic communists and German-haters during the questioning, which lasted many hours. Even during the proper interrogation they continuously tried to lie, and every truthful statement had to be forced out of them with the most brutal methods.

All the civilians mentioned above were executed immediately after their interrogation.[123]

The relations between the German army and the civilian Russian population were thus a product both of the ideological concepts underlying the war in the East which emphasised the 'sub-human' nature of the inhabitants, and of the growing resistance of the population to their conquerors. At the same time there seems to have existed some degree of fraternisation between the troops and the civilians, quite typical of armies occupying large territories of foreign lands. The Nazi authorities, as well as the higher echelons of the army command, made a concerted and consistent effort to dehumanise the Russian population in the eyes of their troops and thereby to prevent any sympathy for them and to make it possible to issue and execute the most brutal orders necessary in order to implement the policies of the regime. Moreover, it would seem that the troops and the junior officers were quite eager to make use of the ideological arguments which helped them in justifying to themselves and to their comrades their own brutality. The process of dehumanising the enemy and his population was probably made easier by the fact that most Germans spoke no Russian and could thus have very little verbal communication with the occupied peoples. The troops were not allowed to make any use of the Jewish population, among which there was a higher proportion of German-speakers, and the few interpreters in the divisions were used mainly for purposes of interrogation and printing notices. The increasing numbers of '*Hiwis*' which the divisions were compelled to conscript owing to a growing lack of manpower, however, further complicated the situation. On the one hand, the army went so far as to provide its Russian 'volunteers' with Nazi propaganda material and to establish so-called '*Russische Betreuungsstaffeln*' (Russian Propaganda Squads).[124] On the other hand, the commanders did their utmost to prevent their troops from fraternising with the population, and developed the arguments we saw above regarding the perfidious character of the Russians, and particularly the women, who were described as both racially inferior (mostly Jewish), physically degenerate (suffering from venereal diseases), dangerous (agents and partisans), malicious (would mutilate German soldiers) and, at the same time, sexually attractive. One cannot avoid noticing the similarity in imagery and psychology between the presentation of Russian women by the commanders on the Eastern Front, and the descriptions of enemy females by the men of the *Freikorps* – 'red', satanic women whom they wanted to possess sexually and at the same time to smash into 'bloody pulp'.[125] Indeed, this may indicate yet another connection between the traditional language of the military, the vocabulary of the *Freikorps*, and the Nazi terminology which increasingly dominated the language of the Wehrmacht.

It is difficult to determine to what degree the commanders succeeded in preventing their men from associating with Russian women. That this was, at best, only partially achieved, can be seen from the endless repetitions of these warnings. It seems, however, that in one way this ideological brainwashing did bear fruit. Whereas the individual German soldier may well have refused to view the individual Russian man, woman or child as an '*Untermensch*', the unit, be it squad, platoon, company or battalion, does not seem to have had any difficulty in identifying the mass of Russians, be they in the form of a village, refugees or POWs, as sub-humans worthy of the most brutal treatment. Thus we find that the dehumanisation of the enemy, which is at the core of the process of barbarisation, hinges upon the enemy's anonymity, facelessness, which is best achieved when he is part of a mass, and most difficult when it is reduced to two individuals facing each other.[126] On the Eastern Front it was possible for at least a significant part of the German troops to fraternise with individual Russians for a while, and then to 'eliminate' them and burn down their houses as part of a mass of dangerous and contemptible '*Untermenschen*' the moment this or that 'security' situation called for such actions.

EXPLOITATION, EVACUATION AND DESTRUCTION

The German army marched into the Soviet Union with explicit orders to 'live off the land', regardless of the effect this would have on the civilian population. This method of supplying the army led to terrible impoverishment, famine and destruction, and caused millions of deaths in the occupied territories. Gradually the army realised that for its own interests it had to improve its methods of exploiting the economic resources of Russia. At the same time, however, the commanders at the front became increasingly eager to make use of the labour force of the civilians for work connected with local military operations in view of the growing shortage of manpower; furthermore, pressure was building up to transport all available civilians for work in the Reich. Side by side with these 'official', albeit contradictory policies, the troops at the front, partly motivated by the ideology underlying the Russian campaign, and partly owing to the harsh conditions on the battlefield, constantly plundered and looted the population. The commanders, though they themselves encouraged and directed the 'organised' exploitation of the conquered lands, were alarmed by what they called 'wild requisitions' on the part of the troops since they constituted a potential threat to discipline and morale. The soldiers, however, found it difficult to distinguish between 'organised' and 'wild' looting, as indeed they had the same disastrous effect on the population. The slow and tortuous retreat of the Wehrmacht from Russia brought in its wake even more suffering and devastation, as the Germans conducted a policy of 'scorched earth', aimed at destroying the economic infrastructure of the evacuated areas and uprooting their population. By the time the German army had been finally driven out of the Soviet Union it left behind it a land of misery and famine, death and desolation, brought about by its criminal, barbarous policies, and implemented to a large extent by its troops at the front.[127]

The ruthless exploitation of Western Russia and its inhabitants is well reflected in the files of the three divisions examined here. Three days before the invasion of the Soviet Union, the 18.Pz.Div., for instance, ordered its troops to take as little supplies as possible, and to rely instead on a 'full exploitation of the land'. Plundering on the troops' own initiative was prohibited; in its place the division established so-called 'booty-registration-units' which listed all economic assets in newly occupied areas. As cattle was also to be requisitioned from the population, the division made it clear that it intended to be dependent on supplies from the rear only for flour for baking bread.[128] By the end of July 1941, however, the 18.Pz.Div. realised that if work in the fields, halted by the war and the evacuation of machinery by the retreating Red Army, were not resumed, the harvest would fail and both the population and the army would suffer from a lack of food supplies. The division therefore appointed an 'Agricultural Officer' whose duty was to regulate and control economic activities in the collective farms (Kolkhoz) occupied by its units.[129] Indeed, as a report by the 'Agricultural Officer' pointed out in early August, the situation among the peasants was very serious, both because most of their cattle had been requisitioned by the troops and since their machines had either been destroyed or taken by the Red Army.[130]

Although the 18.Pz.Div. was aware of the fact that the long-term consequences of its policies would harm its own position at the front,[131] it nevertheless continued to exploit the population to the best of its ability. Between 1 August and 6 November 1941 the division requisitioned 'officially' 519 heads of cattle, 123 pigs, 44 calves and 226 sheep. During August and September alone it consumed 25 tons of meat taken from the population.[132] In early November the division was ordered to rely solely on supplies from the 'land', in spite of its objections that the poverty of the population made this almost impossible.[133] As winter approached, the division also expropriated growing numbers of sledges, snowshoes and other items essential for survivial in the bitter Russian cold.[134] Meanwhile difficulties of supply from the rear compelled the 18.Pz.Div. to squeeze from the peasants a total of 40 tons of meat, consisting of 277 heads of cattle, 53 pigs and 213 sheep during the month of November alone.[135] This last operation seems to have completely impoverished the population; the divisional Quartermaster insisted that the orders from above calling for further exploitation had an 'increasingly theoretical meaning'.[136] Indeed, by 9 December 1941 the division informed its troops that they could no longer hope for supplies either from the rear or from the 'land'; it advised them to resort to 'self-help', namely, to take from the surviving civilians all they could find, regardless of the effect this was bound to have on the peasants.[137]

In the northern sector of the front the 12.I.D. was also living off the property and food of the population. To quote but one example, between 24 July and 31 August 1941, the division 'took from the land' 112 tons of oats, 760 tons of hay, 32 head of cattle, 65 sheep, 94 pigs, 2 tons of potatoes, 350 Kg of butter, 2350 eggs and 2200 litres of milk.[138] Not surprisingly, the economic situation of the civilians rapidly deteriorated. Furthermore, in mid-August the division reported that the peasants were 'completely at a loss' (*völlig ratlos*) because instead of abolishing the collective farms as they had promised, the Germans now appointed new, loyal but clearly incompetent managers to the farms. Worse still, the instruction that only those who worked would receive a share of the crops meant that children, pregnant wives of Red Army soldiers, the sick and the old were all left without any food.[139] Meanwhile, notwithstanding its own assessment in early November that the crops held by the population 'will hardly be sufficient to keep the population alive', the division called upon its troops to rely on 'self-help' owing to the difficulties of bringing up supplies from the rear.[140] Here, too, great amounts of winter equipment were expropriated from the civilians; in January 1942 the division demanded that 'felt-boots be ruthlessly taken off the civilian population'.[141] One of the regiments reported in April 1942 that it had taken forty-eight horses from the villages under its control, and that they had been only left with two horses, one of which could still pull a wagon.[142] The consequences of this policy were described in a report submitted to the division in summer 1942:

> The land had been exploited to the utmost . . . Thereby a situation of a general lack of food supplies for the civilian population arose, which in some cases caused starving Russian civilians to turn to German units and ask for relief or beg to be shot.[143]

The situation did not significantly improve during the summer of 1942. The 12.I.D. did not abolish the collective farms, despite a wide-spread desire among the peasants for such a move, because it felt that their centralised organisation would make economic exploitation much simpler.[144] At the same time, attempts to set the economy in motion were largely unsuccessful both because of the severe after-effects of the winter months and because the population was still being exploited by the units at the front.[145] Thus the paradox arose that in September 1942 the 12.I.D. was supplying the population with food; and when it was decided shortly afterwards to stop these supplies, it was clear that the population was being left to starve, as its reserves of essential items were described as 'infinitely scarce'.[146] Nevertheless, the division continued employing large numbers of civilians as workers at the front while providing them with extremely limited amounts of food, and their dependents had to make do with even less.[147] This naturally led to frequent outbreaks of epidemics, particularly Spotted Fever, but the division refused to concern itself with the health of the civilians beyond isolating them from its own troops.[148] Thus by the time the 12.I.D. retreated from the area of Demyansk it had transformed much of it into an agricultural desert.

The 18.Pz.Div. also continued exploiting the civilian population throughout 1942 and early 1943, till it was transferred to a new area of operations. For a while the division went on with its arbitrary requisitions, taking from the population, for instance, 610 head of cattle between January and March 1942.[149] By late March, however, the division was ordered to try and organise the economic activities of the areas under its control in a manner which would enable it to profit better from the population.[150] This decision does seem to have improved somewhat the conditions of the population as well. A series of 'Agricultural Orders' issued by the division during 1942 indicate that it became intensely involved in the economy of the areas it occupied.[151] However, not only were all civilians over the age of 15 compelled to work, it was also emphasised that the military could make any use of the population and its property according to the demands of the operational situation, regardless of the long-term economic effects of such measures. Indeed, during the winter of 1942/3 the 18.Pz.Div. repeated its policies of the previous winter and requisitioned from the population large numbers of horses, sledges, winter clothing and so forth, to a point where the units reported that the civilians had no winter equipment left at all.[152] Thus whatever good results may have been achieved during the summer, they were again destroyed during the following winter months. By early spring 1943 the division reported outbreaks of epidemics among the population caused by malnutrition which, however, did not prevent it from requisitioning large numbers of cattle; as for the sick, the division ordered their 'ruthless evacuation' and 'complete isolation'.[153] Whatever still remained of the economic and administrative apparatus established by the division was destroyed during the ensuing retreat.

The GD Division was instructed to 'live off the land' while it was still preparing for the summer offensive of 1942.[154] During the autumn of that year the GD requisitioned large numbers of horses, wagons, sledges, argicultural products and houses from the population, while ejecting the civilians from their villages.[155] In preparing for the winter of 1942/3, the division ordered its troops to resort to 'self-help' whenever the need arose, and at the same time recruited increasing numbers of civilians for work at the front.[156] Here the GD also assisted the SD units behind the front by marking Jews and foreigners with the letters 'J' and 'A' respectively.[157] By May 1943 the division was stressing even more emphatically that 'no effort should be spared in fully exploiting the economic resources' of the population,[158] the same resources which it was to destroy shortly afterwards during its retreat to the Dniepr.

The 'official' exploitation of the population was accompanied by what the commanders termed 'wild requisitions', carried out by the troops on their own initiative. Though the officers saw this as a disciplinary problem, they do not seem to have succeeded in controlling it, both because of the large-scale exploitation of the population which they themselves organised, and because whenever the need arose they were quick to sanction 'self-help' policies, which meant in effect precisely the same 'wild requisitions' which they tried at other times to curb. The frequent difficulties of supply, combined with the official ideological view of the Russians as '*Untermenschen*', also encouraged the troops to plunder the civilians and take from them whatever they needed or lacked. Early reports of plundering by the troops indicate that ideology played a role in this phenomenon, in the sense that the troops felt there were things they could do in Russia which they could not have done in France, for instance. The ambiguity of the orders also seems to have accentuated the problem, since requisitions were not forbidden on principle; they had, however, to be carried out by orders of an officer. The fact that punishments for plundering in Russia were far lighter than in the West could have been a further sign to the soldiers that in spite of their commanders' complaints, there were great differences between this war and the campaigns in the West. Thus as early as 11 July 1941 the XXXXVII. Panzer Corps pointed out that 'the wild requisitions of cattle and poultry . . . from the impoverished inhabitants cause extraordinary bitterness among the villagers . . . Requisitions are a matter for the supply officers.'[159] From that date on we find the 18.Pz.Div. repeatedly taking note of plundering by the troops. On 18 July it spoke of numerous 'senseless' slaughtering of cattle, and nine days later pointed out that the soldiers often took from the villagers their last remaining food supplies.[160] The divisional commander attempted to put a stop to this by warning his troops that they would force the population 'back into the Bolshevist camp', and by issuing new instructions forbidding the requisition of the last remaining animal of any particular villager.[161] All this was to no avail, and in September 1941 the 18.Pz.Div. issued another order concerning this problem, which clearly illustrates both the persistence of the phenomenon and the inherent contradictions of the German policy in the East:

> The troops should extensively live off the land. The sense and aim of this regulation is not, however, that individual units and individual members of the Wehrmacht will try to appropriate supplies of their own accord [*auf eigene Faust*].[162]

Not only did such instructions fall on deaf ears; by November the approaching winter increased plundering even further, as the following order pointed out:

> The livestock population in the occupied parts of Russia has already been so frightfully reduced, that if the unsparing taking of cattle from the land by the troops continues . . . it will result in starvation among the population and cause severe problems for the German army owing to the approach of winter.[163]

Throughout the first winter in Russia the troops of the 18.Pz.Div. plundered and looted the population wherever they could lay their hands on their possessions. Boots and furs were particularly high on the soldiers' list of priorities, as also were potatoes, flour and cattle. The men broke into houses and indeed stripped whole villages of all their food reserves, shooting down any person who tried to resist them, as reports reaching the more senior commanders indicated.[164] The same kind of incidents were taking place even while the division was making some efforts to revive the economy of its occupied territories during the following summer, and reached another climax in the winter of 1942/3.[165] This behaviour was not restricted to the central sector of the Eastern Front; in the north the 12.I.D. reported similar incidents as early as 2 July 1941.[166] Here too it was clear that the troops refused to recognise the distinction made by their commanders between 'organised' and 'wild' requisitions, as can be seen from an order of the II. Corps from October 1941:

> Taking from the land food items, cattle, horses, fodder and other sorts of material according to the needs of the units as well as those of the individual is understandably necessary and just, but in no case may it turn into wild robbery and plundering, which are unworthy of the German soldier.[167]

The decision as to what was essential for the troops, and what was necessary for the population, was left to the junior commanders in the field. In November 1941 the 12.I.D. stressed that 'the civilian population is to be allowed to keep what is deemed by the commanders of the units as absolutely necessary for its needs'.[168] It was clear where the priorities of the units would lie, and what disastrous consequences this would have for the population. Clearly, the behaviour of the troops also turned the civilian population against them and forced it to join up with the guerrillas. Though this was recognised by some senior commanders, it failed to make an impression on the troops. In June 1943 the commander of the II. Corps summed up the results of his men's conduct, which, however, could no longer be changed at this late stage of the war:

> In spite of numerous and repeated orders forbidding wild requisitions and exactions, such incidents have been reported to the Corps time and again . . . Our soldiers do not understand in their folly that thereby the population . . . is being driven to indifference and impenitence, because if all that belongs to the Russian is unjustly taken away from him, he will understandably sooner view the German soldier as a thief and a robber than his own countrymen [that is, the partisans].[169]

The Corps commander neglected to mention one essential point; the so-called 'wild requisitions' carried out by the troops were only one, and significantly less crucial, aspect of the general policy of economic exploitation pursued by the army, and were a manifestation of the impact that the '*Untermenschen*' indoctrination had had on the soldiers. Thus the vicious circle of violence and plundering had much deeper roots, and could no longer be broken by explaining to the soldiers what the consequences of their brutality would entail.

Side by side with the exploitation of the economic resources of occupied Russia, the divisions also made extensive use of the labour force of the civilians for work at the front. The harsh winter, the lack of manpower, and the stalemate along many sectors of the front created a need for an increasing conscription of civilian workers. Thus in January 1942 the 12.I.D. ordered its units to 'ruthlessly and mercilessly' recruit civilians for works of fortification and to 'bring the population even to the front-line itself regardless of age and sex.[170] In February the division repeated that, concerning 'work on the roads, the civilian population is to be conscripted still much more extensively and ruthlessly than hitherto'.[171] In June 1942 the division reported that it had under its control 6265 civilians whose work was essential, though it could assure the food supplies of only 3792; a further 2208 had to be evacuated, as they were 'of no value to the Corps and the economy'. This last group included 133 men, 476 women and 219 children, as well as 1380 other civilians incapable of working, presumably the old, the sick and the pregnant women. Altogether 184 single individuals and 493 families were to be driven out of their homes.[172] This policy of evacuating all civilians who could not work for the army was pursued throughout 1942.[173] Those who did remain were often employed in road construction, snow-clearing and fortification works. In October 1942, for instance, the 12.I.D. was employing a total of 935 civilians, of whom 806 were women and children; indeed, whole villages were almost completely emptied of their population.[174] The growing lack of German manpower in the East made for competition between various formations over Russian workers, and the 16. Army called upon its formations to dispense with the 'comfort' of employing 'young childless girls and women' at the front instead of sending them to erect a line of defence in the rear.[175] This 'comfort' can hardly be said to have been shared by the civilians, who received about 13 000 calories per week (just over half of the German soldier's food supply) and were entitled to no medical care. Nevertheless, for many civilians it may have seemed better to take part in this gigantic system of slavery, as those who did not work often received no food at all and were doomed to die of starvation.[176] These policies were pursued by the other two divisions as well. The 18.Pz.Div., for instance, ordered its units in July 1943 to 'ruthlessly conscript . . . all the population', including women and children, with 'all available means'.[177] The GD Division instructed its troops in September 1942 'to conscript the civilian population with ruthless energy for all tasks' of fortification.[178] The enslavement of the civilian population of Russia, part and parcel of the Nazi ideology regarding the East, came to an end only after the Wehrmacht was driven out of the Soviet Union.

Another aspect of the exploitation of Russian civilians and POWs by Nazi Germany was their transportation to the Reich itself to fill the gaps in its war economy. The formations at the front played an important role in recruiting the civilians and transporting them to areas of concentration, from which they were sent to the Reich.[179] Thus in May 1942 the 12.I.D. was ordered to begin recruitment of civilians, initially on a voluntary basis, mainly for agricultural work in Germany. The II. Corps expected some 6000 workers, both males and females between the ages of 16 and 50, as well as families with children over 14 years old. Politically and criminally suspect people, as well as Jews and Asiatics, could not, of course, be accepted.[180] By June 1942 the 12.I.D. completed the first wave of recruitment and launched a second operation.[181] Judging only from reports of the divisional transportation officer, the 12.I.D. sent 2556 men, women and children to a concentration point in the rear between 8 July and 27 November 1942.[182] Another large, but unknown, number of civilians were either sent on foot or on different dates.[183] Thus, for instance, the division became engaged in March 1943 in recruiting Russian women as maids for German housewives.[184] The 18.Pz.Div. also took part in the recruitment of civilians, and began registering volunteers in May 1942. By September that year the division increased its pressure on the population to 'volunteer', while at the same time not allowing parents to take children under the age of 15 with them, thus probably creating a considerable number of orphans.[185] Furthermore, a circular of the OKW suggests that some German soldiers had already developed a private slave trade by 'arranging' Russian maids for their own families in the Reich.[186] The files of the GD Division also provide some evidence on this formation's participation in the recruitment of civilian labour.[187] Here it is interesting to note the reaction of the Operations Officer of the GD to this slave trade in a letter to his wife on 9 June 1942:

> This morning our village filled with screams; some 100 women were sent to Germany; this is bitter, although perhaps they will be better off in Germany.[188]

It may have been possible for von Hobe to brush aside these unpleasant scenes in the Russian villages which his division occupied. It was a very different situation as far as the employment of '*Hiwis*' was concerned, as those 'volunteers' were increasingly important in enabling the dwindling German units to hold their positions. Indeed, by May 1943 the GD Division was using so many Russian *Hiwis* that it considered it worthwhile to issue leaflets and newspapers in their own language.[189] Similarly, the 12.I.D. established a so-called '*Einwohnerkampfabteilung*' (Inhabitants' Fighting Battalion) in April 1943 as part of its campaign against the partisans.[190] The 18.Pz.Div., which suffered from a particularly severe shortage in manpower, went much further. It began by employing so-called '*Hilfskräfte*' in May 1942, and two months later had already established armed units of 'volunteers' to guard its lines of communication. [191] In August it set up 'self-defence' units in villages under its control, and by September there were as many as sixty-five such units under its command.[192] A few weeks later yet another 'Voluntary (Russian) Security Company' numbering 144 *Hiwis* was created, and by December the division was employing two such companies of over 300 Russians.[193] At that time the total number of *Hiwis* employed by the 18.Pz.Div. reached 379 men,[194] but this was still only the beginning. In early 1943 a decision was made to forcibly recruit able-bodied 'volunteers', and in April there were 1659 *Hiwis* serving in the division, apart from a further 1066 Russians employed in fortification works and local guard duties.[195] It is clear that by this stage few of the *Hiwis* were willingly serving the Germans. In June 1943 the division reported how those *Hiwis* were 'created':

A great number of the inhabitants of the region and former POWs who had been enrolled to serve with the troops during the winter battles have been proclaimed as volunteers.[196]

It is indeed striking how high the proportion of *Hiwis* among the total number of soldiers in the division was. In August 1943 the division numbered 7415 German soldiers and 1053 *Hiwis*; that is, every seventh soldier was a Russian '*Untermensch*'.[197] The recruitment of *Hiwis* continued till the division was disbanded in October 1943, and had to be constantly maintained, as the *Hiwis* showed very little enthusiasm to remain in German uniforms, as a report dated 1 October 1943 clearly illustrates:

Desertions of *Hiwis* have become increasingly frequent since mid-August and are related to the retreats, evacuations, changing of the front and the proximity to the bandit [partisan] areas. Nominations of *Hiwis* and the employment of *Hiwi* aspirants are continuing in limited numbers.[198]

As we have seen in this chapter, the attitude of the German army to the Russian POWs and civilian population was based on a mixture of ideological and utilitarian concepts and motivations. The occupied territories had to be 'purged' of all political and racial enemies of the Reich, while the remaining population was to provide for the needs of the Wehrmacht both economically and with its physical man-power. Since the Russians were viewed as nothing more than

'*Untermenschen*', the policy of 'scorched earth' was but a logical conclusion of the ideological basis of the war in the East; it also had its own military rationale of slowing down the advance of the Red Army and depriving it both of the economic resources of the land and of its population which might swell its ranks as it rolled towards Germany.

The 18.Pz.Div. carried out its first 'scorched earth' operation early in the war, when it was forced to retreat in the face of the Russian counter-offensive of December 1941. The division issued orders to arrest all men of military age and send them to the rear, and instructed its troops to drive out the rest of the population from their villages. Livestock not used by the units was to be destroyed, houses to be burned down.[199] Soon afterwards, on 20 December 1941, the division issued further instructions regarding the new defensive line it was erecting. A so-called 'desert zone', nine miles deep, was to be created, from which the men and all their possessions were to be evacuated, and women and children sent to the East, towards the advancing Russians. On 1 January 1942 the division ordered the complete evacuation of a further forty-eight villages,[200] and four weeks later yet another 'desert zone' was declared, in which all houses were burned down, all wells poisoned with dead cattle, all men taken to the rear and all women and children instructed 'to wander off to the area north-west of the desert zone', in the midst of the bitter Russian winter.[201]

These ruthless policies were pursued by the 18.Pz.Div. throughout the war. In February 1943, for instance, the division ordered that all areas about to be given up were to be emptied of their population. Men between the ages of 15 and 65 were to be arrested, all property confiscated and all houses burned down.[202] Similarly, during its retreat from Orel in July and August 1943, the division evacuated all men of 14–55 and women of 14–45 years old, and established a special 'command', whose duty was to destroy all economic assets in the area, such as machinery, agricultural implements, stocks of crops, windmills, and, of course, to burn down the villages.[203] The 12.I.D., retreating from the 'Demyansk Pocket' in February 1943, issued precisely the same orders to its own units. Villages were destroyed and booby-trapped, men arrested, cattle slaughtered, machinery burned.[204] Indeed, the division was singled out for praise by the II. Corps for having successfully evacuated and devastated the area.[205] These operations were continued during subsequent retreats of the 12.I.D. throughout 1943.[206]

The GD Division also took part in numerous evacuation and destruction operations during 1943 in the vicinity of Voltshansk, Belgorod, Kharkov and Orel.[207] By far the largest operation, however, was carried out during the rapid retreat to the Dniepr in September 1943. On 6 September the division established a so-called '*Räumungskommando*' under the command of one lieutenant Kleine. During the following three weeks this unit wrought extensive destruction and suffering upon the population and its land. In a final report on his 'achievements', lieutenant Kleine provided the division with the following figures: his unit had evacuated 13 627 civilians; sent to the rear 9268 livestock; destroyed 1260 agricultural machines; blown up or burned down 165 mills; and taken to the rear 1392 tons of crops. The officer added that these numbers did not include the civilians evacuated and economic assets destroyed by other units of the GD operating independently from his own 'command'.[208] One of the men who had taken part in the retreat wrote in his diary:

> During the retreat we were ordered to destroy all villages, as well as to take to the rear all the cattle. I cannot judge whether this measure was absolutely necessary, but it caused deprivation and misery to the population left behind.[209]

What happened to the many thousands of civilians evacuated from their homes we do not know. It would seem likely, however, that many of them perished in the ensuing chaos of crossing the Dniepr with the Red Army hard on the Wehrmacht's heels, whether during the fighting or from lack of food and shelter. The files of the GD Division are silent on the fate of the people whose homes and lands it had devastated.[210]

Conclusion

In 1954 the former commander of the 12. Infantry Division, the retired general Gerhard Engel, concluded his survey of this formation's history with the following words:

> Thus ended the battles of the 12.I.D., always fairly conducted, though tough and bitter. Its name, its coat of arms and its weapons have remained unsullied till the very last day, as even the enemy has conceded.[1]

The chronicle of the 18. Panzer Division, written after the war by one of its veterans, Wolfgang Paul, contains a similar statement:

> Not one of those who did not return wanted to be in that land; nobody wanted to occupy it. The files of the 18. Panzer Division . . . are devoid of any ideological propaganda on our side. They are files of soldiers.[2]

Helmut Spaeter, a veteran of the Grossdeutschland Division, and one of the editors of its chronicle, wrote in a circular to former soldiers of this formation shortly before the publication of its history:

> I keep hearing the softly voiced complaint . . . Why do you not publicise this [the preparation of the chronicle] more widely? . . . But . . . Do we really want this? – Should this be a chronicle of our history for the public? For everyone – friend and foe?[3]

In this study we have attempted to investigate in greater depth the realities of the Eastern Front, as they were viewed and experienced by the combat soldiers and officers and reflected in their divisional files. It was statements such as those quoted above which have made it seem necessary to examine in detail the contemporary evidence produced by the formations engaged at the front. The realisation, however, that the German army was indeed undergoing a fundamental process of barbarisation during its years of fighting in the

Soviet Union, made it essential to try and analyse at least some of the more significant causes of this phenomenon. Let us first recapitulate the main findings of our research, and then point out a few of the problems involved in interpreting this information both in the context of German society under National Socialism on the whole, and in comparing the conduct of the German Army in the East during the Second World War with the behaviour of other armies in other wars.

In the first chapter of this book we examined the conditions at the front as they were experienced by the combat soldiers. We first demonstrated that the three divisions selected for the study spent the greater part of the war in the East, and took part in the fighting in most major sectors of that front. We then analysed the rate of casualties among these formations, and reached the conclusion that during the war in Russia the three divisions lost between two and three times the number of men and between three and four times the number of officers who had originally filled their ranks when they invaded the Soviet Union. This tremendous rate of casualties also meant that from the very first months of the war the divisions suffered from a chronic lack of manpower, particularly serious as regards officers, a situation which greatly enhanced the suffering of those soldiers who had survived the fighting.

In the second section of Chapter 1 we investigated in greater detail the various elements which played a role in the physical hardship involved in living at the front. Here we pointed out the vast distances which the troops had to march both during the initial months of the war and in the long retreats of later years. We further demonstrated that one of the consequences of the heavy casualties and lack of manpower was a heavy burden of routine operational activities upon the survivors, resulting in a chronic and growing lack of rest and sleep. This, combined with the wretched housing facilities, the harsh climate, the severe lack of appropriate winter clothes and the frequent breakdowns in supplies of food, brought about a serious deterioration in the physical health and mental condition of the troops, clearly observed by both commanders and doctors treating the front-line soldiers. When all the above-mentioned factors were brought to a pitch during heavy and sustained periods of fighting, they occasionally caused individual and, in some cases, group breakdowns described as 'battle fatigue', entailing extreme physical exhaustion and mental disintegration.

In the last section of the first chapter we discussed how the discipline and morale of the troops were affected by the conditions at the front, and what measures were taken by the commanders to maintain the fighting capabilities of their men. We saw that, as opposed to previous campaigns, the war in Russia was accompanied by a growing number of cases involving neglect of duty while on guard, self-mutilation and cowardice in the face of the enemy. Whereas soldiers charged with theft, plundering and sleeping while on guard were treated with some understanding by their officers, those who attempted to get away from the front by deserting or injuring themselves received very severe sentences, and in some cases were even executed. The divisions made a great effort to publicise these harsh punishments among their troops in an attempt to prevent any such future cases. We have observed that morale among the troops was under a severe strain also, because of the rarity of leave and the growing feeling of isolation in a vast, unknown and alien land coupled with a sense of having been forgotten by the so-called 'green table' staff officers in the rear.

In concluding the first chapter we pointed out that the terrible physical and mental hardship at the front must have contributed to some extent to the growing brutalisation of the individual soldier. It was also clear that these same factors made it exceedingly difficult to maintain the fighting spirit of the troops. It is, therefore, particularly interesting to note the remarkable resilience shown by the units we examined during most of the war in the East. One explanation for this, centring on the loyalty of the individual to his 'primary group', that is to his unit, could not be fully accepted. The extraordinarily heavy casualties among the combat units seem to have hindered the formation of such a group loyalty owing to a constant change in the manpower composition of the units.[4] We consequently suggested that part of the explanation for the stubborn determination shown by the German soldier on the Eastern Front may be found in his ideological indoctrination. As this activity was by and large the responsibility of the junior officers, we turned in Chapter 2 of this study to examine the biographies of a sample of officers from the three divisions, in order to establish how susceptible they were to the National Socialist *Weltanschauung*.

The 531 officers of the sample, representing about a quarter of the overall number of officers who had passed through the three divisions during the war, were divided into a number of categories. Only about 15 per cent of the officers in the sample belonged to the aristocracy, the traditional source of officers in the German army. Of all categories of officers, these men were the least susceptible to Nazi influences. Apart from the fact that they stemmed from the social stratum known to have remained relatively aloof from Hitler's rhetoric, they also belonged to the older age groups among the sample officers and a very high proportion of them came from officer families and from the landed gentry. These findings corresponded well with the fact that a much lower percentage of the aristocratic officers were members of the NSDAP. However, the nobles constituted only a small minority among the sample officers.

Over a third of the officers in the sample belonged to the reserve. We found that the men who were already performing their reserve service were nevertheless still very young, and that particularly among the junior ranks there was a gap of only about three years between the regulars and the reservists. On the other hand, the rate of promotion among officers belonging to this second category was much slower, and they could not achieve a higher rank than that of major. These findings were of particular importance in analysing the third and crucial category of National Socialist officers, who constituted close to a third of the sample. This relatively high number of party members was found to possess certain interesting characteristics. National Socialist officers were far better educated than the average officer in the sample; a higher proportion of them came from the upper middle class or from the universities; and the majority of these men belonged to the reserve officer corps. This last characteristic helped to explain why promotion among party members was slower than the average in the sample. It also helps us to understand why there was a relatively higher number of university students among National Socialist officers.

Having examined these three different categories of officers, we then moved on to investigate education, social origins and promotion in the sample as a whole. We found that in comparison with the Imperial Army and the Reichswehr of the Weimar Republic there certainly was a decline in educational standards and requirements from officers, owing to the massive and rapid growth of the Wehrmacht under the Third Reich. We also saw that educational standards were actually on the rise towards the late 1930s and war years, as the army had exhausted its supplies of veteran officers of the First World War and of NCOs and began absorbing large numbers of school graduates to fill the ranks of its officer cadets. The increasing recruitment of young *reserve* officers further improved the general educational level among the officers (as well as the numbers of party members). We pointed out that by and large the officers in our sample still represented a minority within German society as a whole, as relatively well-educated young men. We stressed that as most of those officers had gone to school under Hitler's regime, this meant that their political indoctrination had begun long before they joined the ranks of the Wehrmacht.

Concerning the social background of the officers in the sample, it was clear that the great majority of them came from the middle classes. Compared with the Reichswehr of Weimar, there was a tremendous drop in the number of men who came from officer families, and a rather less striking rise in the percentage of officers belonging to working-class or very-low-middle-class families. Nevertheless, most of the officers stemmed from those social strata which represented only a quarter of the total German population at the time. Here too we find that the most significant lowering of social standards was during the mid-1930s, and that among the youngest officers there was again a gradual rise in social status as increasing numbers of school-leavers were conscripted and the army's biases against the commissioning of NCOs got the upper hand the moment the circumstances made that possible.

Promotion during the late 1930s and the war was faster than at any other time in the history of the German army. The officers stemming from the middle and upper middle strata of the middle class, as well as those belonging to officer families, benefited most from this process. In consequence, most of the officers serving in relatively responsible field commands were very young men. Thus, for example, a third of the lieutenants of 1945 were 13 years old or younger when Hitler came to power, and hardly any of them were over 23, while almost a third of the majors of 1945 were, at the most, 18 in 1933.

Thus we concluded the second chapter by claiming that on the whole the officers of the sample were potentially highly susceptible to National Socialist influences. While the number of aristocratic, hypothetically less Nazi officers was low, a third of the men in the sample were officially members of the party. Moreover, after a temporary drop in the educational and social standards in the mid-to-late 1930s, the army began receiving growing numbers of young, well-educated upper-middle-class officers, of the type who were particularly influenced by the party and who had been indoctrinated in school and at the universities according to the tenets of National Socialism. High rates of promotion meant that these men reached important positions and were, as we saw in the following chapter, responsible not only for leading their men into battle but also for their political education.

Having found that the junior military leaders and ideological instructors of the troops may well have been, by force of their social and educational background as well as their ages, highly supportive of the regime, we proceeded in Chapter 3 to examine the political indoctrination of the troops. Whereas in Chapter 1 we recognised that the difficult conditions at the front may have contributed to the brutalisation of the troops and at the same time put a great stress on discipline and morale, here we wanted to see whether ideological instruction acted both to enhance the *ésprit de corps* and determination of the troops, and to legitimise and encourage the process of barbarisation of the individual. We therefore began by surveying the various forms of ideological instruction and the intensity with which they were employed. We showed that the troops were provided with large numbers of radio receivers, films, newspapers, news-sheets, leaflets and brochures, as well as books. Furthermore, we demonstrated that the most effective form of propaganda, conducted on a personal, face-to-face level, was greatly encouraged by the divisions and carried out on a regular basis by the junior officers, particularly the company commanders. Later on we saw that those activities were further enhanced by the introduction of the special educational officers and, towards the end of the war, by the institution of the National Socialist Leadership Officers, the Nazi equivalent of the Soviet Commissars.

In the second section of this chapter we analysed the content of the stream of propaganda directed at the troops. Here we saw that whatever form of indoctrination was used, it had an increasingly dense National Socialist orientation, blending more common nationalistic and patriotic themes typical of wartime propaganda with the much more extreme racial and genocidal version of the Nazis. This tendency was present in the radio broadcasts, the films and the lectures delivered to the soldiers. Even more significant, it formed an essential part of the news reports contained in the various newspapers and information-sheets supplied to the troops. The greatest propagandistic influence may be ascribed, perhaps, to the fact that the junior officers were ordered by their commanders to stress the ideological nature of the war and to view themselves not only as military leaders but also as ideological instructors of their men. For this purpose they were provided with a large number of brochures which were to serve them as the background for the numerous company sessions intended to stiffen the ideological commitment of the men. Coupled with that, the more senior commanders at the front made increasing use of Nazi terms and concepts in their orders of the day to the soldiers, and stressed that the war against Russia should not be viewed as an ordinary military confrontation but as an ideological and racial struggle to which the rules of war did not, and could not, apply.

The last section of our chapter on indoctrination was an attempt to evaluate the efficacy of ideological education. Here we pointed out first of all the fact that some of the ideas propounded by the Nazis were not an original invention of the party, but had deep-seated roots in cultural and social concepts dating back to the Wilhelmine period, which were given great impetus by the frustration and misery caused by the defeat in the First World War, the economic hardship of the first years of the republic, and the economic depression and political chaos of the early 1930s. We mentioned that recent research had shown a deep desire among wide circles in German society to create a '*Führer Mythos*' even before the Nazi leadership recognised the usefulness of this concept. Furthermore, we pointed out the growing demand among the lower ranks of the military, in the face of increasing difficulties on the Eastern Front, to be supplied with indoctrinational material in order to stiffen the morale of the troops. The men at the front showed a great interest in receiving news from home, and the information with which they were provided was, of course, oriented towards the Nazi *Weltanschauung*. The troops needed pep-talks with their officers, and the young officers read out the National Socialist brochures they received from OKH and OKW. It is difficult to gauge the extent of the success achieved by these constant indoctrinational efforts. We have seen indications that the troops at the front needed a great deal of 'spiritual care' and became increasingly dependent on 'beliefs' which were anything but rational or logical. The Nazi *Weltanschauung* was admirably suited to provide them with just such a set of irrational 'beliefs'. The more hopeless the military situation became, the greater was the need for such 'spiritual', pseudo-religious support. The men were provided with credos and catechisms bearing a close and sinister resemblance to those of the church in form, but of a racist and nihilistic content. In contrast to the opinions of some historians, we have found evidence in the divisional files that the men welcomed these indoctrinational efforts and even demanded their intensification, expressing the need of combat soldiers engaged in a bitter and increasingly hopeless war to be provided with a 'cause' which will put their personal sacrifice within a larger context and make it all 'worth it'. The junior and middle ranking officers agreed with the military and political leadership of the Reich that this indoctrination was essential in keeping the troops at the front and persuading them to go on fighting.

In concluding the third chapter we conceded that it is impossible to quantify precisely the extent and depth of ideological conviction among the troops on the Eastern Front. It seems clear, however, that whatever the men thought of the Nazi party, they were mostly firm believers, almost in a religious sense, in their Führer and, by extension, in many of the ideological and political goals quoted in his name. It thus seems that political indoctrination did achieve two essential purposes: it stiffened the determination of the soldiers at the front and played an important role in preventing disintegration and breakdowns among the ranks of the German army in the East; and at the same time it legitimised and enhanced the barbarisation of warfare in Russia, which, coupled with the brutality emanating from the nature of the war itself described in the first chapter, led to the terrible destruction of western Russia by the German army, which was examined in Chapter 4.

The barbarisation of warfare on the Eastern Front is studied from three different aspects and on two related levels. The first section in Chapter 4 dealt with the maltreatment of Russian POWs as it was expressed both in the policies of the military authorities and in the conduct of the troops towards their captives. The complex of so-called 'criminal orders' instructed the troops to collaborate with the *Einsatzgruppen* of the SS and SD; to eliminate all active and passive civilian resistance and to take collective measures against the population; to shoot all commissars; and to act ruthlessly against all military, political and racial 'enemies' of the Reich. As the files of the three divisions have shown, the units at the front acted in strict accordance with these instructions: commissars were shot, POWs captured behind the front were 'eliminated', and all other prisoners suffered from such a severe shortage of food, clothing, medical care, transport and accommodation facilities, that millions of them perished during the first months of the war. The formations at the front also resorted to conscripting so-called 'volunteers' to their service, and later on to their combat units; and in some cases POWs were also sent on obviously suicidal missions, such as clearing minefields. Along with this 'official' policy of maltreatment, exploitation and murder, we found much evidence of 'wild', undisciplined and indiscriminate shooting of POWs by German troops throughout the war in the Soviet Union. Though opposed by the senior commanders, this phenomenon was a result of the policies and underlying ideological concepts pursued and encouraged by the army, as well as of the general brutal nature of the war.

The second section of the chapter examined the war against the partisans and the resulting mass murder of countless Russian civilians. Here too it was the 'criminal orders' which provided the official legitimation for the barbarous conduct of the army in the East. With the intensification of partisan activities against the army and the growing frustration of the military, anti-partisan operations evolved into large-scale actions in which the main victims were the civilians: villages were burned down, their inhabitants shot, their livestock slaughtered, their food reserves destroyed and their wells poisoned. The evidence indicates that in numerous cases the army failed to lay its hands on real guerrillas and instead took extensive 'collective measures' against the population in areas where partisan activities had taken place. Anti-partisan operations also included activities against 'suspected elements' – that is, people connected in any way with the communist party, and Jews. Moreover, in an attempt to legitimise in their own and their soldiers' eyes the barbarities committed against defenceless civilians, and particularly against women and children, the army invented 'agents', a euphemistic term used both as an excuse for brutality and as a means of preventing fraternisation between the troops and the population. Here too we found that the offical line was even more successful in persuading the troops than the commanders had intended, and the evidence indicates that troops had become so used to indiscriminate shootings of 'agents' that they had to be ordered to cease their activities and to deliver those 'suspected elements' to the GFP or the SD.

The last section of Chapter 4 surveyed the execution of the policies of economic exploitation, evacuation and destruction of the Russian civilian population by the divisions at the front. The German army had been ordered to 'live off the land' even before it marched into the Soviet Union. The results of this policy were the rapid impoverishment of the land and its population and the deaths of millions of civilians caused by starvation, lack of clothing and shelter, as well as a ruthless exploitation of their labour both by the units at the front and by the authorities of the Reich. The divisions requisitioned enormous quantities of food and livestock from the population, confiscated winter clothes and equipment with the approach of winter, and ultimately, as the supply crisis became even more severe, authorised their troops to resort to 'self-help' and to take whatever they needed from the civilians. The population was impoverished to such an extent that indeed even the divisions became worried that they would no longer be able to exploit their economic resources in the future. The efforts to improve economic conditions were hampered, however, by the priority given to urgent military needs regardless of the effects of such further ruthless exploitation on the long-term state of the economy. Furthermore, we again saw that 'official' exploitation was constantly accompanied by 'wild requisitions' by the troops, who seem to have paid little heed to their commanders' warnings against such actions, and refused to differentiate between the official view that the Russians were *Untermenschen* who could be treated in any way conducive to the benefit of the German soldier, and the insistence of the officers that such exploitation should only be carried out in an organised, disciplined manner, reflecting their anxiety that wild looting and plundering might lead to a general breakdown in discipline and morale.

The ambiguity regarding the exploitation of the population was further increased by the use made of their labour force. The army wanted the civilians to work on their fields and provide it with food. At the same time it made extensive use of the population in working on various military installations, fortifications, roads and so forth, thus taking them away from their villages and fields. Moreover, the army played an important role in conscripting labour for the fields and factories of the Reich, which had chosen send its own labour force to fight on the Russian front. The civilians, mostly women and children, were overworked and underfed; yet it was often better to work for the Germans than to die of starvation. The only reaction of the military authorities to the growing incidence of epidemics was to isolate the population from the troops. Civilians who were considered to be 'of no value' to the army were left to their own fate or uprooted from their villages so as not to burden the military with their presence. Others were conscripted to serve the army as *Hiwis*, regardless of their evident reluctance to assist in their 'liberation' by the Wehrmacht.

The final phase in the army's barbarous conduct in Russia came with the great retreats, particularly in the last two years of the war. Here everything was done to execute as fully as possible the policy of 'scorched earth', which included the destruction of vast areas in western Russia and the evacuation, or more precisely, the uprooting, of countless thousands of civilians. Thus the German army in the East, and especially the three formations examined in detail throughout this study, can be said to have acted in strict accordance with the policies and ideology of Hitler's regime: they waged a ruthless war against the Soviet Union and continued fighting even after it had become clear that defeat was inevitable; they made a constant and extensive effort to indoctrinate their soldiers according to the tenets of National Socialism, with the essential assistance of young junior officers who were particularly suitable as ideological instructors; and, finally, they treated the Russian POWs, guerrilla fighters and especially civilians as the *Untermenschen* they had been taught to believe they were, and wreaked destruction, death and misery on millions of men, women and children.

Up to this point we have recapitulated the main findings and conclusions of this study. However, several readers of earlier versions of the work, as well as students and scholars who had heard a number of papers I read on this subject, have raised some important questions regarding the implications of the more general issues addressed here.[5] These questions can be divided into two major and closely connected issues. The first is, can we really say that the individual soldier on the Eastern Front was influenced by the barrage of propaganda directed at him from above? The second is concerned with placing the war in Russia in a larger historical context, and raises the question of whether we can state that the Eastern Front during the Second World War was essentially different from numerous other brutal and barbarous military confrontations. These two issues are connected, because in this study we have claimed that the underlying National Socialist *Untermenschen* ideology regarding the population of Russia played an important role in the barbarisation of the troops. Thus, if one could show that in the absence of such an ideology other wars were just as barbarous, a main component of the thesis offered in this book, namely, that the process of barbarisation was the result of conditions at the front, the susceptibility of the junior officers to National Socialist ideology, and the political indoctrination of the troops, would seem to be unnecessary. Soldiers, it could be claimed, do not need a barbarous ideology in order to behave brutally; it is war itself which brutalises them, whatever the ideology underlying it.

Now, regarding the degree of ideological conviction of the individual soldier, we have already admitted earlier that it is difficult to make any precise evaluation. We have shown that there was a great deal of indoctrination at the front, and that the troops wanted even more of it, in the form of news and pep-talks with their officers. We also feel that there is enough evidence to demonstrate that there was a general and widespread support, if not 'belief', in Hitler. This does not mean that all the soldiers were committed Nazis, but it does indicate that many, if not most of them, were greatly influenced by the Nazi *Weltanschauung* and its implications regarding their conduct in the East. It would probably be unwise to go further than that without a careful study of individual soldiers and their beliefs during the war, which, as far as we know, has not been done. We are therefore still left with the question of the relationship between ideology and action: was there an essential difference between the conduct of the German army in Russia in the Second World War and that of other armies in other wars, and if there was such a difference, was it rooted in the ideology of the Nazi regime?

Questions of this sort compel us, unfortunately, to turn our minds to comparisons between barbarities. One might object and claim that this is unnecessary, as all wars are brutal and there is no substantial difference between massacring thousands or millions. Nevertheless, we believe that some wars are far more brutal than others, and that it is important to try and find out why. Thus, for example, it is often claimed that the Red Army was just as brutal as the Wehrmacht, a particularly convenient assumption for those who say that in Russia one had to behave like the Russians. Now let us look at the figures: during the Second World War Germany lost 3 250 000 soldiers and 3 600 000 civilians on all fronts and in all enemy action, including the invasion of both the Russians and the Western Allies into its territory and the aerial bombardments; the Soviet Union, on the other hand, lost some 13 000 000 soldiers and 7 000 000 civilians, almost all due to German war, extermination and exploitation policies. The total of 20 000 000 Russian deaths constitutes about 40 per cent of the estimated 55 000 000 people killed in the Second World War. Furthermore, the highest estimate of German POWs in Russian hands is 3 155 000, of whom between 1 110 000 and 1 185 000 (35.2–37.4 per cent) died in captivity. Of about 5 700 000 Russian POWs in German hand, on the other hand, some 3 300 000 (57.8 per cent) died in captivity.[6] To this we should add that a recent Soviet publication has hotly contested the figures of German POWs in Russian hands and the number of deaths in captivity, and has claimed, with some degree of conviction, that the main German research on this issue was biased and unconvincing, its mammoth breadth (15 volumes) notwithstanding.[7] We should also keep in mind that not only did the Red Army suffer severe setbacks during the beginning of the war and found it exceedingly difficult to care even for its own soldiers, but the whole of western Russia was occupied by the Wehrmacht, a situation not particularly conducive to good treatment of enemy POWs. The greatest number of deaths of Russian POWs, however, occurred while Germany was at the height of its power and controlled most of Western Europe. Moreover, in spite of the numerous cases of brutality committed by Russian soldiers when they marched into Eastern Germany, it is clear that the Soviet Union had no plans of genocide regarding the German population, though it did play a role in the fundamental change of its political structure. Similarly, though the Allied bombing of Germany can be said to have had an element of vengeance not connected with bringing the end of the war any closer, it was not part of a campaign to exterminate the German people. Even the horrific atomic bombing of Hiroshima and Nagasaki, which would be difficult to defend on any moral basis, had no genocidal aims, as the conduct of the American occupation authorities in Japan after the war clearly demonstrated.

The terrible maltreatment of Allied POWs at the hands of the Japanese in the Second World War is often compared with the much more favourable behaviour of the Germans to their POWs, excluding, of course, the Russians. Indeed, 27 per cent of Anglo-American POWs held by the Japanese forces died while in captivity, compared with only 4 per cent of those held by the German forces.[8] In fact, the latter figure is one of the reasons why some historians tend to praise the conduct of the German military towards their captives and to concentrate on heroic tales of escapes from the camps; the war in the East could just as well have taken place on a different planet. The massacre in the French village of Oradour made more headlines than the destruction of 1710 towns and 70 000 villages (according to the Soviet figures) by the Wehrmacht, let alone the 7 000 000 dead civilians.[9] In any case, it does not seem that the Japanese had any intention of systematically exterminating the Anglo-Americans, or even their POWs, though they certainly demonstrated extraordinary brutality. Even Japan's barbarous policies in countries such as Korea, China and the Philippines cannot be called genocidal, as they were not based on the concept of a total annihilation of a people. In Japan there seems to have been a strange mixture of feelings: an ethnic affinity with other Asian peoples (and particularly an admiration for

Chinese culture), with strong racialist tendencies (and a particular feeling of superiority towards Korea and the Philippines, for instance). The Japanese aimed at economic expansion and exploitation, and it was the bitter war which barbarised their policy-makers, generals and troops. One historian has attempted to explain Japanese brutality in China by the 'absence in the Japanese social system of a generalised code of ethical behaviour', 'relentless destruction of privacy and the extensive use of violence' in Japan's army causing a 'transfer of oppression', but also by 'the deep roots in Japanese history of the view that Japan's defence required the annihilation – or at least the conquest – of China', as well as by 'notions of a greater Japan' which would save 'Oriental Civilisation'.[10]

Examples of brutality in European and colonial history during the last few centuries are not hard to come by. Nevertheless it is interesting to note that wherever wars were accompanied by some version of an *Untermenschen* ideology or, for that matter, religious fanaticism, they quickly developed much stronger genocidal tendencies. In the latter case, the Thirty Years' War can serve as the supreme example. Not only did this war involve terrible massacres of both catholics and protestants, but one of its after-effects was also widespread killing of other religious minorities. Thus, for instance, a sustained pogrom in Poland led to the death of 100 000 Jews during the decade 1648–58.[11] As to colonial wars, suffice it to mention Britain's wars in India, Africa and, more recently, in Malaya; Russia's expansion in Central Asia; France's wars in Africa and Indo-China; and, not least, America's war in Vietnam.[12] In most of these wars an ideological element was involved, and racism was certainly not far from the surface, if not openly expressed. It is interesting to observe that ethnic differences seem to have played an important role in soldiers' attitudes to their enemies. Thus, for example, 42 per cent of a sample of American soldiers said that they felt 'all the more like killing' Japanese soldiers after having seen them, whereas only 18 per cent felt the same way after having seen Germans; 54 per cent thought that the Germans were 'men just like us', but only 20 per cent shared that view regarding the Japanese.[13]

And yet these very examples also indicate the differences between the case of the Eastern Front and that of other wars. Perhaps we should take the Eastern Front of the First World War as one last instance of comparison. This too was a bitter and costly war, fought in harsh weather conditions and with great ruthlessness. The civilian population suffered greatly, and Russian policies of evacuation caused tremendous misery to millions of refugees. However, the Austrians issued orders to treat the Jewish population of Poland well; Russsian POWs in German hands are said to have preferred remaining with the Germans rather than escaping back to their own lines. In short, there was no policy of deliberate extermination in spite of the brutality of the war itself.[14]

Thus we can compare the Eastern Front of 1941–45 to other wars, according to its scale, its intention and the extent to which it was exposed to some sort of public control. As far as scale is concerned, it is difficult to find precedents for the enormous numbers of soldiers, POWs and civilians who died in this confrontation. The only two comparable instances are perhaps Japan's war in China and the Thirty Years' War. But though these wars had a strong element of racial or religious fanaticism, they do not appear to have been conducted with the single-minded intention of exterminating whole peoples, as was the 'war of ideologies' unleashed by Germany in the East. Some colonial wars may well have shared this characteristic, but here they often differed from the Eastern Front in their being subject to much more public criticism at home, which put stricter controls on the conduct of the military. Many wars have led to extreme and widespread acts of brutality, both 'wild' and 'official', as was recently demonstrated in Vietnam. Nevertheless, public opinion in the United States, and the rule of law, however belatedly it may have come into effect, applied great pressure on the military.[15] Such pressure was completely absent in the Third Reich. Thus we cannot accept the arguments of some of the most recent apologists of the defendants in the International Military Tribunal at Nuremberg, however sound their legalistic reservations may be.[16] On the Eastern Front, Nazi Germany exercised barbarism on an unprecedented scale; its declared intention was extermination and enslavement; the only way to prevent her from achieving this goal was to defeat her militarily, for whatever we may think of the resistance, it proved itself incapable of toppling the regime. It was the combination of these elements which made this war into a unique phenomenon in human history. Only by recognising that fact can we hope to prevent it being repeated.

Appendix: Maps

1. RUSSIA: DECEMBER 1941 TO APRIL 1942

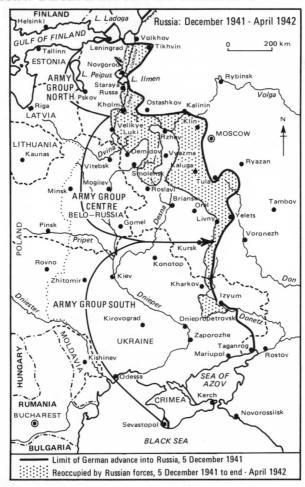

SOURCE: Liddell Hart, *Second World War*, p. 250.

2. MARCH-ROUTE AND AREA OF OPERATIONS OF THE 18.PZ.DIV., 1941–1943

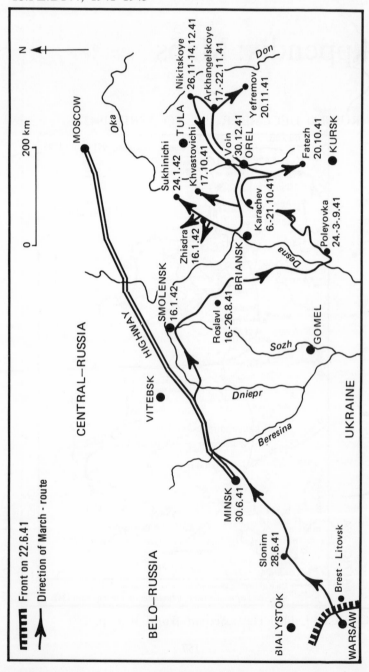

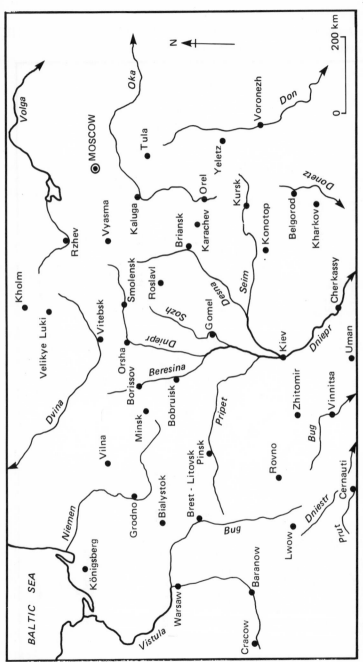

SOURCE: Paul, *18.Pz.Div.*, pp. xii, 166.

3. RETREAT TO THE DNIEPR AND MARCH-ROUTE OF THE GD DIVISION TO RUMANIA

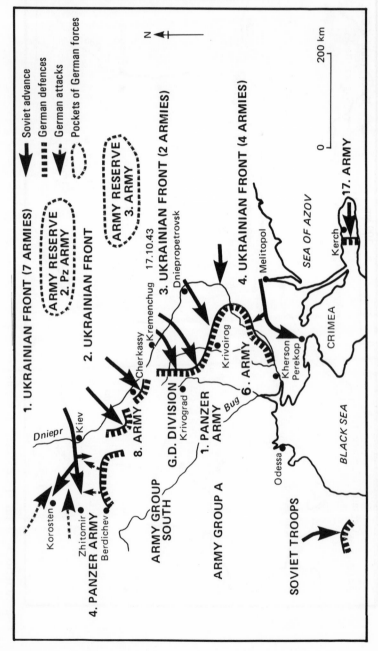

161

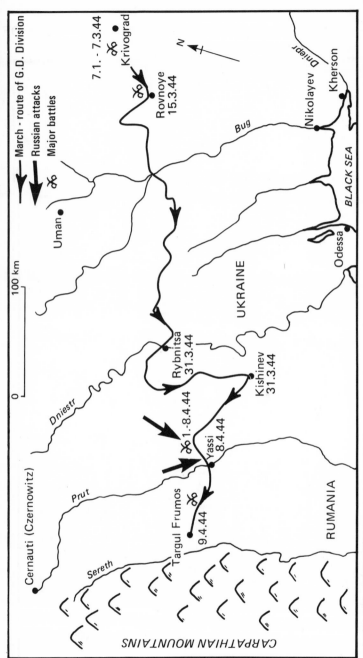

SOURCE: Spaeter/Schramm, *GD*, ii.

4. AREAS OF OPERATION OF THE GD DIVISION, FEBRUARY–MARCH 1945

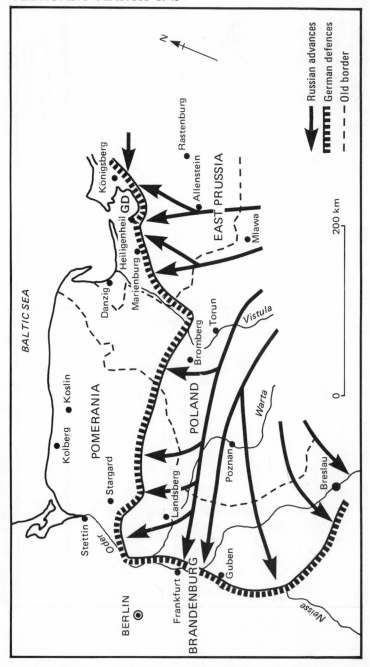

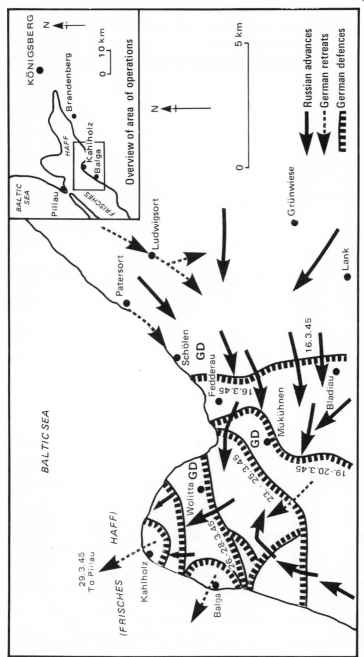

SOURCE: Spaeter/Schramm, *GD*, iii.

Notes and References

INTRODUCTION

1. E. von Manstein, *Aus Einem Soldatenleben* (Bonn, 1958) pp. 353–4. See also his *Verlorene Siege*, 2nd edn (Frankfurt/M., 1964) pp. 7–8; and K. Doenitz, *Memoirs*, 2nd edn (London, 1959) pp. 299–314; H. Guderian, *Panzer Leader*, 3rd edn (London, 1977) pp. 458–64; Kesselring, *The Memoirs* (London, 1953) pp. 314–15; S. Westphal, *The German Army in the West* (London, 1951) pp. 3–18.
2. See, for example, H. Baumann (ed.), *Die 35. Infanterie-Division im 2. Weltkrieg* (Karlsruhe, 1964) pp. 12–14; R. Grams, *Die 14. Panzer-Division* (Bad Nauheim, 1957) p. 8; C. Wagener, *Heeresgruppe Süd* (Bad Nauheim, n.d.) pp. 11, 342; see also Conclusion in this volume. For officers who did oppose these policies, see, for example, H. Teske, *Die Silberne Spiegel* (Heidelberg, 1952); F. von Schlabrendorff, *The Secret War Against Hitler* (London, 1966) *passim*.
3. B. H. Liddell Hart, *The Other Side of the Hill* (London, 1948) p. 29; see also his *History of the Second World War*, 6th edn (London, 1979) *passim*; J. F. C. Fuller, *The Decisive Battles of the Western World*, II, 5th edn (London, 1975) pp. 431–592; A. Seaton, *The Russo-German War* (London, 1971) and his *The German Army* (London, 1982). See also this volume, Chapter 1, n. 1.
4. F. L. Carsten, *The Reichswehr and Politics*, 2nd edn (Berkeley: California, 1973); G. A. Craig, *The Politics of the Prussian Army*, 3rd edn (London, 1978); K-J Müller, *Das Heer und Hitler* (Stuttgart, 1969); R. J. O'Neill, *The German Army and the Nazi Party* (London, 1966); J. W. Wheeler-Bennett, *The Nemesis of Power*, 2nd edn (London, 1980).
5. Discussions of the various Putsch plans and attempts of the military can be found in H. C. Deutsch, *The Conspiracy Against Hitler in the Twilight War* (Minneapolis: Minnesota, 1968) and his *Hitler and his Generals* (Minneapolis: Minnesota, 1974); K-J Müller, *Armee, Politik und Gesellschaft in Deutschland 1933–45* (Padeborn, 1979); N. Reynolds, *Treason was no Crime* (London, 1976); G. Ritter, *Carl Goerdeler und die Deutsche Widerstands-Bewegung* (Stuttgart, 1954).
6. E. Wolf, 'Political and Moral Motives Behind the Resistance', in H. Graml *et al.*, *The German Resistance to Hitler* (London, 1970) p. 232. See also K-J Müller, *General Ludwig Beck* (Boppard am Rhein, 1980).
7. More generally on post-war German historiography, see, in L. Dawidowicz, 'German Historians and National Socialism', *Zmanim*, II (in the Hebrew language, 1979); H. Herzfeld, 'Germany: After the

Catastrophe', *JCH*, II (1967) 79–91; M. Howard, *Studies in War and Peace*, 10th edn (London, 1970) pp. 110–21; D. T. Williams, 'The Historiography of World War II', in E. M. Robertson (ed.), *The Origins of the Second World War*, 5th edn (London, 1979) pp. 40–2.
8. See, for example, B. B. Ferencz, *An International Criminal Court* (London, 1980) pp. 54–77, 83–90, 469–501; G. M. Gilbert, *Nuremberg Diary* (New York, 1947); W. Maser, *Nuremberg* (London, 1979) pp. 93–130.
9. H-A. Jacobsen, 'Kommissarbefehl und Massenexekutionen Sowjetische Kriegsgefangener', in H. Buchheim *et al.*, *Anatomie des SS-Staates* (Olten, 1965) II, pp. 163–279; H. Krausnick, 'Kommissarbefehl und "Gerichtsbarkeitserlass Barbarossa" in Neuer Sicht', *VfZ*, XXV (1977) 682–758, and his and H-H Wilhelm's *Die Truppe des Weltanschauungskrieges* (Stuttgart, 1981); M. Messerschmidt, *Die Wehrmacht im NS-Staat* (Hamburg, 1969); C. Streit, *Keine Kameraden* (Stuttgart, 1978).
10. *Der Spiegel*, no. 16, 13 April 1981, pp. 74–80.
11. *Frankfurter Allgemeine Zeitung*, no. 99, 29 April 1981, p. 10. During the summer of 1981 another public debate took place in Germany concerning the screening of the Soviet/American TV film *'Der Unvergessene Krieg'*. See, for example, B. Martin, 'Badische Zeitung', *Wochenend Magazin*, 5/6 December 1981, pp. 1–2; H. Höhne *et al.*, *Der Spiegel*, no. 38, 14 September 1981, pp. 200–16.
12. Messerschmidt, *Die Wehrmacht*, p. 483
13. Ibid., pp. 354–5.
14. See, for example, K. W. Bird, *Weimar, The German Naval Officer Corps and the Rise of National Socialism* (Amsterdam, 1971); H. H. Herwig, *The German Naval Officer Corps* (Oxford, 1973), for the navy. See K. Demeter, *The German Officer Corps* (London, 1965); and M. Kitchen, *The German Officer Corps* (Oxford, 1968), for the army. Biographies deal, of course, only with the most exceptional officers. See. J. Kramarz, *Stauffenberg* (Frankfurt/M., 1965); C. Müller, *Oberst i.G. Stauffenberg* (Düsseldorf, 1970). For the usefulness of regional studies which, however, do not deal with the army, see W. S. Allen, *The Nazi Seizure of Power* (Chicago, 1965); J. Noakes, *The Nazi Party in Lower Saxony* (London, 1971). An attempt to draw the portrait of the 'typical' (senior) officer is to be found in J. C. Fest, *The Face of the Third Reich,* 3rd edn (Harmondsworth: Middlesex, 1979) pp. 355–75.

1 LIFE, HARDSHIP AND DEATH AT THE FRONT

1. *Findbuch*, BA-MA MSg175; G. Tessin, *Formationsgeschichte der Wehrmacht* (Boppard am Rhein, 1959) pp. 21–2, 28–9, 114–15, 118–19, 128–9, 150–1, 174–5, 190–1; B. Mueller-Hillebrand, *Das Heer* (Darmstadt, 1945) I. 25, 57–9, 68–73, 130–5, 151; W. Deist *et al.*, *Das Deutsche Reich und der Zweite Weltkrieg* (Stuttgart, 1979) I. 415–49. As a general background for the military events of the war, the following

books may be helpful, together with those mentioned above: H. Boog
et al., Das Deutsche Reich und der Zweite Weltkrieg, IV. (Stuttgart,
1983); M. Cooper, *The German Army* (London, 1978); J. Erickson,
The Road to Stalingrad (London, 1975); J. F. C. Fuller, *The Second
World War,* 2nd edn (London, 1948); W. Görlitz, *Der Zweite Weltkrieg*
(Stuttgart, 1951/2); A. Hillgruber, *Hitlers Strategie* (Frankfurt/M.,
1965); A. B. Leach, *German Strategy Against Russia* (London, 1973);
K. A. Maier *et al., Das deutsche Reich und der Zweite Weltkrig,* II.
(Stuttgart, 1979); M. van Crefeld, *Hitler's Strategy* (London, 1973); E.
F. Ziemke, *Stalingrad to Berlin* (Washington DC, 1968).

2. BA-MA, *Heft* 523, p. 11; BA-MA RH26-12/252, 3.11.39.

3. BA-MA, *Heft* 523, p. 12; BA-MA RH26-12/6, 9.5.–23.6.40.

4. BA-MA, *Heft* 523, p. 12; BA-MA RH26-12/16, 1.7.40; BA-MA
   RH26-12/17, 1.9.40; BA-MA RH26-12/21, 16.5.41.

5. BA-MA RH26-12/52, 2.4.42; numerous other reports in files BA-MA
   RH26-12/41, 42, 27, 44, 142 covering the whole period.

6. BA-MA RH26-12/63, 22.4.42; BA-MA RH26-12/59, 21.2.43.

7. BA-MA RH26-12/78, 7.3.43; BA-MA RH26-12/167, '*Abwehrschlacht
   um Witebsk 1943/44*'; BA-MA, *Heft* 523, pp. 12–13.

8. BA-MA RH26-12/168, 27.3.46; BA-MA, *Heft* 523, p. 13; *Findbuch,*
   pp. 1–2. Also: *Supreme Commander*: Operations in Europe of the
   Allied Expeditionary Force (London, 1946).

9. H. Spaeter and W. Ritter von Schramm, *Die Geschichte des Panzer-
   korps Grossdeutschland* (Bielefeld, 1958) I. 45–6; B. Quarrie, *Panzer-
   Grenadier Division 'Grossdeutschland'* (London, 1977) p. 3; BA-MA
   RH26-1005/82.

10. Spaeter/Schramm, *Grossdeutschland,* I. 66–76, 84–92, 194. Generally
    on the French campaign see J. Benoist-Méchin, *Sixty Days that Shook
    the West* (New York, 1963). Contemporary account in W. Durian,
    Infanterieregiment GD Greift An (Berlin, 1942).

11. Spaeter/Schramm, *Grossdeutschland,* I. 199–214.

12. Ibid, 219–23; Quarrie, *Panzer-Grenadier Division,* p. 4; BA-MA
    RH26-1005/85, n.d. p. 21.

13. Spaeter/Schramm, *Grossdeutschland,* I. 220, 247–9, 253, 255–6.

14. Ibid., pp. 271–308.

15. Ibid., pp. 308–17.

16. Ibid., pp. 321–78, 385–400; generally on the fighting in that sector see
    A. Seaton, *The Battle for Moscow* (New York, 1971).

17. Spaeter/Schramm, *Grossdeutschland,* I. 400, 404–12, 414, 429; BA-MA
    RH26-1005/78, *Tagebuch von Hobe,* pp. 1–4; BA-MA RH26-1005/5,
    newspaper clippings of calls for volunteers, May 1942.

18. Spaeter/Schramm, *Grossdeutschland,* I. 431–4, 441–540; BA-MA
    RH26-1005/6, 22.5.42; *von Hobe,* pp. 12–13; RH37/6337, *Tagesbericht
    C. Benes,* pp. 10–12; RH37/6351, *Bericht F. Mebes,* pp. 5–11.

19. Spaeter/Schramm, *Grossdeutschland,* I. 552–666; *von Hobe,* pp. 14–21;
    Benes, pp. 13–14; *Mebes,* pp. 12–26.

20. Spaeter/Schramm, *Grossdeutschland,* I. 667–9 and II. 9–73; Quarrie,
    Panzer-Grenadier Division, p. 9; *Benes,* pp. 14–16; *Mebes,* pp. 26–30;

BA-MA RH26-1005/10, 13.1.43, 27–8.1.43, 6.2.43, 10.2.43, 14–15.2.43.

21. Spaeter/Schramm, *Grossdeutschland*, II. 71–130.
22. Ibid., pp. 130–49, 167–214; *Benes*, p. 17.
23. Spaeter/Schramm, *Grossdeutschland*, II. 233–324; *Benes*, pp. 18–23; BA-MA RH26-1005/70, 1.4.–30.9.43, pp. 102, 115, 148.
24. Spaeter/Schramm, *Grossdeutschland*, II. 324–99, 409–544; *Benes*, pp. 23–8, 31–3, 36–9; BA-MA RH26-1005/82, 2.11.43; BA-MA RH26-1005/82, *Kriegsberichter H. König*, 1944.
25. Spaeter/Schramm, *Grossdeutschland*, II. 590–721; *Benes*, pp. 39–42; BA-MA RH26-1005/84, '*Memel*', '*Frontzeitung: Die Feuerwehr*'.
26. Spaeter/Schramm, *Grossdeutschland*, III. 11–24, 182–261, 381–404, 656–81; *Benes*, pp. 42–53; BA-MA RH26-1005/82, *Bericht: R. Jung*, 1.3.–18.4.45, and '*Neu-Aufstellung der Pz.Gren.Div.GD*'.
27. W. Paul, *Geschichte der 18. Panzer Division* (Freiburg; i.B., n.d.) pp. 1, 3–11; BA-MA RH27-18/2a, 26.9.40; BA-MA RH27-18/1, 27.5.41. On the concept and development of the Panzer arm, see H. Guderian, *Die Panzertruppen*, 2nd edn (Berlin, 1938); R. J. O'Neill, 'Doctrine and Training in the German Army', in M. Howard (ed.), *The Theory and Practice of War* (London, 1965) pp. 143–65.
28. Paul, *18.Pz.Div.*, pp. 14–21, 23–7; 39–31, 33–48, 50–4; BA-MA RH27-18/5, 20.6.41; BA-MA RH27-18/24, 8.7.41 and 9.7.41.
29. Paul, *18.Pz.Div.*, pp. 53, 60–7, 69–72, 87–8, 108–34; BA-MA RH27-18/29, 18.10.41 and 19.10.41; BA-MA RH27-18/73, 3.11.41 and 28.10.41.
30. Paul, *18.Pz.Div.*, pp. 135–49, 151–7, 160–76, 182–6, 193–201, 207–30; BA-MA RH27-18/75, 6.1.42; BA-MA RH27-18/213, 24.1.42 and 28.1.42; BA-MA RH27-18/117, 20.4.42.
31. Paul, *18.Pz.Div.*, pp. 230–51; BA-MA RH27-18/196, 30.4.43 and 1.4.–30.6.43; BA-MA RH27-18/164, 30.6.43. For some background on anti-partisan operations, see M. Cooper, *The Phantom War* (London, 1979); J. A. Armstrong (ed.), *Soviet Partisans in World War II* (Wisconsin, 1964).
32. Paul, *18.Pz.Div.*, pp. 251–89; BA-MA RH27-18/144, 11.7.43, 23.7.43, 1.9.43, 1.10.43; BA-MA RH27-18/150, 5.10.43; BA-MA RH27-18/142, 18.10.43. For some Russian accounts of the war, see V. I. Chuikov, *The End of the Third Reich* (London, 1967) and his *The Battle for Stalingrad* (in the Hebrew language, Tel-Aviv, 1970); M. P. Gallagher, *The Soviet History of World War II* (New York, 1963); V. Petrov, '*June 22, 1941*' (Columbia, 1968); B. S. Telpuchowski, *Die Sowjetische Geschichte des Grossen Vaterländischen Krieges* (Frankfurt/M., 1961); G. K. Zhukov, *Marshall Zhukov's Greatest Battles* (London, 1969). See also R. H. S. Stolfi, 'Barbarossa Revisited; A Critical Reappraisal of the Opening Stages of the Russo-German Campaign', *JCH*, LIV (1982) 27–46.
33. The figures quoted are taken from the following sources: Mueller-Hillebrand, *Das Heer*, I. 70–1; BA-MA RH26-12/252, August 1939, 3.10.39, 12.10.39; BA-MA RH26-12/6, 10.5.40; BA-MA RH26-12/16, 25.6.40; BA-MA RH26-12/22, 1.6.–10.12.41; BA-MA RH26-12/130, 10.12.41; BA-MA RH26-12/265, 24.4.42, 22.5.42, 23.7.42, 16.10.43; BA-MA RH26-12/62, 10.4.42; BA-MA RH26-12/52, 10.4.42; BA-MA

RH26-12/53, 10.5.42; BA-MA RH26-12/54, 1.8.42; BA-MA RH26-12/ 69, 1.10.42; BA-MA RH26-12/92, 16.12.41–28.2.42; BA-MA RH26-12/ 75, 1.3.–21.6.43; BA-MA RH26-12/78, 9.3.43; BA-MA RH26-12/49, 16.12.41–30.4.43; BA-MA RH26-12/168, 27.3.46.

34. BA-MA RH26-12/40, 22.11.41 and 11.12.41.
35. BA-MA RH26-12/142, 24.1.42.
36. BA-MA RH26-12/63, 22.4.42.
37. BA-MA RH26-12/52, 25.4.42.
38. BA-MA RH26-12/261, 31.3.42.
39. BA-MA RH26-12/266, 20.7.42.
40. BA-MA RH26-12/57, 10.12.42.
41. BA-MA RH26-12/56, 26.10.42.
42. The figures quoted have been taken from the following sources: Spaeter/Schramm, *Grossdeutschland,* I. 66–76, 85–6, 194, 199–213, 385, 429; III. 11–24, 381–404; BA-MA RH26-1005/5, 27.6.–31.7.42 and 23.6.–25.7.42; BA-MA RH26-1005/7, 1.7.–31.7.42 and 1.8.42; BA-MA RH26-1005/60, 15.5.–31.7.42; BA-MA RH26-1005/50, 26.4.43, 1.8.42–25.4.43; BA-MA RH26-1005/51, 8.11.43, 1.4.–30.9.43.
43. Spaeter/Schramm, *Grossdeutschland,* I. 556–65, 576–7.
44. Ibid., pp. 606–55.
45. Ibid.
46. Ibid., pp. 655–67.
47. BA-MA RH37/6394, 9.1.43.
48. *Benes,* pp. 18–21, 23–8, 31–3.
49. Spaeter/Schramm, *Grossdeutschland,* II. 270–94.
50. Ibid., pp. 487–544.
51. Ibid., pp. 590–714; BA-MA RH37/6394, 13.6.–31.8.44, 6.10.–15.10.44.
52. Spaeter/Schramm, *Grossdeutschland,* III. 182–261.
53. Ibid., pp. 381–404, 656–65.
54. Ibid., pp. 665–81. For a view of the final defeat from Hitler's bunker, see H. R. Trevor-Roper, *The Last Days of Hitler,* 14th edn (London, 1978).
55. The figures quoted have been taken from the following sources: Mueller-Hillebrand, *Das Heer,* I. 70–1; Paul, *18.Pz.Div.,* pp. 14–15; BA-MA RH27-18/3, 15.3.41; BA-MA RH27-18/26, 22.6.–10.7.41; BA-MA RH27-18/69, 1.10.41, 1.11.41, 1.1.42, 28.2.42, 28.3.42; BA-MA RH27-18/63, 5.11.41, 10.12.41, 22.2.42; BA-MA RH27-18/174, 21.6.41.–31.12.41, 1.1.–31.3.42; BA-MA RH27-18/133, 26.3.43; BA-MA RH27-18/196, 30.4.43; BA-MA RH27-18/169, 1.4.–30.6.43, 14.5.–2.6.43; BA-MA RH27-18/144, 11.7.43, 21.7.43, 1.8.43, 11.8.43, 1.9.43, 1.10.43; BA-MA RH27-18/170, 3.8.43, 1.10.43, 1.7.–30.9.43.
56. Paul, *18.Pz.Div.,* pp. 33–5.
57. Ibid., pp. 36–8.
58. Ibid., pp. 39–42; BA-MA RH27-18/26, 21.7.41.
59. BA-MA RH27-18/26, 27.7.41.
60. Paul, *18.Pz.Div.,* pp. 43–8.
61. Ibid., p. 54; BA-MA RH27-18/24, 11.7.41.
62. Paul, *18.Pz.Div.,* pp. 110–26; BA-MA RH27-18/63, 5.11.41, 10.12.41.
63. Paul, *18.Pz.Div.,* pp. 131–4.

64. Ibid., pp. 209–24.
65. Ibid. Also BA-MA RH27-18/117, 20.6.42.
66. BA-MA RH27-18/144, 1.9.43.
67. BA-MA RH27-18/144, 17.9.43.
68. BA-MA RH27-18/170, 1.7.–30.9.43.
69. BA-MA RH26-12/30, 22.6.–21.7.41; BA-MA RH37/943, 13.6.–13.8.41.
70. Spaeter/Schramm, *Grossdeutschland*, I. 491–510; *Mebes*, pp. 10–11; *Benes*, pp. 11–12.
71. Spaeter/Schramm, *Grossdeutschland*, I. 450–87; *Benes*, pp. 31–3.
72. Paul, *18.Pz.Div.*, pp. 64–7, 135–49; BA-MA RH27-18/27, 14.9.41; BA-MA RH27-18/30, 29.9.41. For some powerful pictorial evidence, see Kameradschaftsbund 16. Panzer-und Infanterie-Division (eds), *Bildband der 16. Panzer-Division* (Bad Nauheim, 1956).
73. BA-MA RH26-12/67, 1.8.42.
74. BA-MA RH26-12/69, 18.11.42.
75. BA-MA RH26-12/56, 1.10.42.
76. Spaeter/Schramm, *Grossdeutschland*, II. 37–42, 48–67.
77. BA-MA RH26-12/38, 28.10.41.
78. BA-MA RH26-12/142, 24.1.42.
79. BA-MA RH27-18/179, 14.11.41–7.1.42.
80. BA-MA RH27-18/63, 22.2.42.
81. BA-MA RH27-18/184, 7.1.–31.3.42.
82. BA-MA RH26-12/212, 21.1.42.
83. BA-MA RH26-12/142, 21.1.42.
84. Ibid., and BA-MA RH26-12/291, 24.1.42.
85. BA-MA RH26-12/246, 28.1.42. See also H. Meier-Welcker, *Aufzeichnungen eines Generalstabsoffiziers* (Freiburg i.B. 1982) pp. 150–9.
86. BA-MA RH27-18/74, 2.12.41.
87. BA-MA RH27-18/74, 21.12.41.
88. BA-MA RH26-12/38, 28.10.41.
89. BA-MA RH26-12/142, 24.1.42; on the general logistical problems of the campaign see M. van Crefeld, *Supplying War*, 3rd edn (London, New York, 1980) pp. 148–54, 166–80.
90. BA-MA RH26-12/85, 5.4.42; BA-MA RH26-12/84, 24.2.42; other reports of cannibalism in O. Buchbender, *Das tönende Erz* (Stuttgart, 1978) p. 108.
91. BA-MA RH26-12/142, 9.5.42.
92. BA-MA RH26-12/85, 24.10.42.
93. BA-MA RH27-18/63, 22.2.42; BA-MA RH27-18/178, 15.2.42, 28.2.42, 17.3.42.
94. BA-MA RH27-18/184, 7.1.–31.3.42; BA-MA RH27-18/188, 1.5.42; BA-MA RH27-18/185, 2.1.42.
95. BA-MA RH26-12/38, 28.10.41.
96. BA-MA RH26-12/142, 24.1.42.
97. BA-MA RH26-12/63, 22.4.42.
98. BA-MA RH26-12/134, 5.8.42; BA-MA RH26-12/69, 18.11.42.
99. Paul, *18.Pz.Div.*, pp. 110–31; see also Table 1.6, this volume.
100. BA-MA RH27-18/63, 22.2.42; BA-MA RH27-18/117, 25.4.42.

101. BA-MA RH27-18/207, 22.8.–21.9.43.
102. BA-MA RH26-12/142, 24.1.42. A recent study of the now newly termed 'combat reaction' was presented at Tel-Aviv University, in a symposium on the war in Lebanon. See *The Sunday Times*, 13 March 1983, p. 14.
103. BA-MA RH26-12/63, 22.4.42.
104. *Mebes*, p. 22.
105. Spaeter/Schramm, *Grossdeutschland,* II. 45–8.
106. BA-MA RH27-18/26, 27.7.41. For a discussion of many of the issues dealt with in this section as they manifested themselves among the troops of the Western Allies in the Second World War, see J. Ellis, *The Sharp End of War* (New York, 1982).
107. Table 1.7 is based on the following sources: BA-MA RH26-12/99, 25.10.40; BA-MA RH26-12/235, 2.10.40; BA-MA RH26-12/108, 9.4.41; BA-MA RH26-12/131, 25.12.41; BA-MA RH26-12/139, 4.5.43; BA-MA RH26-12/151, 24.9.43.
108. BA-MA RH26-12/45, 5.10.41. During the whole of the First World War the German army sentenced 150 soldiers to death, of whom only 48 were executed, whereas during the Second World War, according to van Crefeld's estimates, 11 753 men were executed. See M. van Crefeld, *Fighting Power* (Westport: Connecticut, 1982) pp. 113–5.
109. BA-MA RH26-12/262, 27.12.41; BA-MA RH26-12/267, 7.5.42.
110. Ibid.
111. BA-MA RH26-12/85, 27.5.42.
112. BA-MA RH26-12/134, 30.7.42.
113. BA-MA RH26-12/85, 24.10.42.
114. BA-MA RH26-12/139, 4.5.43.
115. Ibid.
116. BA-MA RH26-12/54, 1.8.42.
117. BA-MA RH26-12/267, 9.7.42.
118. BA-MA RH26-12/54, 1.8.42.
119. BA-MA RH26-12/57, 2.11.–1.12.42.
120. BA-MA RH26-12/57, 10.12.42.
121. Table 1.8 is based on the following sources: BA-MA RH26-1005/5, 27.6.–18.8.42; BA-MA RH26-1005/60, 27.3.–18.8.42; BA-MA RH26-1005/61, 7.4.43; BA-MA RH26-1005/75, 15.11.43.
122. Spaeter/Schramm, *Grossdeutschland,* I. 348–52.
123. Ibid., pp. 365–6.
124. Ibid., p. 385.
125. Ibid., III. 665–81.
126. Table 1.9 is based on the following sources: BA-MA RH27-18/172, 1.1.–30.4.41; BA-MA RH27-18/76, 5.1.42; BA-MA RH27-18/178, 2.1.43, Januar 1943; BA-MA RH27-18/194, Februar–Juni 1943; BA-MA RH27-18/207, Juli–18 Oktober 1943.
127. BA-MA RH27-18/24, 26.6.41.
128. BA-MA RH27-18/28, 18.8.41.
129. BA-MA RH27-18/73, 29.11.41.
130. BA-MA RH27-18/74, 16.12.41.
131. BA-MA RH27-18/63, 10.12.41.

132. BA-MA RH27-18/76, 19.3.42.
133. BA-MA RH27-18/147, 12.7.43.
134. BA-MA RH27-18/142, 17.7.43.
135. E. A. Shils and M. Janowitz, 'Cohesion and Disintegration in the Wehrmacht in World War II', *POQ*, XII (1948) 280–1; this issue is also discussed in E. P. Chodoff, 'Ideology and Primary Groups', *AFS*, IX, 4 (1983) 569–93; van Crefeld, *Fighting Power*, pp. 83–7, 163–6.
136. Spaeter/Schramm, *Grossdeutschland*, I. 338–41.
137. Ibid., pp. 341–6.
138. Ibid., pp. 365–6.
139. Ibid., II. 251–70.
140. G. Sajer, *The Forgotten Soldier*, 2nd edn (London, 1977) pp. 263–7.

2 THE OFFICERS: BACKBONE OF THE ARMY

1. Mueller-Hillebrand, *Das Heer*, I. 69–71; II. 102; Seaton, *Russo-German War*, pp. 74–5.
2. R. Absolon, 'Das Offizierkorps des Deutschen Heeres, 1935–45', in H. H. Hofmann (ed.), *Das deutsche Offizierkorps, 1860–1960* (Boppard am Rhein, 1980) pp. 247–50, 253; see tables in van Crefeld, *Fighting Power*, pp. 155–7, including comparison to First World War.
3. See this volume: Introduction, and Chapter 1 ('Military Events'). For manpower, this volume Chapter 1 ('Manpower and Casualties').
4. For the numbers of the files, see Bibliography, A. I. in this volume.
5. For details see Bibliography, A. II., this volume.
6. Ibid.
7. Ibid.
8. Special thanks are due to Mr John Ridge of the Department of Social and Administrative Studies at Oxford University for greatly assisting me with the computer analysis. I have also learned a great deal from R. Floud, *An Introduction to Quantitative Methods for Historians* (London, 1973).
9. One important category, that of the religion of the officers, has not been analysed at all, owing to lack of sufficient data.
10. M. Kitchen, *The German Officer Corps*, (London, 1968) p. 22; D. Bald, *Der deutsche Generalstab* (München, 1977) pp. 108, 120. On attempts to retain the high proportion of noble officers before the First World War, see V. R. Berghahn, *Germany and the Approach of War in 1914*, 4th edn (London, 1979) pp.6–9; G. A. Craig, 'Portrait of a Political General', *POQ*, LXVI (1951) 1–36.
11. As 'aristocrats' I have defined all officers whose names were prefixed with the title 'von' and other noble prefixes. The fact that the 18.Pz.Div. had a smaller number of aristocrats than the GD may be accounted for by the overall smaller number of officers from the former formation in this sample. The ratio of noble/non-noble officers in absolute numbers was: 12.I.D.–41/161; GD–22/184; 18.Pz.Div.–18/105; total–81/450.

12. R. Absolon, *Die Personnelle Ergänzung der Wehrmacht im Frieden und im Kriege* (Bundesarchiv-Zentralnachweisstelle, 1972) pp. 5, 8; and his *Wehrgesetz und Wehrdienst* (Boppard am Rhein, 1960) pp. 78–93, 108–11, 151–64, 173–83, 186–202; 223–41, 245–52; Deist, *Das Deutsche Reich*, pp. 400–49. See also E. W. Bennet, *German Rearmament and the West* (Princeton: N.J., 1979); M. Geyer, *Aufrüstung oder Sicherheit* (Wiesbaden, 1980). On the difficulties of dividing German society into 'classes' and the problem of overlapping categories, see M. H. Kater, *The Nazi Party* (Cambridge, Mass., 1983) pp. 1–16. Figures of officers' background during Weimar are taken from Bald, *Generalstab*, pp. 121–3. The nobility comprised only 0.14 per cent of the population; on the other hand, in 1930, 95 per cent of the officers came from social strata which had been considered eligible before 1914. See Carsten, *Reichswehr and Politics*, pp. 214–16.

13. Among the officers whose first known rank was second lieutenant, 36.2 per cent of the nobles remained 'stuck' in it, as opposed to 42.8 per cent of the non-nobles; 6.4 per cent of the nobles reached the rank of colonel, as opposed to only 1.9 per cent of the non-nobles. See also G. H. Kleine, 'Adelgenossenschaft und Nationalsozialismus', *VfZ*, XXVI (1978) 100–43.

14. Absolon, *Das deutsche Offizierkorps*, p. 250.

15. On promotion and the 'Offizierlaufbahn', see ibid., pp. 254–60; reserve officers could not be promoted above the rank of major, according to R. Absolon, *Die Wehrmacht im Dritten Reich* (Boppard am Rhein, 1975) III. 291–3; also see G. Papke, 'Offizierkorps und Anciennität', in H. Meier-Welcker (ed.), *Untersuchungen zur Geschichte des Offizierkorps* (Stuttgart, 1962) pp. 202–6; M. Messerschmidt, 'Werden und Prägung des preussischen Offizierkorps', in Militärgeschichtliches Forschungsamt (eds), *Offiziere im Bild von Dokumenten* (Stuttgart, 1964) pp. 97–104; on promotion in the Reichswehr, see H. J. Gordon (Jr), *The Reichswehr and the German Republic* (Princeton: N.J., 1957) pp. 169–216.

16. T. Geiger, *Die Soziale Schichtung des Deutschen Volkes,* 2nd edn (Stuttgart, 1967) pp. 20–1. It is also interesting to point out that the GD had the lowest number of Nazi officers; this division was mistakenly mentioned by some historians as an SS formation. See Seaton, *Russo-German War*, p. 349 n. 27; R. A. Beaumont, *Military Elites* (London, 1976) p. 73.

17. T. Mason, 'Women in Germany', Part 1, *HWJ*, I. (1976) p. 78.

18. D. Schoenbaum, *Hilter's Social Revolution* (London, 1967) pp. 71–2. The occupations are: white collar, independent, civil servants including teachers, farmers and students. Further discussed later in this chapter. Also see note 39 below.

19. Schoenbaum, *Social Revolution,* p. 73.

20. German generals were, as has been conclusively shown, always involved in politics, however '*überparteilich*' they claimed to be. See, apart from works quoted earlier, also M. Geyer, 'Professionals and Junkers: German Rearmament and Politics in the Weimar Republic', in R. Bessel and E. J. Feuchtwanger (eds), *Social Changes and Political*

Development in Weimar Germany (London, 1981) pp. 77–133; F. L. Carsten, 'Germany: From Scharenhorst to Schleicher: the Prussian Officer Corps in Politics', in M. Howard (ed.) *Soldiers and Governments* (London, 1957); G. Ritter, *The Sword and the Sceptre* (London, 1972) I–IV.

21. P. H. Merkl, *The Making of a Stormtrooper* (Princeton: N.J., 1980) p. 156; T. Abel, *Why Hitler Came into Power* (New York, 1938) p. 312. Also T. Segev, 'From Dachau to Bergen-Belsen: Concentration Camp Commanders', *Zmanim,* II (Hebrew, 1981).

22. Krausnick/Wilhelm, *Die Truppe,* pp. 644–6; infiltration of Nazis into the universities of Baden is described in J. H. Grill, *The Nazi Movement in Baden* (Chapel Hill: North Carolina, 1983) pp. 217–2; also see G. C. Boehnert, 'The Third Reich and the Problem of "Social Revolution" ', in V. R. Berghahn and M. Kitchen (eds), *Germany in the Age of Total War* (London, 1981) pp. 203–17; K. D. Bracher, *The German Dictatorship* (New York, 1970) pp. 266–72; G. A. Craig, *Germany* (New York, 1978) pp. 638–72; G. J. Giles, 'The Rise of the National Socialist Students' Association', in P. D. Stachura (ed), *The Shaping of the Nazi State* (London, 1978) pp. 160–85; F. Meinecke, *The German Catastrophe* (Boston, 1963) pp. 43–6; W. Zorn, 'Student Politics in the Weimar Republic', *JCH,* V (1970) 128–44.

23. Our findings certainly correspond with those of another historian who has recently pointed out 'the consistency of elite over-representation in the Nazi party from 1919 to 1945'. See Kater, *The Nazi Party,* p. 237.

24. See further on this subject E. Y. Hartshorne (Jr), *The German Universities and National Socialism* (Cambridge, Mass., 1937); M. H. Kater, *Studentenschaft und Rechtsradikalismus in Deutschland* (Hamburg, 1975), and his 'The Work Student', *JCH,* X (1975) 71–94; H. P. Bleuel and E. Klinnert, *Deutsche Studenten auf dem Weg ins Dritte Reich* (Gütersloh, 1967).

25. D. Orlow, *The History of the Nazi Party* (Newton Abbot: Pittsburgh, 1973) II. 48, 66, 136–8, 202–8, 253; in 1941–3 youngsters preferred to become officers in the Waffen SS rather than joining the party (p. 342). On the 'Vorzeitig dienende Freiwillige', see Absolon, *Personelle Ergänzung,* p. 14.

26. As Giles and Grill, quoted above, point out, apathy was spreading among students; this did not mean that they opposed the regime ideologically, but rather that they reacted to the institutionalisation of the *Weltanschauung.* Instances of real resistance among students were rare. See K-H. Jahnke, *Weisse Rose contra Hakenkreuz* (Frankfurt/M., 1969) and his *Entscheidungen* (Frankfurt/M., 1970); I. Scholl, *Die Weisse Rose,* 3rd edn (Frankfurt/M., 1952). Stauffenberg, the bravest of the 'Putschists' of 1944, seems to have begun his relationship with the Nazis as an enthusiastic supporter. See H. Foertsch, *Schuld und Verhängnis* (Stuttgart, 1951) pp. 22, 181–5.

27. On transferring to regular status, see Absolon, *Die Wehrmacht,* III. 226. Some officers in this sample actually did change status during the war.

28. D. Bald, *Vom Kaiserheer zur Bundeswehr* (Frankfurt/M., 1981) p. 14;

see also his *Der deutsche Offizier* (München, 1982); I. Welcker and F. F. Zelnika, *Qualifikation zum Offizier?* (Frankfurt/M., 1982) p. 113; C. Barnett, 'The Education of Military Elites', *JCH*, II (1967) 15–35.

29. Bald, *Kaiserheer*, p. 21: in 1899, 77 per cent of the officers came from the '*erwünschte Kreise*'. See also Demeter, *Officer Corps*, pp. 103–6; Carsten, *Reichswehr*, pp. 216–7; on Seeckt, see H. Meier-Welcker, *Seeckt* (Frankfurt/M., 1967) and F. v. Rabenau, *Hans von Seeckt* (Leipzig, 1938).

30. On Hitler's order regarding the promotion of officers of 4.11.1942, see Papke, *Offizierkorps*, pp. 205–6; van Crefeld, *Fighting Power*, p. 143; Demeter, *Officer Corps*, pp. 13, 81.

31. Bald, *Kaiserheer*, pp. 41–3.

32. Ibid., pp. 43–4; see also D. Bald, *Die Soziale Auswahl des Militärs* (transcript of a lecture, given me by the author, n.d.) pp. 9–10; the *Abitur* was given up as a requirement for officer aspirants by 1942; in July 1944, 64 per cent of the total of 240 000 officers were former NCOs. I would like to thank Dr Bald for his assistance.

33. Deist, *Das Deutsche Reich*, I. 420–3, 433–4, 437, 444; also his *The Wehrmacht and German Rearmament* (London, 1981); Mueller-Hillebrand, *Das Heer*, I. 57–64, 29–31; Absolon, *Offizierkorps*, pp. 247–53. In 1922 there were 35 644 NCOs and 40 000 lance corporals in the 100 000-man army; but in 1928 only 117 officers had been promoted from the ranks. See Craig, *The Politics*, p. 398 n. 1; Carsten, *Reichswehr*, p. 217; on 'rankers', also in H. Rosinski, *The German Army* (London, 1939) pp. 185–6.

34. V. R. Berghahn, *Modern Germany* (London, New York, 1982) pp. 13–14, 253, 281; Welcker, *Qualifikation*, pp. 36–7, 40.

35. Absolon, *Die Wehrmacht*, IV. 49–53. On the HJ in Baden, see Grill, *The Nazi Movement*, pp. 216–17.

36. Absolon, *Die Wehrmacht*, IV. 54, 98–100. General background in M. Broszat, *The Hitler State* (New York, 1981); W. Laqueur, *Young Germany* (London, 1962); E. Mann, *School for Barbarians* (London, 1939); H. Siemsen, *Hitler Youth* (London, 1940); D. P. Stachura, 'The ideology of the Hitler Youth in the Kampfzeit', *JCH*, VIII (1973) 155–67, and his *Nazi Youth in the Weimar Republic* (Santa Barbara: California, 1975).

37. See J. W. Baird, *The Mythical World of Nazi War Propaganda* (Minneapolis: Minnesota, 1974); E. K. Bramsted, *Goebbels and National Socialist Propaganda* (London, 1965); H. T. Burden, *The Nuremberg Party Rallies* (London, 1967); H. Brenner, *Die Kunstpolitik des Nationalsozialismus* (Hamburg, 1963); K. Vondung, *Magie und Manipulation* (Göttingen, 1971). On Hitler and the '*Führerkult*', see A. Bullock, *Hitler*, rev. edn (New York, 1964) pp. 372–410; J. C. Fest, *Hitler*, 4th edn (Harmondsworth: Middlesex, 1982) pp. 511–38; J. P. Stern, *Hitler*, 5th edn (Glasgow, 1979) pp. 85–8; and especially I. Kershaw, *Der Hitler-Mythos* (Stuttgart, 1980). On Nazi educational institutions, see H. Ueberhorst (ed), *Elite für die Diktatur* (Düsseldorf, 1969); on a very different development in France, see B. Singer, 'From Patriots to Pacifists', *JCH*, XII (1977) 413–34.

38. Geiger, *Soziale Schichtung,* pp. 20–3. Kater, *The Nazi Party,* p. 12, analysed 27 047 899 socially classifiable persons in 1933 with the following results; 54.56 per cent belonged to the 'lower class', 42.65 per cent to the 'lower middle class', and 2.78 per cent to the 'elite'.
39. Berghahn, *Germany,* pp. 263, 282. For other possible social classifications, see A. H. Halsey *et al., Origins and Destinations* (London, 1980) p. 18; H. Kaelbe, 'Social Mobility in Germany', *JMH,* III (1978) 439–61; B. Wegner, 'Das Führerkorps der Waffen-SS im Kriege', in Hofmann, *Offizierkorps,* p. 340; *Organisation der Deutschen Arbeitsfront und der NS Gemeinschaft Kraft durch Freude* (Leipzig, n.d.) pp. 30–67. See also note 48 below.
40. We have the professions of 165 officers and 126 fathers; in case both were known, we preferred the officer's profession, thereby reaching a final figure of 271.
41. On overlapping categories, see note 12, this chapter.
42. Bald, *Generalstab,* p. 121; in 1913, 28 per cent of the officers came from officer families: Bald, *Kaiserheer,* p. 21.
43. Bald, *Kaiserheer,* p. 21; Bald, *Generalstab,* p. 121.
44. Regarding 'self-recruitment' among generals: in 1925, 52 per cent came from an officer family; in 1944–29 per cent; in 1965–37 per cent. See Dahrendorf, *Gesellschaft und Demokratie in Deutschland* (München, 1965) pp. 281–2. On similar 'self-recruitment' among students, see Zorn, '*Student Politics*', pp. 128–9. Yet a new 'Officer-Ideal' was developing after the First World War, centring on professional rather than social qualifications. See H. Kurzke, 'Das Bild des Offiziers in der Deutschen Literatur', in Hofmann, *Offizierkorps,* pp. 431–5.
45. Mueller-Hillebrand, *Das Heer,* I. 29–30. This reluctance to promote NCOs was maintained in spite of the greatly accelerated promotion of officers. Also see note 47 below.
46. Merkl, *Stormtrooper,* p. 186.
47. E. Graf von Matuschka, 'Die Beförderung in Praxis', in Meier-Welcker, *Offizierkorps,* pp. 175–6. See also, van Crefeld, *Fighting Power,* pp. 141–5. On complaints among junior officers on slow promotion in the Reichswehr, see S. E. Finer, *The Man on Horseback,* 2nd rev. edn (Harmondsworth: Middlesex, 1975) pp. 51–2.
48. The discussion regarding the question of who voted for Hitler is still very much in the centre of numerous social studies of the Third Reich. It is impossible to pursue it further within the limits of this work. The traditional thesis according to which the supporters of the Nazis came mainly from the middle class has been strongly criticised; nevertheless, it seems to me that recent research has been more successful in showing the over-representation of the elite among Nazi voters than of the working class or of the traditional aristocracy. See T. Childers, 'The Social Bases of the National Socialist Vote', *JCH,* II (1976) 17–42, and his *The Nazi Voter* (Chapel Hill: North Carolina, 1983); R. Hamilton, *Who Voted for Hitler?* (Princeton, 1982); Kater, *The Nazi Party;* S. M. Lipset, *Political Man,* rev. edn (Baltimore, 1981); P. H. Merkl, *Political Violence under the Swastika* (Princeton: N.J., 1975); A. J. Mayer, 'The Lower Middle Class as Historical Problem', *JMH,* III (1975) 409–36; D.

Mühlberger, 'The Sociology of the NSDAP', *JCH*, XV (1980) 493–511; K. O'Lessker, 'Who Voted for Hitler?, *AJS*, VIII, 74 (1968) 63–9; H. Winkler, 'Extremismus der Mitte?', *VfZ*, XX, 2 (1972) 175–91, and his *Mittelstand, Demokratie und Nationalsozialismus* (Köln, 1972). A good discussion of this debate is in S. Gordon, *Hitler, Germans, and the 'Jewish Question'* (Princeton: N.J., 1984) pp. 71–87; on 'big-business' and the Nazis in Weimar, see D. Abraham, *The Collapse of the Weimar Republic* (Princeton: N.J., 1981); on labour's opposition, see T. Mason, 'Labour in the Third Reich', *P&P*, XXXIII (1966) 112–41; his *Sozialpolitik im Dritten Reich* (Opladen, 1977), and his 'The Workers' Opposition in Nazi Germany', *HWJ*, XI (1981) 120–37; also S. Salter, 'Structures of Concensus and Coercion', in D. Welch (ed.), *Nazi Propaganda* (London, 1983) pp. 88–116.

49. For another aspect of social, political and ideological tensions in Weimar, see in J. M. Diehl, *Paramilitary Politics in Weimar Germany* (Bloomington, 1977). Further on the propagandistic preparation of the German population for war, see J. Sywottek, *Mobilmachung für den Krieg* (Opladen, 1976); W. Wette, 'Ideologien, Propaganda und Innenpolitik als Voraussetzungen der Kriegspolitik des Dritten Reiches', in Deist, *Das Deutsche Reich*, I. 25–173; Z. A. B. Zeman, *Nazi Propaganda* (London, 1964).

3　INDOCTRINATION AND THE NEED FOR A CAUSE

1. BA-MA RH26-12/227, 1.5.40, which adds that since the beginning of the war over 20 000 radios had been sent to the troops at the front 'from donations and former Jewish ownership'. See also E. Kris and H. Speier, *German Radio Propaganda* (New York, 1944); P. M. Taylor, 'Propaganda in International Politics, 1919–39', in K. R. M. Short (ed.), *Film & Radio Propaganda in World War II* (Knoxville, 1983) pp. 29–32; R. Taylor, 'Goebbels and the Function of Propaganda', in Welch, *Nazi Propaganda*, pp. 39–40; Zeman, *Nazi Propaganda*, pp. 51–2: by 1939 some 3 500 000 *Volksempfänger* had been sold and 70 per cent of all German households owned a wireless set–the highest percentage anywhere in the world.

2. BA-MA RH26-12/225. 11.11.39.

3. BA-MA RH26-12/82, 1.6.–15.12.41.

4. BA-MA RH26-1005/5, 10.4.–10.8.42.

5. BA-MA RH27-18/151, 1.1.–25.5.41; BA-MA RH27-18/158, 7.4.42–3.2.43.

6. On films in the Third Reich, see D. Hollstein, *Anti-semitische Filmpropaganda* (München-Pullach, 1971); D. S. Hull, *Film in the Third Reich* (Berkeley: California, 1969); M. S. Phillips, 'The German Film Industry and the New Order', in Stachura, *Nazi State*; D. Welch, 'Educational Film Propaganda and the Nazi Youth', in Welch, *Nazi Propaganda*, pp. 65–87; D. Welch, 'Nazi Wartime Newsreel Propaganda', in Short, *Propaganda*, pp. 201–19.

7. BA-MA RH26-12/225, 11.11.39; BA-MA RH26-12/226, 22.1.40.
8. BA-MA RH26-12/80, 23.6.40–31.3.41; BA-MA RH26-12/81, 1.4.–31.5.41.
9. BA-MA RH26-12/82, 1.6.–15.12.41.
10. BA-MA RH26-12/86, 1.3.–30.6.43.
11. BA-MA RH26-1005/5, 10.4.–10.8.42; BA-MA RH26-12/47, 5.5.–5.6.43.
12. BA-MA RH27-18/151, 1.1.–25.5.41; BA-MA RH27-18/158, 7.4.42–3.2.43; BA-MA RH27-18/165, 3.6.–18.10.43.
13. Generally on the press in the Third Reich, see Bramsted, *Goebbels*, pp. 88–123; J. Hagemann, *Die Presselenkung im Dritten Reich* (Bonn, 1970); O. J. Hale, *The Captive Press in the Third Reich* (Princeton: N.J., 1964). On Goebbels's direction of propaganda, see also W. A. Boelcke (ed), *The Secret Conferences of Dr Goebbels*, 2nd edn (New York, 1970) especially Introduction, pp. vii–xxii.
14. BA-MA RH26-12/225, 11.11.39; BA-MA RH26-12/226, 22.1.40 and 21.11.39, according to which each company received ten newspapers daily.
15. BA-MA RH26-12/80, 23.6.40–31.3.41.
15. BA-MA RH26-12/80, 23.6.40–31.3.41.
16. Ibid. On the Communiqué, see E. Murawski, *Der deutsche Wehrmachtbericht* (Boppard am Rhein, 1962); also see Messerschmidt, *Die Wehrmacht*, pp. 347–53.
17. BA-MA RH26-12/81, 1.4.–31.5.41.
18. BA-MA RH26-12/229; see also Messerschmidt, Die Wehrmacht, p. 322.
19. BA-MA RH26-12/236, 17.11.39; BA-MA RH26-12/227, 11.7.40 and 18.7.40.
20. For example, BA-MA RH26-12/228, 6.8.40; BA-MA RH26-12/195, 28.1.41.
21. BA-MA RH26-12/82, 1.6.–15.12.41; BA-MA RH26-12/83, 16.12.41–28.2.43.
22. BA-MA RH26-12/86, 1.3.–30.6.43.
23. Numerous copies of these news-sheets in BA-MA RH26-12/294, April 1942.
24. BA-MA RH26-1005/5, 10.4.–10.8.42.
25. BA-MA RH26-1005/47, 5.5.–5.6.43.
26. BA-MA RH27-17/151, 26.10.–31.12.40 and 1.1.–25.5.41; BA-MA RH27-18/158, 7.4.42–3.2.43.
27. BA-MA RH27-18/162, 4.2.–2.6.43; BA-MA RH27-18/165, 3.6.–18.10.43.
28. See generally Messerschmidt, *Die Wehrmacht*, pp. 156–71, 315–26.
29. BA-MA RH26-12/225, 12.12.39, 13.12.39, *Erster Jahrgang 1939, Heft 1,* and so forth. Also BA-MA RH26-12/226, 1939/40, *Erster Jahrgang, Heft 5.*
30. BA-MA RH26-12/182, *Schulungshefte für den Unterricht über Nationalsozialistische Weltanschauung und Nationalpolitische Zielsetzung, Zweiter Jahrgang 1940, Heft 1.*

31. BA-MA RH26-12/227, *Für den Kompanie-Führer, Merkblatt zum Unterricht*, Nr.1/März 1940 (for example).
32. BA-MA RH26-12/80, 23.6.40–31.3.41.
33. See, for example, BA-MA RH26-12/231, *Sonderschrift des OKW, 1940*; BA-MA RH26-12/89, 26.6.43. See also V. R. Berghahn, 'NSDAP und "Geistige Führung" der Wehrmacht', *VfZ*, XVII (1969) p. 40.
34. BA-MA RH26-1005/47, 5.5.–5.6.43.
35. BA-MA RH27-18/158, 7.4.42–3.2.43; BA-MA RH27-18/165, 3.6.–18.10.43.
36. BA-MA RH26-12/225, 11.11.39; BA-MA RH26-12/226, 22.1.40. On Max Amann's takeover of German publishing houses, see Zeman, *Propaganda*, pp. 46–7.
37. BA-MA RH26-12/80, 23.6.40–31.3.41; BA-MA RH26-12/82, 1.6.–15.12.41; BA-MA RH26-12/86, 1.3.–30.6.43.
38. BA-MA RH26-1005/5, 10.4.–10.8.42.
39. BA-MA RH26-1005/42, 6.9.42; BA-MA RH26-1005/47, 5.5.–5.6.43. On Rosenberg's role in the indoctrination of the army, see Berghahn, '*Geistige Führung*', pp. 17–71.
40. BA-MA RH27-18/158, 7.4.42–3.2.43.
41. For example, BA-MA RH26-12/226, 15.1.40, and 20.1.40.
42. BA-MA RH26-12/194, 24.1.41; BA-MA RH26-12/80, 23.6.40–31.3.41.
43. BA-MA RH26-1005/5, 10.4.–10.8.42; BA-MA RH26-1005/42, 6.9.42.
44. BA-MA RH27-18/151, 1.1.–25.5.41; BA-MA RH27-18/158, 7.4.42–3.2.43.
45. Berghahn, '*Geistige Führung*', pp. 17–19.
46. BA-MA RH26-12/274, 18.12.38.
47. BA-MA RH26-12/16, 8.7.40.
48. BA-MA RH26-12/18, 29.10.40.
49. BA-MA RH26-1005/7, 3.4.–3.7.42.
50. BA-MA RH26-1005/39, 22.9.42.
51. BA-MA RH26-1005/47, 26.4.43.
52. BA-MA RH27-18/151, 22.5.41.
53. These developments are described at length in Berghahn, '*Geistige Führung*', and Messerschmidt, *Die Wehrmacht*, pp. 441–80. See also, G. L. Weinberg, 'Dokumentation: Adolf Hitler und der NS-Führungsoffizier (NSFO)', *VfZ*, XII (1964) 443–56.
54. BA-MA RH27-18/159, 27.10.42; Berghahn, '*Geistige Führung*', P. 37.
55. BA-MA RH26-1005/47, 11.5.43.
56. BA-MA RH26-12/298, 6.6.43.
57. BA-MA RH26-12/301, 20.2.45.
58. Some of the most important works dealing with these issues are Berghahn, '*Geistige Führung*'; Messerschmidt, *Die Wehrmacht*; Müller, *Das Heer*; O'Neill, *The German Army*. For a typical contemporary interpretation, see R. Donnevert (ed.), *Wehrmacht und Partei* (Leipzig, 1938).
59. I. Kershaw, 'How Effective was Nazi Propaganda?', in Welch, *Propaganda*, pp. 183–7.
60. Messerschmidt, *Die Wehrmacht*, pp. 216–25, discusses this point.

61. For example, see BA-MA RH26-12/182, 25.4.40. See also, J. Wulf, *Presse und Funk im Dritten Reich* (Gütersloh, 1964).
62. BA-MA RH26-12/226, November 1939.
63. Welch, *'Newsreel Propaganda'*, pp. 206–11.
64. H. Boberach (ed), *Meldungen aus dem Reich* (Neuwied, 1965) pp. 47–8.
65. See discussion of Riefenstahl's works in S. Sontag, 'Fascinating Fascism', in her *Under the Sign of Saturn*, 7th edn (New York, 1981) pp. 73–105.
66. BA-MA RH26-12/226, 20.1.40.
67. BA-MA RH26-12/226, 15.1.40.
68. BA-MA RH26-12/182, *Zweiter Jahrgang 1940, Heft 1.*
69. BA-MA RH26-12/229, 5.10.40.
70. BA-MA RH26-12/225, 22.11.39.
71. Apart from the works by Bramsted, Hagemann, Hale and Wulf quoted above, see also F. Sänger, *Politik der Täuschungen* (Wien, 1975). In 1933 the Nazis ran only 2.5 per cent of all German newspapers; by 1944, 82 per cent of the remaining 977 newspapers were controlled by them. See Zeman, *Propaganda*, p. 47.
72. BA-MA RH26-12/225, 22.10.39, Nr. 45.
73. BA-MA RH26-12/228, August 1940, Nr. 29.
74. BA-MA RH26-12/229, 1.10.40.
75. BA-MA RH26-12/227, *Mitteilungen für die Truppe*, Juni 1940, Nr. 17.
76. BA-MA RH26-12/230, 14.11.40. See also U. Tal, 'Territory and Space (Raum) in the Nazi Ideology', *Zmanim*, I (in the Hebrew language, 1979).
77. BA-MA RH26-12/227, 20.7.40, Nr. 4; BA-MA RH26-12/228, Nr. 8/Juli 1940; BA-MA RH26-12/298, Nr. 26/Februar 1943 and Nr. 27/Februar 1943 and Nr. 28/April 1943.
78. BA-MA RH26-12/298, *Nationalpolitischer Unterricht im Heere*, IV. Hauptthema: Der Nationalsozialismus, Thema 13: *Die Grossen Deutschen bis zu Adolf Hitler*, für den kompanie-Führer *(Merkblatt zum Unterricht)*, Nr. 26/Februar 1943.
79. BA-MA RH26-12/18, 29.10.40.
80. *MfT*, Nr. 116, quoted in Messerschmidt, *Die Wehrmacht*, pp. 326–7. On anti-Slav propaganda even before 1914, see F. Fischer, *War of Illusions* (London, 1975) pp. 191, 198, 386; see also M. Broszat, *Der Nationalsozialismus* (Stuttgart, 1960). Further on anti-Soviet propaganda, see Baird, *Nazi War Propaganda*, ch. IX, 'The Soviet War', pp. 147–65; Kershaw, *Nazi Propaganda*, p. 192, writes that 'Given the extent of pre-existing anti-Polish and anti-Russian sentiment, the level of anti-Bolshevik propaganda, and the ignorance about the Polish and especially the Russian people, it is a fair assumption that Nazi propaganda was successful in confirming and reinforcing prevailing stereotypes.'
81. BA-MA RH27-18/4, 21.6.41.
82. BA-MA RH26-12/34, 24.8.41.
83. BA-MA RH26-12/82, 17.11.41; German original also in H-A. Jacobsen, *1939–45, Der Zweite Weltkrieg in Chronik und Dokumenten*, 4th

edn (Darmstadt, 1961) pp. 416–17; full English translation in Cooper, *Phantom War*, pp. 171–2, and for Manstein's equally notorious order, pp. 173–4; for a peculiar defence of Manstein's orders, R. T. Paget, *Manstein*, (London, 1951).

84. BA-MA RH26-12/262, 28.12.41.
85. BA-MA RH26-12/297, 27.1.43.
86. BA-MA RH26-1005/39, 22.9.42.
87. BA-MA RH26-1005/47, 10.4.43. It is interesting to note how little of this fanaticism we find in post-war memoirs of German generals. Apart from works quoted in notes 1, 2 in Introduction (this volume), see also G. Blumentritt, *Von Rundstedt* (London, 1952); F. von Senger und Etterlin, *Neither Fear nor Hope* (London, 1963); as well as W. Görlitz (ed.), *Generalfeldmarschall Keitel* (Göttingen, 1961) and his *Paulus und Stalingrad* (Frankfurt/M., 1964); also D. Irving, *Hitler's War* (London, 1977).
88. G. L. Mosse, *The Crisis of German Ideology* (New York, 1964); F. Stern, *The Politics of Cultural Despair* (Berkeley: California, 1961).
89. On the background of the new nationalism and some of its intellectual and political roots, see G. A. Craig, *The Germans* (New York, 1982) pp. 190–210; G. L. Mosse, *The Nationalisation of the Masses* (New York, 1975) and his 'National Cemeteries and National Revival', *JCH*, XIV (1979) 1–20; F. Stern, *The Failure of Illiberalism* (London, 1972).
90. For some recent works on anti-Semitism, see S. Almog (ed.), *Antisemitism Through the Ages* (in the Hebrew language, Jerusalem, 1980); L. Dawidowicz, *The War Against the Jews*, 3rd edn (Harmondsworth: Middlesex, 1979); Gordon, *'Jewish Question'*; J. Katz, *Anti-Semitism* (In the Hebrew language, Tel-Aviv, 1979); I. Kershaw, *Popular Opinion and Political Dissent in the Third Reich* (London, 1983) pp. 224–77, 358–72; K. Kwiet, 'Zur Historiographischen Behandlung der Judenverfolgung im Dritten Reich', *MGM*, I (1980) 149–92; E. Schulin (ed.), *Die Juden als Minderheit in der Geschichte* (München, 1981); S. Volkov, 'On Anti-semitism and its Investigation', *Zmanim*, II (in the Hebrew language, 1981). On German universities, see C. E. McClelland, *State, Society and University in Germany* (London, New York, 1980); F. K. Ringer, *The Decline of the German Mandarins* (Cambridge, Mass., 1969). On racism among leaders of the Second Reich, see note 80, this chapter.
91. Apart from works quoted already, see also V. R. Berghahn, *Der Stahlhelm* (Düsseldorf, 1966); F. L. Carsten, ' "Volk Ohne Raum", A Note on Hans Grimm', *JCH*, II (1967) 221–27; A. J. Nicholls, *Weimar and the Rise of Hitler*, 3rd edn (London, 1981); R. G. L. Waite, *Vanguard of Nazism* (Cambridge, Mass., 1952). On the communists, see E. Rosenhaft, *Beating the Fascists?* (London, New York, 1983).
92. P. Bucher, *Der Reichswehrprozess* (Boppard am Rhein, 1967).
93. Apart from works quoted previously, see further on the reactions and indoctrination of various groups in German society under the Nazis, in H. Becker, *German Youth: Bond or Free* (London, 1946); A. D. Beyerchen, *Scientists under Hitler* (New Haven, London, 1977); J. Caplan, 'The Civil Servant in the Third Reich' (Oxford Univ. D. Phil.

thesis, 1973); H. Seier, 'Der Rektor als Führer, zur Hochschulpolitik des Reichserziehungsministeriums 1934–45', *VfZ*, XII (1964) 105–46; G. Ziemer, *Education for Death* (London, 1941).

94. Most important on this issue are Kershaw's *Der Hitler-Mythos* and *Popular Opinion*; see also, R. Cecil, *The Myth of the Master Race* (London, 1972); H. Hatfield, 'The Myth of Nazism', in H. A. Murray, *Myth and Mythmaking*, 2nd edn (Boston, 1969) pp. 199–220. On police terror, see E. K. Bramsted, *Dictatorship and Political Police* (London, 1945).

95. On pressure from below for more propaganda in winter 1941/2, see Berghahn, *'Geistige Führung'*, pp. 34–7.

96. BA-MA RH27-18/159, 7.5.42.

97. Zeman, *Nazi Propaganda*, pp. 176–8.

98. A report on the troops of Army Group Centre said that the men were interested in four main issues: wife, profession, party and religion. See Berghahn, *'Geistige Führung'*, p. 36. The 12.I.D. launched an investigation regarding a group of its officers alleged to have listened to a foreign broadcasting station. See BA-BA, RH26-12/233, 26.3.40. As far as propaganda was concerned, 'immigration into the army', discussed by Messerschmidt, *Die Wehrmacht*, pp. 245–58, can hardly have been useful.

99. Messerschmidt, *Die Wehrmacht*, pp. 326–36. The most comprehensive study of German propaganda towards the Red Army, including numerous documents and leaflets, is Buchbender, *Das tönende Erz*.

100. BA-MA RH26-12/294, *Mitteilungen für das Offizierkorps*, April 1942, Nr. 4. Russian generals did emphasise in their memoirs the political content of their soldiers' indoctrination, since changes of leadership notwithstanding, the 'communist man' was shown as having beaten the fascists and, indeed, Soviet Russia had not been compelled to adopt a different political system, as Nazi Germany did. Apart from works already quoted, see S. Bialer (ed.), *Stalin and his Generals* (London, 1970); Ponomarenko *et al.*, *Behind the Front Line* (London, n.d.).

101. BA-MA RH27-18/174, 1.5.41–31.3.42.

102. BA-MA RH27-18/207, 1.10.43.

103. BA-MA RH27-18/178, 1.7.–30.9.42, 7.10.42.

104. BA-MA RH27-18/178, 1.1.43.

105. BA-MA RH27-18/207, 1.10.43.

106. Messerschmidt, *Die Wehrmacht*, p. 325, citing *MfT*, April 1941, Nr. 89. The development of the 'officer-ideal' of the *Kaiserheer* to that of the Wehrmacht is discussed by Messerschmidt, *Die Wehrmacht*, pp. 422–40. Compare with the ideal SS officer, strikingly similar, in B. Wegner, *Hitlers Politische Soldaten* (Paderborn, 1982) pp. 38–56.

107. Messerschmidt, *Die Wehrmacht*, pp. 326–36, citing *MfO*, März 1943.

108. Messerschmidt, *Die Wehrmacht*, pp. 354–7.

109. Ibid.

110. English translation in Craig, *Germany*, p. 750.

111. Messerschmidt, *Die Wehrmacht*, pp. 465–7.

112. Ibid.

113. Ibid., pp. 331–2, citing *MfT*, Januar 1945, Nr. 389.

114. Berghahn, *'Geistige Führung'*, p. 36.
115. BA-MA RH26-12/89, 18.6.43.
116. BA-MA RH26-12/89, 26.6.43. The same officer stressed, however, that 'The bombing terror creates a great mental strain': Ibid. On Hitler's indifference to the bombing, see H. Trevor-Roper (ed.), *The Goebbels Diaries*, 2nd edn (London, 1979) p. 18; and his (ed.), *Hitler's Table Talk*, 2nd edn (London, 1973) pp. 668–9; also A. Speer, *Inside the Third Reich*, 6th edn (London, 1979) pp. 408–9.
117. BA-MA RH27-18/159, 27.10.42.
118. Ibid.
119. On the mutinies in the French army in 1917, see G. Pedrocini, *Les Mutinerie de 1917* (Paris, 1976); J. Williams, *Mutiny 1917* (London, 1962). On the German collapse and revolution, see Nicholls, *Weimar*, pp. 1–19.
120. Further on the intensification of the indoctrination in the winter of 1941/2, see Messerschmidt, *Die Wehrmacht*, pp. 307–8, and, after Stalingrad, pp. 329–30.
121. Propaganda and criminality among the Western allies were, of course, not completely absent; studying them, however, only further emphasises the difference between them and the Eastern Front. See, on propaganda, M. Balfour, *Propaganda in War* (London, 1979) and I. McLaine, *Ministry of Morale* (London, 1979); on discipline, morale and patriotism, Ellis, *The Sharp End*, pp. 212–66, 314–57; on Allied brutality, A. M. de Zayas, *Die Wehrmacht-Untersuchungsstelle*, 3rd edn (München, 1980); on Allied failure to bomb death camps, W. Z. Laqueur, *The Terrible Secret*, 2nd edn (Harmondsworth: Middlesex, 1982) and D. S. Weiman, 'Why was Auschwitz not Bombed?', *Zmanim*, II (in the Hebrew language, 1981). As for the SS, it has indeed been pointed out recently that it served as 'an alibi of a nation', most of all, it would seem to me, regarding the Wehrmacht who could blame everything on the 'black coats'. See R. L. Koehl, *The Black Corps* (Madison, 1983) p. 245.
122. V. Klemperer, *Die Unbewältigte Sprache*, 3rd edn (Darmstadt, n.d.) pp. 23, 27, 105–8, 208–19, 238–9.
123. E. E. Evans-Pritchard, *Theories of Primitive Religion*, 8th edn (Oxford, 1977) p. 7.
124. Quoted in R. Needham, *Belief, Language and Experience* (Oxford, 1972) p. 7.
125. Ibid.
126. Ibid.
127. Ibid., p. 56.
128. Ibid., p. 6.
129. Kershaw, *Hitler-Mythos*, pp. 90–1; and his *Popular Opinion*.
130. On the alienation of the catholics from the NSDAP, see Kershaw, *Popular Opinion*, pp. 185–223; on the workers, see, for example, Mason, *The Workers' Opposition*, as well as his other publications quoted earlier.
131. Both Kershaw, *Popular Opinion*, and Gordon, *'Jewish Question'*, have concluded that most of the German population was indifferent to

persecution of Jews rather than rabidly anti-Semitic. On anti-Slav and anti-Bolshevik sentiments, see note 80, this chapter.

132. P. Fussel, *The Great War and Modern Memory*, 3rd edn (Oxford, 1979) p. 115.

133. Messerschmidt, *Die Wehrmacht*, pp. 245–58. See also, Cecil, *The Myth of the Master Race*; J. W. Baird, 'The Myth of Stalingrad', *JCH*, IV, 3 (1969) 187–204. On another myth, see G. Kirwin, 'Waiting for Retaliation', *JCH*, XVI, 16 (1981) 565–83. M. Howard, *War in European History*, 2nd edn (Oxford, 1977) p. 134 describes The Second World War as 'a struggle in which every individual felt his value system as well as his physical survival to be threatened by alien forces with which there could be neither communication nor compromise'.

134. Kershaw, *Popular Opinion*, p. 1.

135. Religious and pseudo-religious or ideological fanaticism have played an important role in motivating soldiers throughout history, both in Europe and in numerous others civilizations. See, for example, J. A. Aho, *Religious Mythology and the Art of War* (Westport, 1981); P. H. Merkl and N. Smart (eds), *Religion and Politics in the Modern World* (New York, 1983); and a highly original and interesting theory on the relationship between religion and violence, in R. Girard, *Violence and the Sacred*, 2nd edn (Baltimore, 1979).

136. *Last Letters from Stalingrad* (London, 1956) pp. 27–8. Also see A. Werth, *The Year of Stalingrad* (London, 1946). The need of the professional soldier, and particularly the German officer corps of the new Wehrmacht, to find a set of ideological principles as to 'why we fight' is analysed in M. Janowitz, *The Professional Soldier* (New York, 1960) pp. 401–3. Further on this point, see M. D. Feld, 'Professionalism, Nationalism and the Alienation of the Military', in J. van Doorn (ed.), *Armed Forces and Society* (The Hague, 1968) pp. 55–70; and J. van Doorn, 'Political Change and the Control of the Military', in J. van Doorn (ed.), *Military Profession and Military Regimes* (The Hague, 1969) pp. 11–31.

137. M. I. Gurfein and M. Janowitz, 'Trends in Wehrmacht Morale', in D. Lerner (ed.), *Propaganda in War and Crisis* (New York, 1951) pp. 200–8; Shils/Janowitz, 'Cohesion and Disintegration', p. 304.

138. Trevor-Roper, *Goebbels Diaries*, p. 95.

139. Ibid., p. 113. When Hitler expressed worry about opposition in the army to the NSFOs, Keitel assured him: 'Nein, mein Führer, das ist nicht zu erwarten . . . Wir sind der Erziehung schon so weit.' See Messerschmidt, *Die Wehrmacht*, pp. 448–52. However, on the army's anxiety regarding civilian morale, see V. Berghahn, 'Meinungsforschung im "Dritten Reich" ', *MGM*, I (1967) 83–119.

140. Needham, *Belief*, p. 53. On the impact of the changing vocabulary in Nazi Germany as an essential aspect of the conversion of the population to National Socialism and the Führer-Myth, see, apart from Klemperer's work, also C. Berning *Vom 'Abstammungsnachweis' zum 'Zuchtwart', Vokabular des Nationalsozialismus* (Berlin, 1964). Very revealing is the chapter 'Ich Glaube an Ihm', in Klemperer, *Sprache*, pp. 115–32.

4 BARBARISM AND CRIMINALITY

1. Streit, *Kameraden,* pp. 28–61; Jacobsen, '*Kommissarbefehl*', pp. 170–82; Jacobsen, *1939–45,* pp. 441–516; Krausnick, '*Kommissarbefehl*'. See also A. Roberts and R. Guelff (eds), *Documents on the Laws of War* (Oxford, 1982) pp. 1–22, 43–59, 153–6; D. Schindler and J. Toman (eds), *The Laws of Armed Conflicts* (Geneva, 1973) pp. 247–88. Military aspects of the Barbarossa Orders in H. R. Trevor-Roper (ed.), *Hitler's War Directives,* 4th edn (London, 1978).
2. BA-MA RH26-12/82, 1.6.–15.12.41.
3. BA-MA RH26-12/203, 17.6.41.
4. BA-MA RH26-12/201, 12.6.41.
5. Streit, *Kameraden,* p. 10; a slightly lower figure in A. Streim, *Die Behandlung sowjetischer Kriegsgefangener im 'Fall Barbarossa'* (Heidelberg, 1981) pp. 246–7; Mason, '*Women in Germany*'; See also, A. Rosas, *The Legal Status of Prisoners of War* (Helsinki, 1976) pp. 69–80; W. Anders, *Hitler's Defeat in Russia* (Chicago, 1953) pp. 168–72; A. Dallin, *German Rule in Russia,* 2nd edn (London, 1981) pp. 68–70, 409–27, 533–52; G. H. Davis, 'Prisoners of War in Twentieth-Century War Economies', *JCH,* XII (1977) 623–34.
6. BA-MA RH26-12/34, 24.8.41; BA-MA RH26-12/142, 22.12.41; BA-MA RH26-12/262, 25.12.41 and 31.12.41.
7. BA-MA RH27-18/24, 8.7.41; BA-MA RH27-18/72, 19.10.41; BA-MA RH27-18/30, 23.9.41; BA-MA RH27-18/29, 18.10.41 and 19.10.41.
8. Baird, *Nazi War Propaganda,* p. 159. Dallin, *German Rule,* pp. 71–2, expresses the same opinion and says that 'Official directives notwithstanding, this attitude was an exception in the Army rather than the rule.'
9. See this volume, Introduction, note 9.
10. BA-MA RH27-18/4, 19.6.41; BA-MA RH26-12/244, 22.6.41; Krausnick-Wilhelm, *Die Truppe,* pp. 251–4; Streit, *Kameraden,* pp. 83–7; Dallin, *German Rule,* pp. 30–4; Jacobsen, '*Kommissarbefehl*', pp. 182–5, 230–78.
11. See documents quoted above as well as BA-MA RH27-18/27, 9.9.41.
12. BA-MA RH26-1005/42, 19.9.42.
13. BA-MA RH27-18/154, 4.11.41.
14. BA-MA RH27-18/157, 6.3.42 and BA-MA RH26-12/85, 21.5.42, for examples of POWs in whose interrogation report it was stated that they were Jews. Also see Krausnick/Wilhelm, *Die Truppe,* pp. 251–4; Streit, *Kameraden,* p. 109; Dallin, *German Rule,* pp. 410–18.
15. BA-MA RH26-12/243, 13.9.41.
16. BA-MA RH26-12/56. See also Streit, *Kameraden,* pp. 106–8.
17. Streit, *Kameraden,* pp. 128–30, 137ff, 162ff, 171ff, 177ff, 183ff.
18. BA-MA RH26-12/236, 21.6.40; BA-MA RH26-12/283, 18.4.40; BA-MA RH26-12/237, 13.8.40; BA-MA RH26-12/277, 13.8.40. Streit, *Kameraden,* pp. 187–8, stresses the wide-ranging measures taken to ensure the well-being of POWs in the French campaign, and points out that such orders were '*a priori undenkbar*', not only in the Nazi leadership but also among the military command regarding Russia.

19. Streit, *Kameraden*, p. 66. On 2 May 1941 a meeting between the Leader of the Economic Staff of Oldenburg, General Dr Schubert, and the State Secretaries of various ministries concluded that the third year of the war could only be conducted if the whole Wehrmacht lived off Russia: 'Hierbei werden zweifellos zig Millionen Menschen verhungern.' It was further stressed that in the forest areas and industrial cities in the north alone, 'viele 10 Millionen Menschen werden . . . überflüssig und werden sterben'. Attempts to save them would 'nur auf Kosten der Versorgung Europas gehen'. Rosenberg spoke of the decimation of a few dozen millions of Russians 'in order to free the German people for the next centuries from the terrible pressure of 180 millions'. See Streit, pp. 63–6.
20. Streit, *Kameraden*, pp. 162–71.
21. BA-MA RH26-12/211, 31.7.41.
22. BA-MA RH27-18/27, 17.8.41.
23. BA-MA RH26-1005/6, 3.4.–3.7.42.
24. BA-MA RH27-18/189, 30.7.42.
25. Dallin, *German Rule*, p. 416.
26. BA-MA RH27-18/175, 17.6.41; Streit, *Kameraden*, pp. 137–62.
27. BA-MA RH26-12/288, 6.8.41; BA-MA RH27-18/176, 2.9.41.
28. BA-MA RH26-12/290, 21.10.41; calory tables in Streit, *Kameraden*, pp. 138–40.
29. BA-MA RH27-18/74, 21.12.41; BA-MA RH26-12/246, 28.1.42.
30. BA-MA RH26-12/291, 24.1.42; BA-MA RH27-18/184, 8.3.42; BA-MA RH27-18/27, 14.9.41. See also Meier-Welcker, *Aufzeichnungen*, p. 157.
31. BA-MA RH27-18/194, 25.9.42.
32. BA-MA RH27-18/202, 8.7.43.
33. Streit, *Kameraden*, pp. 177–83; according to Streim, *Sowjetischer Kriegsgefangene*, pp. 163–79, sick and wounded POWs were delivered to the SS and 'liquidated' by its troops. Generally on the liquidation of 'potential enemies', see Streim, pp. 33–155; and of other categories of POWs Streim, pp: 156–87.
34. Streit, *Kameraden*, pp. 183–7.
35. BA-MA RH27-18/26, 6.8.41.
36. BA-MA RH26-12/287, 21.8.41.
37. Further on Russians serving in the Wehrmacht, see Dallin, *German Rule*, pp. 533–52, 553–659 (on Vlasov); Anders, *Hilter's Defeat*, pp. 173–204; B. Wegner, 'Auf dem Wege zur Pangermanischen Armee', *MGM*, II (1980) 101–36; and his *Hitlers Politische Soldaten*, pp. 291–4, 310–16; G. H. Stein, *The Waffen SS*, 4th edn (London, 1977) pp. 165–96.
38. BA-MA RH26-12/295, 14.11.41.
39. BA-MA RH27-18/177, 8.–15.11.41.
40. BA-MA RH26-12/51, 6.3.42.
41. BA-MA RH26-1005/6, 3.4.–3.7.42.
42. BA-MA RH27-18/124, 26.7.42.
43. BA-MA RH27-18/194, 19.8.42.
44. BA-MA RH26-1005/37, 21.9.42.
45. BA-MA RH26-1005/63, 20.11.42.

46. Ibid.
47. BA-MA RH27-18/76, 2.11.41.
48. BA-MA RH27-18/73, 11.11.41.
49. BA-MA RH27-18/76, 7.3.42.
50. BA-MA RH26-1005/5, 19.6.42.
51. BA-MA RH26-12/220, 8.12.42.
52. BA-MA RH26-12/220, 14.12.42.
53. BA-MA RH26-1005/47, 11.6.43.
54. Most of the material referred to will be quoted in the following pages. On the ideological instruction carried out by the officers see Chapter 3. An example of the attempts made by the commanders to restrict the spreading of news regarding their own brutal measures against the Russian population, is an order forbidding the taking of photographs of executions, though as we know these orders were often not carried out. See BA-MA RH26-12/200, 16.12.41. On the 'lack' of 'moral offences' and 'plundering' owing to 'Russian conditions', see, for instance, BA-MA RH26-12/131, 1.4.–15.12.41.
55. BA-MA RH27-18/24, 25.6.41.
56. BA-MA RH27-18/175, 30.6.41.
57. Ibid.
58. BA-MA RH26-12/27, 5.7.41.
59. BA-MA RH26-12/27, 17.7.41.
60. BA-MA RH27-18/157, 14.2.42.
61. BA-MA RH26-1005/42, 23.9.42.
62. BA-MA RH26-1005/67, 1.12.42.
63. BA-MA RH26-1005/47, 26.4.43; see also Streit, *Kameraden,* pp. 106–8, 239–44; Krausnick/Wilhelm, *Die Truppe,* pp. 205–9, 217–23, 232–43, 249–78.
64. For secondary literature on the partisans, apart from works already quoted in Chapter 1, note 31 (this volume), see: M. R. D. Foot, *Resistance,* 2nd edn (London, 1978) pp. 286–92, 313–16; H. Kühnrich, *Der Partisanenkrieg in Europa* (Berlin, 1965); W. Z. Laqueur, *Guerrilla* (London, 1977) pp. 207–14, 232–8; F. M. Osanka (ed.), *Modern Guerrilla Warfare* (New York, 1962) pp. 57–127; P. Vershigora, *Kopvak's Campaigns* (in the Hebrew language, Tel-Aviv, 1953); G. Wright, *The Ordeal of Total War* (New York, 1968) pp. 154–61.
65. BA-MA RH26-12/244, 22.6.41.
66. BA-MA RH26-12/211, 31.7.41.
67. BA-MA RH27-18/26, 4.8.41.
68. BA-MA RH26-12/84, 20.1.–30.1.42.
69. BA-MA RH26-12/32, 5.8.41.
70. See this volume, Chapter 4 ('Introduction').
71. BA-MA RH26-12/126, 4.7.41.
72. For instance, BA-MA RH26-12/128, 12.8.41.
73. BA-MA RH26-12/287, 15.8.41.
74. BA-MA RH27-18/28, 14.8.41.
75. BA-MA RH27-18/154, September 1941; BA-MA RH26-12/242, 25.8.41.
76. BA-MA RH26-12/123, 18.9.41.

77. B'A-MA RH26-12/128, 27.9.41.
78. BA-MA RH26-12/243, 4.10.41.
79. BA-MA RH27-18/154, 8.10.41.
80. BA-MA RH26-12/128, 11.10.41.
81. BA-MA RH26-12/245, 13.10.41.
82. BA-MA RH26-12/244, 31.10.41.
83. BA-MA RH26-12/206, 1.11.41.
84. BA-MA RH26-12/244, 14.11.41.
85. BA-MA RH26-12/245, 17.11.41; they were not to be photographed, however. See this volume, Chapter 4, note 54.
86. BA-MA RH26-12/245, 20.11.41.
87. BA-MA RH26-12/245, 2.12.41.
88. BA-MA RH26-12/200, 5.12.41.
89. BA-MA RH26-12/246, 29.11.–5.12.41.
90. BA-MA RH26-12/245, 3.12.41 and 7.12.41.
91. BA-MA RH26-12/245, 14.12.41.
92. BA-MA RH26-12/294, 9.1.42.
93. BA-MA RH26-12/246, 19.12.41.
94. BA-MA RH26-12/246, 24.12.41.
95. BA-MA RH26-12/246, 4.1.42 and 8.1.42.
96. For instance, BA-MA RH26-12/245, 11.12.41 on the shooting or hanging of twelve civilians, including two women, between 4 and 9 December 1941.
97. BA-MA RH26-12/246, 5.12.41.
98. BA-MA RH26-12/246, 31.1.42.
99. For instance, BA-MA RH27-18/158, 7.4.42–3.2.43, especially entries for 7.4.–1.7.42 on evacuations; BA-MA RH27-18/115, 13.4.42; BA-MA RH27-18/157, 11.2.42.
100. BA-MA RH26-1005/6, 15.4.42.
101. For example, BA-MA RH27-18/76, 21.3.42. Further on lists of Jews, communist party members and Soviet bureaucrats prepared by the 18.Pz.Div. for the SD, as well as executions and taking of hostages, see, for instance, BA-MA RH27-18/194, 23.9.42; BA-MA RH27-18/164, 19.3.43.
102. BA-MA RH27-18/162, 4.2.–2.6.43, especially entry for 12.5.–16.5.43; BA-MA RH27-18/132, 10.5.43.
103. BA-MA RH27-18/164, 13.5.43; BA-MA RH27-18/196, 16.5.43; BA-MA RH27-18/130, 16.5.43.
104. BA-MA RH27-18/132, 9.6.43; BA-MA RH27-18/135, 2.6.43.
105. Krausnick/Wilhelm, *Die Truppe,* pp. 243–9.
106. BA-MA RH27-18/164, *Anlage* 426; BA-MA RH27-18/166, 8.6.43.
107. On continued partisan activities, see, for instance, BA-MA RH26-12/86, 1.3.–30.6.43; BA-MA RH26-12/78, 8.6.43; on a visit to Orel shortly after its liberation see A. Werth, *Russia at War* (London, 1964) pp. 688–99; on Russian atrocities while occupying Germany, see Jacobsen, *1939–45,* pp. 598–600; in defence of the 'decency' of the Wehrmacht as opposed to the 'atrocities' of the partisans, see V. Redelis, *Partisanenkrieg* (Heidelberg, 1958) pp. 86–90.
108. BA-MA RH27-18/24, 24.6.41.

109. BA-MA RH27-18/24, 8.7.41.
110. BA-MA RH27-18/123, 31.7.41.
111. BA-MA RH26-12/244, 11.7.41.
112. BA-MA RH27-18/26, 4.8.41.
113. BA-MA RH26-12/246, 9.1.42; see also, L. Goure, *The Siege of Leningrad* (Stanford, 1962) p. 141, H. E. Salisbury, *The Siege of Leningrad* (London, 1969) p. 331; M. Walzer, *Just and Unjust Wars,* 3rd edn (Harmondsworth: Middlesex, 1980) pp. 165–70; and, more generally, G. Best, *Humanity in Warfare* (London, 1980) pp. 224–44; Y. Dinstein, 'Just and Unjust War', *Zmanim,* I (in the Hebrew language, 1980).
114. BA-MA RH27-18/159, 8.6.42.
115. BA-MA RH26-1005/42, 23.9.42.
116. See, for example, Krausnick/Wilhelm, *Die Truppe,* p. 236.
117. BA-MA RH26-12/245, 13.10.41.
118. BA-MA RH27-18/154, 4.11.41.
119. BA-MA RH27-18/177, 17.11.41.
120. BA-MA RH26-1005/42, 22.10.42.
121. BA-MA RH26-1005/42, 31.10.42.
122. BA-MA RH27-18/164, 30.4.43.
123. BA-MA RH26-12/246, 11.1.42; further on executions of 'agents', see, for instance, BA-MA, RH26-12/83, 16.12.41–28.2.43; on the army's involvement in the killing of Jewish children, see, for example, H. Krausnick and H. C. Deutsch (eds), *Helmut Groscurth: Tagebücher Eines Abwehroffiziers* (Stuttgart, 1970) pp. 234–42.
124. On instructions not to use Jews as interpreters, see, for example, BA-MA RH27-18/73, 4.11.41; on propaganda among '*Hiwis*', see, for instance, BA-MA RH26-1005/47, 11.5.43; BA-MA RH26-12/89, 17.6.43, 22.6.43 and 26.6.43.
125. See L. Niethammer, 'Male Fantasies', *HWJ,* VII (1979) 176–86, on Klaus Theweleit's study *Männerphantasien* (Frankfurt, 1977/8).
126. This point is made in recent studies on public reactions in Germany to anti-Semitism. Kershaw, *Popular Opinion,* p. 360, writes that 'the Jews, a generally unloved minority, had become . . . almost totally isolated from the rest of German society. For most people, "the Jew" was now a completely depersonalized image. The abstraction of the Jew had taken over more and more from the real "Jew" who, whatever animosity he had caused, had been a flesh-and-blood person. The depersonalization of the Jew had been the real area of success of Nazi policy and propaganda on the Jewish Question.' Similarly, Gordon, '*Jewish Question*', pp. 185–6, says that 'Jews had in most instances been segregated from Germans physically, occupationally, sexually, socially, and psychologically.' She shows that Germans could often help Jews on a personal level, but were, as Kershaw would agree, quite indifferent to their fate as a mass of dehumanised beings.
127. In general on the economic exploitation of Russia, see Dallin, *German Rule,* pp. 305–408; Krausnick/Wilhelm, *Die Truppe,* pp. 380–400; L. M. Wheeler, 'The SS and the Administration of Nazi Occupied Eastern Europe' (Oxford Univ. D.Phil. thesis 1981); on Poland, see M.

Broszat, *Nationalsozialistische Polenpolitik* (Stuttgart, 1961); on preparations for this policy, see N. Rich, *Hitler's War Aims* (London, 1973) pp. 211–23.
128. BA-MA RH27-18/4, 19.6.41.
129. BA-MA RH27-18/153, 28.7.41; BA-MA RH27-18/26, 5.8.41; BA-MA RH27-18/176, 6.8.41.
130. BA-MA RH27-18/153, 10.8.41.
131. BA-MA RH27-18/27, 17.8.41.
132. BA-MA RH27-18/181, August and September 1941.
133. BA-MA RH27-18/176, 7.11.41.
134. BA-MA RH27-18/177, 8.11.–15.11.41.
135. BA-MA RH27-18/181, November 1941.
136. BA-MA RH27-18/177, 7.12.41.
137. BA-MA RH27-18/78, 9.12.41.
138. BA-MA RH26-12/129, 26.5.–15.12.41.
139. BA-MA RH26-12/129, 11.8.41.
140. BA-MA RH26-12/129, 7.11.41.
141. BA-MA RH26-12/291, 24.1.42.
142. BA-MA RH26-12/288, 2.4.42.
143. BA-MA RH26-12/140, 16.12.41–31.8.42; Compare with Guderian, *Panzer Leader,* pp. 193–4, who speaks of the 'more benevolent military administration'; and numerous accounts of looting and brutality in Meier-Welcker, *Aufzeichnungen,* pp. 120–80.
144. BA-MA RH26-12/211, 17.8.41.
145. BA-MA RH26-12/294, 22.4.42.
146. BA-MA RH26-12/133, 3.9.42 and 17.9.42; BA-MA RH26-12/295, 10.11.42.
147. BA-MA RH26-12/295, 10.11.42.
148. BA-MA RH26-12/134, 5.8.42.
149. BA-MA RH27-18/184, January, February, March 1942.
150. BA-MA RH27-18/76, 24.3.42.
151. For example, BA-MA RH27-18/188, 17.4.42, and many others in files BA-MA RH27-18/188, 194 and 196.
152. BA-MA RH27-18/194, 31.7.42; BA-MA RH27-18/178, 17.2.43.
153. BA-MA RH27-18/133, 26.3.43; BA-MA RH27-18/199, 7.6.43.
154. BA-MA RH26-1005/6, 3.4.–3.7.43.
155. BA-MA RH26-1005/62, 1.9.–31.10.42.
156. BA-MA RH26-1005/62, 16.9.42 and 23.9.42.
157. BA-MA RH26-1005/42, 15.10.42.
158. BA-MA RH26-1005/71, 19.5.43.
159. BA-MA RH27-18/24, 11.7.41.
160. BA-MA RH27-18/24, 18.7.41; BA-MA RH27-18/175, 27.7.41.
161. BA-MA RH27-18/175, 30.7.41; BA-MA RH27-18/26, 7.8.41.
162. BA-MA RH27-18/27, 14.9.41.
163. BA-MA RH27-18/181, 2.11.41.
164. BA-MA RH27-18/75, 15.1.42; BA-MA RH27-18/178, 28.2.42; BA-MA RH27-18/76, 24.3.42.
165. For instance, BA-MA RH27-18/188, 10.4.42; BA-MA RH27-18/194, 9.11.42.

166. BA-MA RH26-12/128, 2.7.41.
167. BA-MA RH26-12/294, 8.10.41.
168. BA-MA RH26-12/126, 7.11.41.
169. BA-MA RH26-12/298, 29.6.43.
170. BA-MA RH26-12/246, 14.1.42; BA-MA RH26-12/42, 16.1.42.
171. BA-MA RH26-12/62, 27.2.42.
172. BA-MA RH26-12/292, 25.6.42.
173. For instance, BA-MA RH26-12/295, 9.11.42.
174. BA-MA RH26-12/295, 11.10.42 and 22.10.42.
175. BA-MA RH26-12/298, 1.7.43.
176. BA-MA RH26-12/128, 21.9.41. These were instructions of OKH given to all German formations. See Streit, *Kameraden,* p. 140.
177. BA-MA RH27-18/142, 24.7.43.
178. BA-MA RH26-1005/37, 21.9.42.
179. On Russian civilian labour at the front and in the Reich, see Dallin, *German Rule,* pp. 428–53; Speer, *Third Reich,* pp. 306–9, 436–8, 504–5; Krausnick/Wilhelm, *Die Truppe,* pp. 400–8; Werth, *Russia,* pp. 607–8, 800–10; A. S. Milward, *The German Economy at War* (London, 1965) pp. 96–9, 111–13; B. A. Carroll, *Design for Total War* (The Hague, 1968) pp. 232–50.
180. BA-MA RH26-12/292, 25.5.42.
181. BA-MA RH26-12/294, 12.6.42.
182. BA-MA RH26-12/137, reports between 8.7.42 and 27.11.42.
183. Whereas those civilians transported in the division's vehicles were registered, we cannot establish the precise number of those sent on foot; various lists and forms, as well as notices meant to attract the population to volunteer, attest to the fact that this recruitment of civilian labour continued on a rather large scale.
184. BA-MA RH26-12/148, 17.3.43.
185. BA-MA RH27-18/188, 14.5.42; BA-MA RH27-18/189, 8.6.42.
186. BA-MA RH27-18/191, 13.11.42.
187. BA-MA RH26-1005/71, 18.5.43.
188. *von Hobe,* pp. 10–11.
189. BA-MA RH26-1005/47, 22.5.43.
190. BA-MA RH26-12/78, 20.4.43.
191. BA-MA RH27-18/188, 2.5.42; BA-MA RH27-18/189, 25.6.42.
192. BA-MA RH27-18/159, 5.9.42.
193. BA-MA RH27-18/124, 25.11.42 and 6.12.42.
194. BA-MA RH27-18/124, 15.12.42.
195. BA-MA RH27-18/196, 30.4.43.
196. BA-MA RH27-18/164, 1.4.–30.6.43.
197. BA-MA RH27-18/144, 24.8.43.
198. BA-MA RH27-18/170, 1.7.–30.9.43.
199. BA-MA RH27-18/179, 9.12.41.
200. BA-MA RH27-18/74, 20.12.41, 21.12.41; BA-MA RH27-18/78, 29.12.41; BA-MA RH27-18/157, 1.1.42.
201. BA-MA RH27-18/82, 28.1.42.
202. BA-MA RH27-18/131, 13.2.43.
203. BA-MA RH27-18/203, 3.8.43; see also, Dallin, *German Rule,* pp.

363–4; Seaton, *Russo-German War*, p. 376; Speer, *Third Reich*, pp. 537–9; Werth, *Russia*, pp. 189–97.

204. BA-MA RH26-12/133, 12.2.43; BA-MA RH26-12/72, 14.2.43, 15.2.43.
205. BA-MA RH26-12/76, 1.3.43; BA-MA RH26-12/141, 28.2.43.
206. BA-MA RH26-12/297, 16.5.–22.5.43; BA-MA RH26-12/210, 26.7.43.
207. BA-MA RH26-1005/68, 15.1.–27.2.43; BA-MA RH26-1005/71, 2.8.43; BA-MA RH26-1005/70, 1.4.–30.9.43.
208. BA-MA RH26-1005/71, 6.9.–28.9.43.
209. *Benes*, pp. 22–3, entry for 17.9.43.
210. For apologetic accounts of the retreat to the Dniepr, see Manstein, *Verlorene Siege*, pp. 539–40; Wagener, *Heeresgruppe Süd*, pp. 245–54; and P. Carell, *Scorched Earth* (London, 1970) pp. 323–33, who says that the GD had 'no time for elaborate demolition' (!).

CONCLUSION

1. BA-MA *Heft* 523, p. 13.
2. Paul, *18.Pz.Div.*, p. xx.
3. BA-MA RH26-1005/81, letter by H. Spaeter to veterans of the division: *Kleine Plauderei um das 'Errinerungsbuch GD'*, n.d.
4. Van Crefeld, *Fighting Power*, p. 163, emphasises much more the army's internal organisation and goes on to say (p. 166) that this organisation also explains its brutality. To some extent, this is true; but it seems to me that on the Eastern Front, in any case, this organisation would have broken down had it not been for the massive indoctrinational effort. As we have shown, the officers at the front themselves were quite aware of this and consequently asked for even more propaganda. As van Crefeld's own data show (pp. 156–7), officer casualties were so great that 'organisation' as such cannot serve as a sufficient explanation for the Wehrmacht's resilience, let alone its brutality.
5. Here I sould like to mention, apart from Dr Tim Mason and Mr Tony Nicholls, who supervised the writing of my D.Phil. thesis, and Professors Michael Howard and Volker Berghahn who examined me, also the participants of the Tuesday Noon Seminar at the School of History of Tel-Aviv University and of the Davis Seminar of the Department of History at Princeton University, who made numerous useful suggestions and criticisms of papers I had delivered there while working on the manuscript of this book.
6. Streit, *Kameraden*, pp. 9–10. See also this volume, Chapter 4, note 5. Streit takes his figures regarding German POWs from K. W. Böhme, *Die deutschen Kriegsgefangenen in Sowjetischer Hand, Eine Bilanz*, VII (München, 1966) p. 151 and *Errata* page. This book is a highly detailed, though not necessarily accurate, description of the fate of German POWs in the Soviet Union.
7. A. Blank, *Die deutschen Kriegsgefangenen in der UdSSR* (Köln, 1979) pp. 36–49, and 'Open Letter' pp. 198–208. I wish to thank Professor Arno Mayer of Princeton University who brought these books to my notice, as well as Buchbender's above-quoted *Das tönende Erz*.

8. P. R. Piccigallo, *The Japanese on Trial* (Austin, 1979) p. 27; the German and Italian armies took 235 000 American and British POWs during The Second World War, whereas the Japanese took 132 000 (p. 27).

9. On the conduct of two infamous Waffen-SS divisions in France, in 1940 and in 1944, see C. W. Sydnor (Jr), *Soldiers of Destruction* (Princeton: N.J., 1977) and M. Hastings, *Das Reich* (London, 1981). Russian figures taken from Blank, *Kriegsgefangenen,* p. 199. A book which, though it is interesting and at times helpful, tends to sentimentalise POW life in The Second World War, and passes over the fate of the Red Army troops with a few sentences (which it certainly does not do concerning Japanese, Korean and Vietnamese treatment of American POWs) is R. Garrett, *P.O.W.* (Newton Abbot: Pittsburgh, 1981).

10. The *Chinese People's Daily* claimed in 1960 that 'Japanese militarism inflicted on this country a loss of more than 10 million lives and the destruction and burning of property worth at least 50 000 million US dollars.' See R. K. Jain, *China and Japan* (London, 1977) p. 4; same figure quoted in C. J. Argyle, *Japan at War* (London, 1976) p. 120. Explanation of Japanese brutality quoted from J. H. Boyle, *China and Japan at War* (Stanford: California, 1972) pp. 341–9. On 'Thought Control and Indoctrination' in Japan, see S. Ienaga, *The Pacific War* (New York, 1978) pp. 13–32; and, ibid., pp. 181–202 on 'The Horrors of War'–Japanese atrocities in China. On the 'Rape of Manila' and the massacre of some 60 000 Filipinos, see L. Taylor, *A Trial of Generals* (South Bend, 1981) pp. 114–26, and slightly lower estimates in R. L. Lael, *The Yamashita Precedent* (Wilmington, 1982) pp. 37, 140. On Japanese expansion in Asia, see the very recent R. H. Myers and M. R. Peattie (eds), *The Japanese Colonial Empire* (Princeton: N.J., 1984), with a very interesting contribution by M. R. Peattie, 'Japanese Attitudes Toward Colonialism, 1895–45', pp. 80–127. Also on the ideological motivations behind the military insurrection of February 1936, see B-A Shillony, *Revolt in Japan* (Princeton: N.J., 1973) pp. 56–80; his 'The February 26 Affair: Politics of a Military Insurrection', in G. M. Wilson (ed.), *Crisis Politics in Prewar Japan* (Tokyo, 1970) pp. 25–50; and on the domestic scene during the war, his *Politics and Culture in Wartime Japan* (Oxford, 1981). I wish to thank Dr S. Garon of Princeton University for bringing many of these books to my knowledge and discussing these issues with me at great length.

11. G. Parker, *Europe in Crisis, 1598–1648* (Glasgow, 1979) p. 293. Generally on the Thirty Years' War and its historiography, see D. Maland, *Europe at War, 1600–50* (Totowa: N.J., 1980) and T. K. Rabb (ed.), *The Thirty Years' War,* 2nd edn (Lanham, 1981); a particularly bloody incident during that war can be found in G. Mann, *Wallenstein* (New York, 1976) pp. 306–7; examples of barbarities in warfare between the Thirty Years' War and the French Revolution, in J. Childs, *Armies and Warfare in Europe, 1648–1789* (New York, 1982) pp. 1–27; armies living 'off the land' and destroying it during the following generation, in G. Best, *War and Society in Revolutionary Europe* (Bungay: Suffolk, 1982) pp. 34–6, 174–7; treatment of the '*Francs-*

Tirers' by the Prussian army in 1870–71, in M. Howard, *The Franco-Prussian War,* 3rd edn (New York, 1981) pp. 249–56, 379–81.
12. See V. G. Kiernan, *European Empires from Conquest to Collapse, 1815–1960* (Leicester UP, 1982) which abounds with descriptions of brutality and barbarism; for American atrocities in Vietnam, see P. Karsten, *Law, Soldiers and Combat* (Westport, 1978) particularly ch. 2; see also, M. Herr, *Dispatches,* 5th edn (New York, 1978).
13. Karsten, *Law,* p. 57.
14. N. Stone, *The Eastern Front, 1914–17* (London, 1975) pp. 82, 168, 183–4; W. Rutherford, *The Russian Army in World War I* (London, 1975) pp. 135, 149–53, 157; S. Washburn, *On the Russian Front in World War I* (New York, 1982) pp. 143–5.
15. Regarding Britain in the Second World War, see, for instance, A. Goldman, 'Germans and Nazis', *JCH,* XIV (1979) 155–91; M. Howard, *War and the Liberal Conscience* (Oxford, 1981) p. 109; also see Introduction to his *Restraints on War* (Oxford, 1979) pp. 1–14; also T. Wilson, 'Lord Bryce's Investigation into Alleged German Atrocities in Belgium, 1914–15', *JCH,* XIV (1979) 369–83; a very early example of European pangs of conscience, in M. Eliav-Feldon, 'Humanitarian Scruples in the Early Stages of the Age of Colonialism', *Zmanim,* IV (in the Hebrew language, 1984); an example of the feeling of shock experienced by American troops when faced with a German atrocity (which was commonplace in the East) in A. H. Mick (ed.), *With the 102nd Infantry Division Through Germany* (Washington, 1974) pp. 211–16.
16. Maser, *Nuremberg,* pp. 259–87. Recent works reviewing the Japanese war trials are R. H. Minear, *Victors' Justice* (Princeton: N.J., 1971), and Piccigallo, *The Japanese on Trial.* Further on atrocities in China, L. E. Eastman, 'Facets of an Ambivalent Relationship', in A. Iriye (ed.), *The Chinese and the Japanese* (Princeton: N.J., 1980). A short and interesting study of genocide is I. L. Horowitz, *Genocide* (New Brunswick, 1976) with numerous unsettling examples from contemporary history. For recent interpretations and analyses of National Socialism and its historiography, see T. Mason, 'Intention and Explanation', in G. Hirschfeld *et al.,* (eds). *Der Führerstaat* (Stuttgart, 1981) pp. 23–40; Craig, *The Germans,* pp. 61–80; see also, H. Arendt, *Eichmann in Jerusalem,* 23rd edn rev. (Harmondsworth: Middlesex, 1979), especially pp. 278, 283. For a Marxist analysis of 'Japanese Fascism' intermingled with ancient myths, see J. Yamamoto, *Die Struktur der Selbstzerstörung* (Bochum, 1982).

Bibliography

A. MANUSCRIPT SOURCES

I. Bundesarchiv-Militärarchiv in Freiburg

12. Infantry Division:
Findbuch MSg 175
Heft 523
RH37/943, RH37/944, RH37/4979, RH37/6023
All files from RH26-12/1 to RH26-12/305
Grossdeutschland Division:
RH71/v.320, RH37/888, RH37/343, RH37/6337, RH37/6351,
RH37/6387, RH37/6391, RH37/6392, RH37/6394.
All files from RH26-1005/1 to RH26-1005/87
18. Panzer Division:
MSg 175/46
All files from RH27-18/1 to RH27-18/233

II. The personal files of 201 officers in the Bundesarchiv-Zentralnachweisstelle in Kornelimünster; the index catalogue cards of 341 officers in the Deutsche Dienststelle in Berlin; the party membership cards of 155 officers in the Berlin Document Centre in West Berlin. The names of these officers can be found in the bibliography in: O. Bartov, 'The Barbarisation of Warfare 1941–45' (Oxford Univ. D.Phil. thesis, 1983).

B. PRINTED SOURCES

I. Primary Sources

Boberach, H. (ed.), *Meldungen aus dem Reich* (Neuwied, 1965).
Boelcke, W. A. (ed.), *The Secret Conferences of Dr Goebbels,* 2nd edn (New York, 1970).
Buchbender, O., *Das tönende Erz, Deutsche Propaganda gegen die Rote Armee im Zweiten Weltkrieg* (Stuttgard, 1978).
Ferencz, B. B., *An International Criminal Court* (London, 1980).
Görlitz, W. (ed.), *Generalfeldmarschall Keitel, Verbrecher oder Offizier?* (Göttingen, 1961).
——, *Paulus und Stalingrad* (Frankfurt/M., 1964).
Jacobsen, H-A, *1939–45, Der Zweite Weltkrieg in Chronik und Dokumenten,* 4th edn (Darmstadt, 1960).

Krausnick, H. and Deutsch, H. C. (eds), *Helmuth Groscurth, Tagebücher Eines Abwehroffiziers* (Stuttgart, 1970).
Last Letters from Stalingrad (London, 1956).
Meier-Welcker, H., *Aufzeichnungen eines Generalstabsoffiziers* (Freiburg i.B., 1982).
Murawski, E., *Der deutsche Wehrmachtbericht* (Boppard am Rhein, 1962).
Roberts, A. and Guelff, R. (eds). *Documents on the Laws of War* (Oxford, 1982).
Schindler, D. and Toman, J. (eds). *The Laws of Armed Conflicts* (Geneva, 1973).
Streim, A., *Die Behandlung sowjetischer Kriegsgefangener im 'Fall Barbarossa'* (Heidelberg, 1981).
Supreme Commander: Report of the Combined Chiefs of Staff on the Operations in Europe of the Allied Expeditionary Force, 6.6.1944–8.5.1945 (London, 1946).
Trevor-Roper, H. R. (ed.) *Hitler's Table Talk, 1941–44*, 2nd edn (London, 1973).
——, (ed.), *Hitler's War Directives, 1939–45*, 4th edn (London, 1978).
——, (ed.), *The Goebbels Diaries: The Last Days*, 2nd edn (London, 1979).
Ueberhorst, H. (ed.), *Elite für die Diktatur* (Düsseldorf, 1969).
Weinberg, G. L., 'Dokumentation: Adolf Hitler und der NS-Führungsoffizier (NSFO)', *VfZ*, XII (1964) 443–56.
Wulf, J., *Presse und Funk im Dritten Reich* (Gütersloh, 1964).

II. Secondary Sources

Abel, T., *Why Hitler Came into Power* (New York, 1938).
Abraham, D., *The Collapse of the Weimar Republic* (Princeton: N.J., 1981).
Absolon, R., *Wehrgesetz und Wehrdienst, 1935–45* (Boppard am Rhein, 1960).
——, *Die Personelle Ergänzung der Wehrmacht im Frieden und im Kriege* (Bundersarchiv-Zentralnachweisstelle, 1972).
——, *Die Wehrmacht im Dritten Reich*, III (Boppard am Rhein, 1975).
——, *Die Wehrmacht im Dritten Reich*, IV (Boppard am Rhein, 1979).
——, 'Das Offizierkorps des Deutschen Heeres, 1935–45', in H. H. Hofmann (ed.), *Das deutsche Offizierkorps, 1860–1960* (Boppard am Rhein, 1980).
Aho, J. A., *Religious Mythology and the Art of War* (Westport, 1981).
Allen, W. S., *The Nazi Seizure of Power* (Chicago, 1965).
Almog, S. (ed.), *Antisemitism Through the Ages* (in the Hebrew language, Jerusalem, 1980).
Anders, W., *Hitler's Defeat in Russia* (Chicago, 1953).
Arendt, H., *Eichmann in Jerusalem,* 23rd edn rev. (Harmondsworth: Middlesex, 1979).
Argyle, C. J., *Japan at War, 1937–45* (London, 1976).
Armstrong, J. A. (ed.), *Soviet Partisans in World War II* (Wisconsin, 1964).
Baird, J. W., 'The Myth of Stalingrad', *JCH*, IV (1969) 187–204.

——, *The Mythical World of Nazi War Propaganda, 1939–45* (Minneapolis: Minnesota, 1974).

Bald, D., *Der deutsche Generalstab 1859–1939* (München, 1977).

——, *Vom Kaiserheer zur Bundeswehr* (Frankfurt/M., 1981).

——, *Der deutsche Offizier* (München, 1982).

——, *Die Soziale Auswahl des Militärs* (transcript of a lecture given me by the author, n.d.).

Balfour, M., *Propaganda in War, 1939–45* (London, 1979).

Barnett, C., 'The Education of Military Elites', *JCH*, II (1967) 15–35.

Baumann, H. (ed.), *Die 35. Infanterie-Division im 2. Weltkrieg* (Karlsruhe, 1964).

Beaumont, R. A., *Military Elites* (London, 1976).

Becker, H., *German Youth: Bond or Free* (London, 1946).

Bennet, E. W., *German Rearmament and the West, 1932–33* (Princeton: N.J., 1979).

Benoist-Méchin, J., *Sixty Days that Shook the West* (New York, 1963).

Berghahn, V. R., *Der Stahlhelm* (Düsseldorf, 1966).

——, 'Meinungsforschung im "Dritten Reich" ', *MGM*, I (1967) 83–119.

——, 'NSDAP und "Geistige Führung" der Wehrmacht, 1939–45', *VfZ*, XVII (1969) 17–71.

——, *Germany and the Approach of War in 1914*, 4th edn (London, 1979).

——, *Modern Germany* (London, New York, 1982).

Berning, C., *Vom 'Abstammungsnachweis' zum 'Zuchtwart', Vokabular des Nationalsozialismus* (Berlin, 1964).

Best, G., *Humanity in Warfare* (London, 1980).

——, *War and Society in Revolutionary Europe, 1770–1870* (Bungay: Suffolk, 1982).

Beyerchen, A. D., *Scientists Under Hitler* (New Haven, London, 1977).

Bialer, S. (ed.), *Stalin and his Generals* (London, 1970).

Bird, K. W., *Weimar, the German Naval Officer Corps and the Rise of National Socialism* (Amsterdam, 1977).

Blank, A., *Die deutschen Kriegsgefangenen in der UdSSR* (Köln, 1979).

Bleuel, H. P. and Klinnert, E., *Deutsche Studenten auf dem Weg ins Dritte Reich* (Gütersloh, 1967).

Blumentritt, G., *Von Rundstedt* (London, 1952).

Boehnert, G. C., 'The Third Reich and the Problem of "Social Revolution": German Officers and the SS', in V. R. Berghahn and M. Kitchen (eds), *Germany in the Age of Total War* (London, 1981) pp. 203–17.

Böhme, K. W., *Die deutschen Kriegsgefangenen in Sowjetischer Hand, Eine Bilanz* (München, 1966).

Boog, H. *et al.*, *Das Deutsche Reich und der Zweite Weltkrieg*, IV (Stuttgart, 1983).

Boyle, J. H., *China and Japan at War, 1937–45* (Stanford: California, 1972).

Bracher, K. D., *The German Dictatorship* (New York, 1970).

Bramsted, E. K., *Dictatorship and Political Police* (London, 1945).

——, *Goebbels and National Socialist Propaganda, 1925–45* (London, 1965).

Brenner, H., *Die Kunstpolitik des Nationalsozialismus* (Hamburg, 1963).

Broszat, M., *Der Nationalsozialismus* (Stuttgart, 1960).

——, *Nationalsozialistische Polenpolitik, 1939–45* (Stuttgart, 1961).

——, *The Hitler State* (New York, 1981).

Bucher, P., *Der Reichswehrprozess* (Boppard am Rhein, 1967).

Bullock, A., *Hitler, a Study in Tyranny*, rev. edn (New York, 1964).

Burden, H. T., *The Nuremberg Party Rallies: 1923–39* (London, 1967).

Caplan, J., 'The Civil Servant in the Third Reich' (Oxford University D.Phil. thesis 1973).

Carell, P., *Scorched Earth* (London, 1970).

Carroll, B. A., *Design for Total War* (The Hague, 1968).

Carsten, F. L., 'Germany. From Scharnhorst to Schleicher: the Prussian Officer Corps in Politics, 1806–1933', in M. Howard (ed.), *Soldiers and Governments* (London, 1957).

——, ' " Volk Ohne Raum", A Note on Hans Grimm', *JCH*, II (1967) 221–27.

——, *The Reichswehr and Politics, 1918–33*, 2nd edn (Berkeley: California, 1973).

Cecil, R., *The Myth of the Master Race* (London, 1972).

Childers, T., 'The Social Bases of the National Socialist Vote', *JCH*, II (1976) 17–42.

——, *The Nazi Voter* (Chapel Hill: North Carolina, 1983).

Childs, J., *Armies and Warfare in Europe, 1648–1789* (New York 1982).

Chodoff, E. P., 'Ideology and Primary Groups', *AFS*, IX, 4 (1983) 569–93.

Chuikov, V. I., *The End of the Third Reich* (London, 1967).

——, *The Battle for Stalingrad* (in the Hebrew language, Tel-Aviv, 1970).

Cooper, M., *The German Army, 1933–45* (London, 1978).

——, *The Phantom War* (London, 1979).

Craig, G. A., 'Portrait of a Political General: Edwin von Manteuffel and the Constitutional Conflict in Prussia', *PSQ*, LXVI (1951) 1–36.

——, *The Politics of the Prussian War, 1640–1945*, 3rd edn (London, 1978).

——, *Germany, 1866–1945* (New York, 1978).

——, *The Germans* (New York, 1982).

Dahrendorf, R., *Gesellschaft und Demokratie in Deutschland* (München, 1965).

Dallin, A., *German Rule in Russia, 1941–45*, 2nd edn (London, 1981).

Davis, G. H., 'Prisoners of War in Twentieth-Century War Economies', *JCH*, XII (1977) 623–34.

Dawidowicz, L., *The War Against the Jews, 1933–45*, 3rd edn (Harmondsworth: Middlesex, 1979).

——, 'German Historians and National Socialism', *Zmanim*, II (in the Hebrew language, 1979).

Deist, W., *et al.*, *Das Deutsche Reich und der Zweite Weltkrieg*, I. (Stuttgart, 1979).

——, *The Wehrmacht and German Rearmament* (London, 1981).

Demeter, K., *The German Officer Corps* (London, 1965).

Deutsch, H. C., *The Conspiracy Against Hitler in the Twilight War* (Minneapolis: Minnesota, 1968).

——, *Hitler and his Generals* (Minneapolis: Minnesota, 1974).

Diehl, J. M., *Paramilitary Politics in Weimar Germany* (Bloomington, 1977).

Dinstein, Y., 'Just and Unjust War', *Zmanim*, I (in the Hebrew language, 1980).

Doenitz, K., *Memoirs*, 2nd edn (London, 1959).

Donnevert, R. (ed.), *Wehrmacht und Partei* (Leipzig, 1938).

Durian, W., *Infanterieregiment Grossdeutschland Greift An* (Berlin, 1942).

Eastman, L. E., 'Facets of an Ambivalent Relationship: Smuggling, Puppets, and Atrocities During the War, 1937–45', in A. Iriye (ed.), *The Chinese and the Japanese* (Princeton: N.J., 1980).

Eliav-Feldon, M., 'Humanitarian Scruples in the Early Stages of the Age of Colonialism', *Zmanim*, IV (in the Hebrew language, 1984).

Ellis, J., *The Sharp End of War* (New York, 1982).

Erickson, J., *The Road to Stalingrad* (London, 1975).

Evans-Pritchard, E. E., *Theories of Primitive Religion*, 8th edn (Oxford, 1977).

Feld, M. D., 'Professionalism, Nationalism and the Alienation of the Military', in J. van Doorn (ed.), *Armed Forces and Society* (The Hague, 1968) pp. 55–70.

Fest, J. C., *The Face of the Third Reich*, 3rd edn (Harmondsworth: Middlesex, 1979).

——, *Hitler*, 4th edn (Harmondsworth: Middlesex, 1982).

Finer, S. E., *The Man on Horseback*, 2nd rev. edn (Harmondsworth: Middlesex, 1975).

Fischer, F., *War of Illusions* (London, 1975).

Floud, R., *An Introduction to Quantitative Methods for Historians* (London, 1973).

Foertsch, H., *Schuld und Verhängnis* (Stuttgart, 1951).

Foot, M. R. D., *Resistance*, 2nd edn (London, 1978).

Fuller, J. F. C., *The Second World War, 1939–45*, 2nd edn (London, 1948).

——, *The Decisive Battles of the Western World, 1792–1944*, II, 5th edn (London, 1975).

Fussel, P., *The Great War and Modern Memory*, 3rd edn (Oxford, 1979).

Gallagher, M. P., *The Soviet History of World War II* (New York, 1963).

Garrett, R., *P.O.W.* (Newton Abbot: Pittsburgh, 1981).

Geiger, T., *Die Soziale Schichtung des Deutschen Volkes*, 2nd edn (Stuttgart, 1967).

Geyer, M., *Aufrüstung oder Sicherheit* (Wiesbaden, 1980).

——, 'Professionals and Junkers: German Rearmament and Politics in the Weimar Republic', in R. Bessel and E. J. Feuchtwanger (eds), *Social Changes and Political Development in Weimar Germany* (London, 1981).

Gilbert, G. M., *Nuremberg Diary* (New York, 1947).

Giles, G. J., 'The Rise of the National Socialist Students' Association and the Failure of Political Education in the Third Reich', in P. D. Stachura (ed.), *The Shaping of the Nazi State* (London, 1978) pp. 160–85.

Girard, R., *Violence and the Sacred*, 2nd edn (Baltimore, 1979).

Goldman, A., 'Germans and Nazis: the Controversy over "Vanisttartism" in Britain During the Second World War', *JCH*, XIV (1979) 155–91.

Gordon, H. J. (Jr), *The Reichswehr and the German Republic, 1919–26* (Princeton: N.J., 1957).

Gordon, S., *Hitler, Germans, and the 'Jewish Question'* (Princeton: N.J., 1984).

Görlitz, W., *Der Zweite Weltkrieg, 1939–45*, I and II (Stuttgart, 1951/2).

——, *The German General Staff, 1657–1945* (London, 1953).

Goure, L., *The Siege of Leningrad* (Stanford: California, 1962).

Graml, H. *et al.*, *The German Resistance to Hitler* (London, 1970).

Grams, R., *Die 14. Panzer-Division, 1940–45* (Bad Nauheim, 1957).

Grill, J. H., *The Nazi Movement in Baden, 1920–45* (Chapel Hill: North Carolina, 1983).

Guderian, H., *Die Panzertruppen*, 2nd edn (Berlin, 1938).

——, *Panzer Leader*, 3rd edn (London, 1977).

Gurfein, M. I. and Janowitz, M., 'Trends in Wehrmacht Morale', in D. Lerner (ed.), *Propaganda in War and Crisis* (New York, 1951) pp. 200–208.

Hagemann, J., *Die Presselenkung im Dritten Reich* (Bonn, 1970).

Hale, O. J., *The Captive Press in the Third Reich* (Princeton: N.J., 1964).

Halsey, A. H., *et al.*, *Origins and Destinations* (London, 1980).

Hamilton, R., *Who Voted for Hitler?* (Princeton: N.J., 1982).

Hartshorne, E. Y. (Jr), *The German Universities and National Socialism* (Cambridge: Mass., 1937).

Hastings, M., *Das Reich* (London, 1981).

Herr, M., *Dispatches*, 5th edn (New York, 1978).

Herwig, H. H., *The German Naval Officer Corps, 1890–1918* (Oxford, 1973).

Herzfeld, H., 'Germany: After the Catastrophe', *JCH*, II (1967) 79–91.

Hillgruber, A., *Hitlers Strategie* (Frankfurt/M., 1965).

Hochhut, R., *Der Stellvertreter*, 16th edn (Reinbek bei Hamburg, 1981).

Hollstein, D., *Antisemitische Filmpropaganda* (München-Pullach, 1971).

Horowitz, I. L., *Genocide* (New Brunswick, 1976).

Howard, M., *Studies in War and Peace*, 10th edn (London, 1970).

——, *War in European History*, 2nd edn (Oxford, 1977).

——, *Restraints on War* (Oxford, 1979).

——, *The Franco-Prussian War*, 3rd edn (New York, 1981).

——, *War and the Liberal Conscience* (Oxford, 1981).

Hull, D. S., *Film in the Third Reich* (Berkeley: California, 1969).

Ienaga, S., *The Pacific War, 1931–45* (New York. 1978).

Irving, D., *Hitler's War* (London, 1977).

Jacobsen, H-A, 'Kommissarbefehl und Massenexekutionen Sowjetische Kriegsgefangener', in H. Buchheim *et al.*, *Anatomie des SS-Staates* (Olten, 1965) II. 163–279.

Jahnke, K-H, *Weisse Rose contra Hakenkreuz* (Frankfurt/M., 1969).

——, *Entscheidungen* (Frankfurt/M., 1970).

Jain, R. K., *China and Japan, 1949–76* (London, 1977).

Janowitz, M., *The Professional Soldier* (New York, 1960).

Kaelbe, H., 'Social Mobility in Germany, 1900–1960', *JMH*, III (1978) 439–61.

Kameradschaftsbund 16. Panzer- und Infanterie-Division, Kameradenhilfswerk e.V. (eds), *Bildband der 16. Panzer-Division, 1939–45* (Bad Nauheim, 1956).

Karsten, P., *Law, Soldiers, and Combat* (Westport, 1978).

Kater, M. H., 'The Work Student: A Socio-Economic Phenomenon of Early Weimar Germany', *JCH*, X (1975) 71–94.

——, *Studentschaft und Rechtsradikalismus in Deutschland, 1918–33* (Hamburg, 1975).

——, *The Nazi Party*, (Cambridge: Mass., 1983).

Katz, J., *Anti-Semitism* (in the Hebrew language, Tel-Aviv, 1979).

Kershaw, I., *Der Hitler-Mythos* (Stuttgart, 1980).

——, *Popular Opinion and Political Dissent in the Third Reich: Bavaria 1933–45* (London, 1983).

Kesselring, *The Memoirs of Field-Marshall Kesselring* (London, 1953).

Kiernan, V. G., *European Empires from Conquest to Collapse, 1815–1960* (Leicester UP, 1982).

Kirwin, G., 'Waiting for Retaliation–A Study in Nazi Propaganda Behaviour and German Civilian Morale', *JCH*, XVI (1981) 565–83.

Kitchen, M., *The German Officer Corps, 1890–1914* (London, 1968).

Kleine, G. H., 'Adelgenossenschaft und Nationalsozialismus', *VfZ*, XXVI (1978) 100–43.

Klemperer, V., *Die Unbewältigte Sprache*, 3rd edn (Darmsatdt, n.d.).

Koehl, R. L., *The Black Corps* (Madison, 1983).

Kramarz, J., *Stauffenberg* (Frankfurt/M., 1965).

Krausnick, H., 'Kommissarbefehl und "Gerichtsbarkeitserlass Barbarossa" in Neuer Sicht', *VfZ*, XXV (1977) 682–758.

——, and Wilhelm, H-H, *Die Truppe des Weltanschauungskrieges* (Stuttgart, 1981).

Kris, E. and Speier, H., *German Radio Propaganda* (New York, 1944).

Kühnrich, H., *Der Partisanenkrieg in Europa, 1939–45* (Berlin, 1965).

Kurzke, H., 'Das Bild des Offiziers in der Deutschen Literatur', in H. H. Hofmann (ed.), *Das deutsche Offizierkorps, 1860–1960* (Boppard am Rhein, 1980) pp. 413–35.

Kwiet, K., 'Bericht: Zur historiographischen Behandlung der Judenverfolgung im Dritten Reich', *MGM*, I (1980) 149–92.

Lael, R. L., *The Yamashita Precedent* (Wilmington, 1982).

Laqueur, W. Z., *Young Germany* (London, 1962).

——, *Guerrilla* (London, 1977).

——, *The Terrible Secret*, 2nd edn (Harmondsworth: Middlesex, 1982).

Leach, A. B., *German Strategy against Russia, 1939–41* (London, 1973).

Liddell Hart, B. H., *The Other Side of the Hill* (London, 1948).

——, *History of the Second World War*, 6th edn (London, 1979).

Lipset, S. M., *Political Man: The Social Bases of Politics*, rev. edn (Baltimore, 1981).

Maier, K. A. *et al.*, *Das deutsche Reich und der Zweite Weltkrieg*, II (Stuttgart, 1979).

Maland, D., *Europe at War, 1600–50* (Totowa: N.J., 1980).

Mann, Erika, *School for Barbarians* (London, 1939).

Mann, Golo, *Wallenstein* (New York, 1976).

Manstein, E. von, *Aus Einem Soldatenleben* (Bonn, 1958).

——, *Verlorene Siege*, 2nd edn (Frankfurt/M., 1964).

Maser, W., *Nuremberg* (London, 1979).

Mason, T. W., 'Labour in the Third Reich, 1933–39', *P&P*, XXXIII (1966) 112–41.

——, 'Women in Germany, 1925–40: Family, Welfare and Work', Parts 1–2, *HWJ*, I (1976) 74–113; II (1976) 5–32.

——, *Sozialpolitik im Dritten Reich* (Opladen, 1977).

——, 'The Workers' Opposition in Nazi Germany', *HWJ*, XI (1981) 120–37.

——, 'Intention and Explanation: A Current Controversy about the Interpretation of National Socialism', in G. Hirschfeld and L. Kettenacker (eds), *Der 'Führer-Staat': Mythos und Realität* (Stuttgart, 1981) pp. 23–40.

Matuschka, E. Graf von, 'Die Beförderung in Praxis', in H. Meier-Welcker (ed.), *Untersuchungen zur Geschichte des Offizierkorps* (Stuttgart, 1962) pp. 153–76.

Mayer, A. J., 'The Lower Middle Class as Historical Problem, *JMH*, III (1975) 409–36.

McClelland, C. E., *State, Society and University in Germany, 1700–1914* (London, New York, 1980).

McLaine, I., *Ministry of Morale* (London, 1979).

Meier-Welcker, H., *Seeckt* (Frankfurt/M., 1967).

Meinecke, F., *The German Catastrophe* (Boston, 1963).

Merkl, P. H., *Political Violence under the Swastika* (Princeton: N.J., 1975).

——, *The Making of a Stormtrooper* (Princeton: N.J., 1980).

——, and Smart, N. (eds), *Religion and Politics in the Modern World* (New York, 1983).

Messerschmidt, M., 'Werden und Prägung des preussischen Offizierkorps– Ein Überblick', in Militärgeschichtliches Forschungsamt (eds), *Offiziere im Bild vom Dokumenten aus drei Jahrhunderten* (Stuttgart, 1964) pp. 11–104.

——, *Die Wehrmacht im NS-Staat* (Hamburg, 1969).

Mick, A. H. (ed.), *With the 102d Infantry Division Through Germany* (Washington D.C., 1974).

Milward, A. S., *The German Economy at War* (London, 1965).

Minear, R. H., *Victors' Justice* (Princeton: N.J., 1971).

Mosse, G. L., *The Crisis of German Ideology* (New York, 1964).

——, *The Nationalisation of the Masses* (New York, 1975).

——, 'National Cemeteries and National Revival: The Cult of the Fallen Soldiers in Germany', *JCH*, XIV (1979) 1–20.

Mueller-Hillebrand, B., *Das Heer, 1933–45: Das Heer bis zum Kriegsbeginn*, I (Darmstadt, 1954); *Die Blitzfeldzüge*, II (Frankfurt/M., 1956); *Der Zweifrontkrieg*, III (Frankfurt/M., 1969).

Mühlberger, D., 'The Sociology of the NSDAP: The Question of Working Class Membership', *JCH*, XV (1980) 493–511.

Müller, C., *Oberst i.G. Stauffenberg* (Düsseldorf, 1970).

Müller, K-J, *Das Heer und Hitler* (Stuttgart, 1969).

——, *Armee, Politik und Gesellschaft in Deutschland, 1933–45* (Padeborn, 1979).

——, *General Ludwig Beck* (Boppard am Rhein, 1980).

Murray, H. A. (ed.), *Myth and Mythmaking*, 2nd edn (Boston, 1969).

Myers, R. H. and Peattie, M. R. (eds), *The Japanese Colonial Empire, 1895–1945* (Princeton: N.J., 1984).

Needham, R., *Belief, Language and Experience* (Oxford, 1972).

Nicholls, A. J., *Weimar and the Rise of Hitler*, 3rd edn (London, 1981).

Niethammer, L., 'Male Fantasies: An Argument For and Against with an Important New Study in History and Psychoanalysis', *HWJ*, VII (1979) 176–86.

Noakes, J., *The Nazi Party in Lower Saxony, 1921–33* (London, 1971).

O'Lessker, K., 'Who Voted for Hitler? A New Look at the Class Basis of Nazism', *AJS*, VIII, 74 (1968) 63–9.

O'Neill, R. J., 'Doctrine and Training in the German Army, 1919–39', in M. Howard (ed.), *The Theory and Practice of War* (London, 1965) pp. 143–65.

——, *The German Army and the Nazi Party, 1933–39* (London, 1966).

Organisation der Deutschen Arbeitsfront und der NS Gemeinschaft Kraft durch Freude (Leipzig, n.d., about 1934).

Orlow, D., *The History of the Nazi Party, 1933–45* (Newton Abbot: Pittsburgh, 1973) II.

Osanka, F. M. (ed.), *Modern Guerrilla Warfare* (New York, 1962).

Paget, R. T., *Manstein* (London, 1951).

Papke, G., 'Offizierkorps und Anciennität', in H. Meier-Welcker (ed.), *Untersuchungen zur Geschichte des Offizierkorps* (Stuttgart, 1962) pp. 177–206.

Parker, G., *Europe in Crisis, 1598–1648* (Glasgow, 1979).

Paul, W., *Geschichte der 18. Panzer Division, 1940–43* (Freiburg, i.B., n.d.).

Pedrocini, G., *Les Mutinerie de 1917* (Paris, 1967).

Petrov, V., *'June 22, 1941'* (Columbia, 1968).

Phillips, M. S., 'The German Film Industry and the New Order', in P. D. Stachura (ed.), *The Shaping of the Nazi State* (London, 1978).

Piccigallo, P. R., *The Japanese on Trial* (Austin: Texas, 1979).

Ponomarenko *et al.*, *Behind the Front Line* (London, n.d.).

Quarrie, B. *Panzer-Grenadier Division 'Grossdeutschland'* (London, 1977).

Rabb, T. K., (ed.), *The Thirty Years' War*, 2nd edn (Lanham, 1981).

Rabenau, F. von, *Hans von Seeckt* (Leipzig, 1938).

Redelis, V., *Partisanenkrieg* (Heidelberg, 1958).

Reynolds, N., *Treason was no Crime* (London, 1976).

Rich, N., *Hitler's War Aims* (London, 1973).

Ringer, F. K., *The Decline of the German Mandarins* (Cambridge: Mass., 1969).

Ritter, G., *Carl Goerdeler und die Deutsche Widerstands-Bewegung* (Stuttgart, 1954).

——, *The Sword and the Sceptre* (London, 1972) I–IV.

Rosas, A., *The Legal Status of Prisoners of War* (Helsinki, 1976).

Rosenhaft, E., *Beating the Fascists?* (London, New York, 1983).

Rosinski, H., *The German Army* (London, 1939).

Rutherford, W., *The Russian Army in World War I* (London, 1975).

Sajer, G., *The Forgotten Soldier*, 2nd edn (London, 1977).

Salisbury, H. E., The Siege of Leningrad (London, 1969).

Sänger, F., *Politik der Täuschungen,* (Wien, 1975).

Schlabrendorff, F. von, *The Secret War Against Hitler* (London, 1966).

Schoenbaum, D., *Hitler's Social Revolution* (London, 1967).

Scholl, I., *Die Weise Rose*, 3rd edn (Frankfurt/M., 1952).

Schulin, E., (ed.), *Die Juden als Minderheit in der Geschichte* (München, 1981).

Seaton, A., *The Russo-German War, 1941–45* (London, 1971).

——, *The Battle for Moscow, 1941–43* (New York, 1971).

——, *The German Army, 1933–45* (London, 1982).

Segev, T., 'From Dachau to Bergen-Belsen: Concentration Camp Commanders', *Zmanim*, II (in the Hebrew language, 1981).

Seier, H., 'Der Rektor als Führer, zur Hochschulpolitik des Reichserziehungsministeriums 1934–45', *VfZ*, XII (1964) 105–46.

Senger und Etterlin, F. von, *Neither Fear nor Hope* (London, 1963).

Shillony, B-A, 'The February 26 Affair: Politics of a Military Insurrection', in G. M. Wilson (ed.), *Crisis Politics in Prewar Japan* (Tokyo, 1970) pp. 25–50.

——, *Revolt in Japan* (Princeton: N.J., 1973).

——, *Politics and Culture in Wartime Japan* (Oxford, 1981).

Shils, E. A. and Janowitz, M., 'Cohesion and Disintegration in the Wehrmacht in World War II', *POQ*, XII (1948) 280–315.

Short, K. R. M., (ed.), *Film & Radio Propaganda in World War II* (Knoxville: Tennessee, 1983).

Siemsen, H., *Hitler Youth* (London, 1940).

Singer, B., 'From Patriots to Pacifists: The French Primary School Teachers, 1880–1940', *JCH*, XII (1977) 413–34.

Sontag, S., *Under the Sign of Saturn*, 7th edn (New York, 1981).

Spaeter, H. and Schramm, W. Ritter von, *Die Geschichte des Panzerkorps Grossdeutschland* (Bielefeld, 1958) II–III.

Speer, A., *Inside the Third Reich*, 6th edn (London, 1979).

Stachura, P. D., 'The Ideology of the Hitler Youth in the Kampfzeit', *JCH*, VIII (1973) 155–67.

——, *Nazi Youth in the Weimar Republic* (Santa Barbara: California, 1975).

Stein, G. H., *The Waffen SS, 1939–45*, 4th edn (London, 1977).

Stern, F., *The Politics of Cultural Despair* (Berkeley: California, 1961).

——, *The Failure of Illiberalism* (London, 1972).

Stern, J. P., *Hitler*, 5th edn (Glasgow, 1979).

Stolfi, R. H. S., 'Barbarossa Revisited: A Critical Reappraisal of the Opening Stages of the Russo-German Campaign (June–December 1941)', *JCH*, LIV (1982) 27–46.

Stone, Norman, *The Eastern Front, 1914–17* (London, 1975).

Streit, C., *Keine Kameraden* (Stuttgart, 1978).

Sydnor, C. W. (Jr), *Soldiers of Destruction* (Princeton: N.J., 1977).

Sywottek, J., *Mobilmachung für den Krieg* (Opladen, 1976).

Tal, U., 'Territory and Space (Raum) in the Nazi Ideology', *Zmanim*, I (in the Hebrew language, 1979).

Taylor, L., *A Trial of Generals* (South Bend, 1981).

Telpuchowski, B. S., *Die Sowjetische Geschichte des Grossen Vaterländischen Krieges, 1941–45*, ed. A. Hillgruber and H-A Jacobsen (Frankfurt/M., 1961).

Teske, H., *Die Silberne Spiegel* (Heidelberg, 1952).

Tessin, G., *Formationsgeschichte der Wehrmacht, 1933–39* (Boppard am Rhein, 1959).

Trevor-Roper, H. R., *The Last Days of Hitler*, 14th edn (London, 1978).
van Crefeld, M., *Hitler's Strategy 1940–41* (London, 1973).
——, *Supplying War*, 3rd edn (Cambridge, 1980).
——, *Fighting Power* (Westport, 1982).
van Doorn, J., 'Political Change and the Control of the Military: Some German Remarks', in J. van Doorn (ed.), *Military Profession and Military Regimes* (The Hague, 1969) pp. 11–31.
—— 'Armed Forces and Society: Patterns and Trends' in J. van Doorn (ed.), *Armed Forces and Society* (The Hague, 1968).
Vershigora, P., *Kopvak's Campaigns* (in the Hebrew language, Tel-Aviv, 1953).
Volkov, S., 'On Antisemitism and its Investigation', *Zmanim*, II (in the Hebrew language, 1981).
Vondung, K., *Magie und Manipulation* (Göttingen, 1971).
Wagener, C., *Heeresgruppe Süd* (Bad Nauheim, n.d.).
Waite, R. G. L., *Vanguard of Nazism* (Cambridge: Mass., 1952).
Walzer, M., *Just and Unjust Wars*, 3rd edn (Harmondsworth: Middlesex, 1980).
Washburn, S., *On the Russian Front in World War I* (New York, 1982).
Wegner, B., 'Auf dem Wege zur Pangermanischen Armee', *MGM*, II (1980) 101–36.
——, 'Das Führerkorps der Waffen-SS im Kriege', in H. H. Hofmann (ed.), *Das deutsche Offizierkorps, 1860–1960* (Boppard am Rhein, 1980) pp. 327–50.
——, *Hitlers Politische Soldaten: Die Waffen-SS 1933–45* (Paderborn, 1982).
Weiman, D. S., 'Why was Auschwitz not Bombed?', *Zmanim*, II (in the Hebrew language, 1981). See also *'Commentary'* (May, 1978).
Welch, D. (ed.), *Nazi Propaganda* (London, 1983).
Welcker, I. and Zelinka, F. F., *Qualifikation zum Offizier?* (Frankfurt/M., 1982).
Werth, A., *The Year of Stalingrad* (London, 1946).
——, *Russia at War, 1941–45* (London, 1964).
Westphal, S., *The German Army in the West* (London, 1951).
Wheeler, L. M., 'The SS and the Administration of Nazi Occupied Eastern Europe, 1939–45' (Oxford Univ. D.Phil. thesis 1981).
Wheeler-Bennett, J. W., *The Nemesis of Power*, 2nd edn (London, 1980).
Williams, D. T., 'The Historiography of World War II', in E. M. Robertson (ed.), *The Origins of the Second World War*, 5th edn (London, 1979).
Williams, J., *Mutiny 1917* (London, 1962).
Wilson, T., 'Lord Bryce's Investigation into Alleged German Atrocities in Belgium, 1914–15', *JCH*, XIV (1979) 369–83.
Winkler, H., 'Extremismus der Mitte? Sozialgeschichtliche Aspekte der nationalsozialistischen Machtergriefung', *VfZ*, XX, 2 (1972) 175–91.
——, *Mittelstand, Demokratie und Nationalsozialismus* (Köln, 1972).
Wright, G., *The Ordeal of Total War, 1939–45* (New York, 1968).
Yamamoto, J., *Die Struktur der Selbstzerstörung* (Bochum, 1982).
De Zayas, A. M. and Rabus, W., *Die Wehrmacht-Untersuchungsstelle*, 3rd edn (München, 1980).

Zeman, Z. A. B., *Nazi Propaganda* (London, 1964).
Zhukov, G. K., *Marshall Zhukov's Greatest Battles* (London, 1969).
Ziemer, G., *Education for Death* (London, 1941).
Ziemke, E. F., *Stalingrad to Berlin* (Washington D.C., 1968).
Zorn, W., 'Student Politics in the Weimar Republic', *JCH,* V (1970) 128–44.

Index

Aachen, 8
Abel Sample, 50
Absence without leave, 27–9, 33
Aerial bombardments, 153–4
Africa, 155
'Agricultural Officers', 131–2
Akhtyrka, 10
Alarmeinheiten, 15
Alsace, 9
Amman, Captain, 20–1
Anschluss, 79
Anti-partisan units, 123–4
Anti-Semitism, xi, 79, 88, 103
Ardennes Offensive, 8
Army
  conduct compared with First
    World War, xi, 2
  exploitation of Russia by, 130, 139
  Gleichschaltung of, 77
  Goebbels and, 58
  historiography of, xi–xii, 1–4
  ideological affinity to Nazism of,
    78, 80, 83, 88
  image in propaganda films of, 78
  implementation of Nazi policies
    by, 3–4, 153
  mood in 1939 of, 87
  Nazification of, xi, 2, 75, 77,
    83–4, 100
  oath to Hitler of, 77
  opposition to Hitler in, 1, 99
  promotion in, 146
  'purity' of, 3
  radios in, 69
  role in Third Reich of, 77
  Second Reich's *Kaiserheer,* 5,
    54–5, 76, 87, 99, 145
  size and growth of, 40–1, 60, 77,
    145

Army—*cont.*
  Weimar's *Reichswehr,* 5, 43, 46,
    54–5, 59, 63, 66, 145–6
Army Group Centre, 8, 75, 95, 108
Army Group North, 10, 108, 123
Aryans, 80, 88
Asiatics, 85, 95, 138
Austria, 80, 156

Balga-Kahlholz, 10
'Bandits', 125, 139
Barbarisation
  in colonial wars, 155
  comparison between types of, 153
  correlation with indoctrination,
    of, 99, 110, 115–16, 149,
    152–6
  and Eastern Front 1914–17, 155–6
  and the Japanese, 154–6
  legitimation for, 98, 117, 127–9,
    149
  in the Red Army, 153–4
  in the Thirty Years' War, 155
  in the US Army, 155–6
  in Vietnam, 155–6
Barbarossa Operation, 3, 120
'Barred Zones', 122
Bavaria, 102
BBC, 91
Beck, Ludwig, 77
Belgium, 8
Belgorod, 10, 141
Belgrade, 9
Berghahn, V. R., 58
Berlin, 9
Biscay, 8
Blitzkrieg, 87
Blomberg, Werner von, 2
Bohemia-Moravia, 10

207